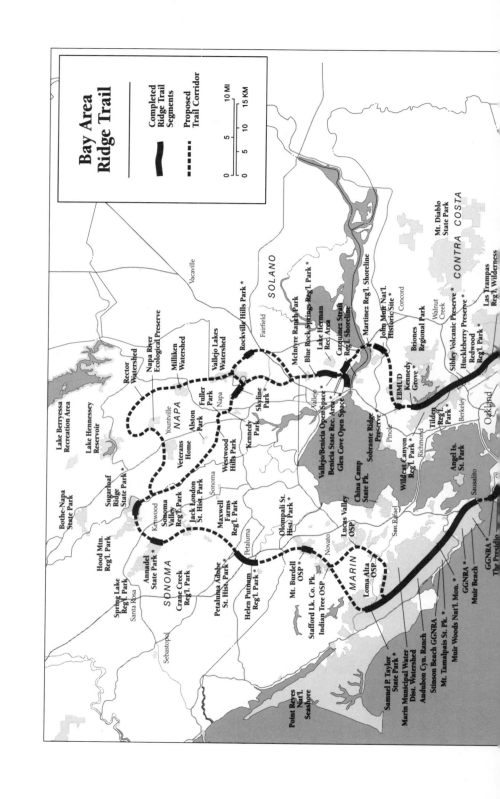

Bay Area Ridge Trail

— Completed Ridge Trail Segments

- - - Proposed Trail Corridor

| 0 | 5 | 10 MI |
| 0 | 5 | 10 | 15 KM |

SOLANO

NAPA

Vacaville

Lake Berryessa Recreation Area

Bothe-Napa State Park

Lake Hennessey Reservoir

Hood Mtn. Regl. Park

Sugarloaf Ridge State Park *

Rector Watershed

Napa River Ecological Preserve

Milliken Watershed

Vallejo Lakes Watershed

Rockville Hills Park *

Fairfield

McIntyre Ranch Park

Blue Rock Springs Regl. Park *

Lake Herman Rec Area

Carquinez Strait Regl. Shoreline

Martinez Regl. Shoreline

John Muir Nat'l. Historic Site *

Concord

CONTRA COSTA

Mt. Diablo State Park

Yountville

Fuller Park

Alston Park

Napa

Skyline Park *

Kennedy Park

Vallejo

Vallejo/Benicia Open Space *

Benicia State Rec. Area *

Glen Cove Open Space

Sobrante Ridge Preserve

Pinole

EBMUD

Kennedy Grove *

Briones Regional Park

Walnut Creek

Sibley Volcanic Preserve *

Huckleberry Preserve *

Redwood Regl. Park *

Las Trampas Regl. Wilderness

Spring Lake Regl. Park

Santa Rosa

Annadel State Park *

Crane Creek Regl. Park *

SONOMA

Kenwood

Sonoma Valley Regl. Park *

Jack London St. Hist. Park *

Sonoma

Westwood Hills Park *

Maxwell Farms Regl. Park *

Petaluma

Olompali St. Hist. Park *

Richmond

Wildcat Canyon Regl. Park *

Tilden Regl. Park *

Berkeley

Angel Is. St. Park

Oakland

Sebastopol

Petaluma Adobe St. Hist. Park *

Helen Putnam Regl. Park *

Mt. Burdell OSP *

Novato

Stafford Lk. Co. Pk. *

Indian Tree OSP

Lucas Valley OSP

MARIN

Loma Alta OSP

China Camp State Pk.

San Rafael

Sausalito

GGNRA * The Presidio

Point Reyes Nat'l. Seashore

Samuel P. Taylor State Park *

Marin Municipal Water Dist. Watershed

Audubon Cyn. Ranch

Stinson Beach GGNRA

Mt. Tamalpais St. Pk. *

Muir Woods Nat'l. Mon. *

GGNRA *

Muir Beach

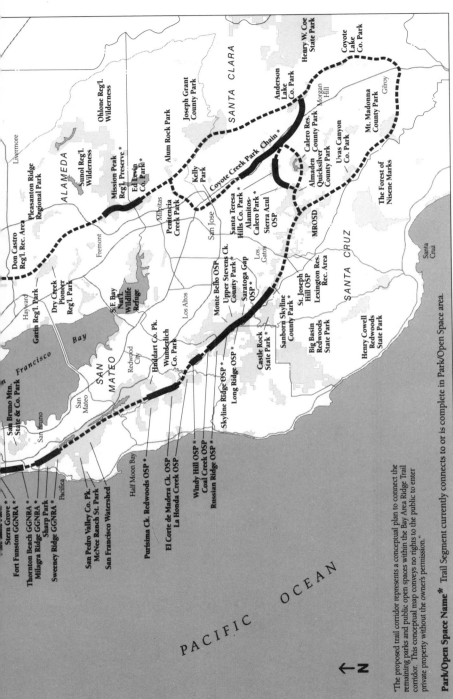

PACIFIC OCEAN

←N

The proposed trail corridor represents a conceptual plan to connect the remaining parks and public open spaces within the Bay Area Ridge Trail corridor. This conceptual map conveys no rights to the public to enter private property without the owner's permission.

Park/Open Space Name* Trail Segment currently connects to or is complete in Park/Open Space area.

SANTA CLARA

ALAMEDA

SAN MATEO

SANTA CRUZ

San Francisco Bay

Livermore

Ohlone Reg'l. Wilderness

Sunol Reg'l. Wilderness

Pleasanton Ridge Regional Park

Mission Peak Reg'l. Preserve *

Ed Levin Co. Park *

Joseph Grant County Park

Alum Rock Park

Henry W. Coe State Park

Coyote Lake Co. Park

Anderson Lake Co. Park

Morgan Hill

Gilroy

Calero Res.

Almaden Quicksilver County Park

Uvas Canyon Co. Park

Mt. Madonna County Park

Santa Teresa Hills Co. Park *

Alamitos-Calero Park *

Sierra Azul OSP *

MROSD

The Forest of Nisene Marks

Kelly Park

Coyote Creek Park Chain *

Santa Cruz

Don Castro Reg'l. Rec. Area

Hayward

Garin Regl. Park

Dry Creek Pioneer Regl. Park

Fremont

Milpitas

San Jose

Penitencia Creek Park

S.F. Bay Nat'l. Wildlife Refuge

Los Altos

Los Gatos

Monte Bello OSP *

Upper Stevens Ck. County Park *

Saratoga Gap OSP *

St. Joseph Hill OSP

Lexington Res. Rec. Area

Sanborn Skyline County Park *

Big Basin Redwoods State Park

Castle Rock State Park *

Henry Cowell Redwoods State Park

Redwood City

San Mateo

Half Moon Bay

Huddart Co. Pk.

Wunderlich Co. Park

Skyline Ridge OSP *

Long Ridge OSP *

Pacifica

San Bruno

Stern Grove *

Fort Funston GGNRA *

Thornton Beach GGNRA *

Milagra Ridge GGNRA *

Sharp Park

Sweeney Ridge GGNRA *

San Pedro Valley Co. Pk.

McNee Ranch St. Park

San Francisco Watershed

Purisima Ck. Redwoods OSP *

El Corte de Madera Ck. OSP *

La Honda Creek OSP

Windy Hill OSP *

Coal Creek OSP

Russian Ridge OSP *

San Bruno Mtn. State & Co. Park

DEDICATION

To the memory of
Karen B. Nilsson,
who led the way to many a ridgetop

The Bay Area Ridge Trail

Ridgetop Adventures Above San Francisco Bay

Jean Rusmore

in cooperation with the
Bay Area Ridge Trail Council

Foreword by
Congressman George Miller

WILDERNESS PRESS
BERKELEY

Library of Congress Card Number 95-35393
ISBN 0-89997-166-0

Manufactured in the United States of America
Published by Wilderness Press
                    2440 Bancroft Way
                    Berkeley, CA 94704

              Write for free catalog

Library of Congress Cataloging-in-Publication Data

Rusmore, Jean.
      The Bay Area Ridge Trail : ridgetop adventures
   above San Francisco Bay / Jean Rusmore ; maps
   by the Bay Area Ridge Trail Council.
          p.   cm.
      Includes index.
      ISBN 0-89997-166-0
      1. Hiking—California—Bay Area Ridge Trail—Guidebooks.
   2. Cycling—California—Bay Area Ridge Trail—Guidebooks.
   3. Horsemanship—California—Bay Area Ridge Trail—Guidebooks.
   4. Bay Area Ridge Trail (Calif.)—Guidebooks. I. Title.
   GV199.42.C22B387   1995
   917.94'6—dc20   95-35393

ACKNOWLEDGMENTS

Since the Bay Area Ridge Trail concept was first proposed, many people have contributed their efforts and enthusiasms into completing more than 200 miles of the trail. Leading this achievement have been Bay Area Ridge Trail Council Chairman Brian O'Neill and the Council's Board of Directors. To these dedicated people who have given their energies and talents to guide the Ridge Trail along its successful way, I offer my thanks. I also extend to them my appreciation for approving the idea of this book and for funding its maps and the original trail guides.

For the splendid support and considerable skills of the Bay Area Ridge Trail Council staff I am most grateful. Barbara Rice, Executive Director since 1988, has been unfailingly resourceful, far-sighted, and good-humored. It has been a pleasure to know and work with her. To the very helpful field coordinators, Peter Bluhon, Ron Brown, Margaret Marshall, and Dee Swanhuyser, and to the capable and friendly office staff, I offer many thanks. I am especially grateful to Wendy Ragsdale, who skillfully produced the maps for this guidebook and who coordinated the production of the Ridge Trail pamphlet trail guides.

The directors, superintendents, and planners of the park and open space agencies through whose lands the Bay Area Ridge Trail trips travel were most cooperative. I extend my appreciation for their specialized knowledge, for their maps and background materials, and for their helpful comments on the trip descriptions. To the rangers, many of whom hiked the trails with me, and to all the field staff who shared their special knowledge of the trails and the natural, historic, and cultural features of their parks, watersheds, and preserves, I offer my thanks. Their love of the lands in their care was truly inspiring.

I salute and thank Larry Orman and Mark Evanoff whose pioneering work at Greenbelt Alliance stimulated Bay Area leaders to reactivate William Penn Mott's dream of a ridgetop trail around San Francisco Bay.

It's been a pleasure to work with the able members of the San Mateo County Committee of the Bay Area Ridge Trail Council. I thank them for their volunteer leadership in exploring, planning, and promoting the Bay Area Ridge Trail in this county and by extension, in the entire Bay Area, and for their longterm efforts to complete the Ridge Trail down the Peninsula.

Many friends hiked the trails with me: Doris Lindfors, a delightful companion who generously contributed her firsthand knowledge of Bay Area trails and shuttled cars to trailheads, cheerfully hiked almost every mile of the Bay Area Ridge Trail route with me. My monthly hiking friends, the Walkie-Talkies, heartened me with their pleasure in exploring most of the South Bay and the Peninsula segments of the Bay Area Ridge Trail. To these and all who shared the Bay Area Ridge Trail trips, I extend my appreciation for their company and their delight in the beautiful country we traveled through.

To my friend and longtime co-author Frances Spangle, I extend my appreciation for contributing her research and writing skills to four Marin County trips and the

Wunderlich to Huddart county parks trip.

During the process of producing this guidebook, the staff of Wilderness Press efficiently managed a significant part of the work—my thanks to Noelle Impera- tore, Anne Iverson, and Larry Van Dyke. To Wilderness Press publisher Tom Winnett, I owe my thanks and appreciation for his unfailing interest and patience and for his expertise in producing *The Bay Area Ridge Trail*.

—Jean Rusmore
Portola Valley, California
July 15, 1995

Foreword by Congressman George Miller

The Bay Area Ridge Trail represents the first major effort to implement the recommendations of the President's Commission on Americans Outdoors to establish trails connecting our nation's communities. The public-private partnerships created by the Bay Area Ridge Trail have generated broad citizen support, and serve as a model for other projects throughout the country. The Bay Area has shown how a major metropolitan region can capitalize on its unique natural assets and bring to all its residents the opportunity to hike, cycle, and horseback ride close to their homes.

The spectacular 400-mile trail links residents of nine Northern California counties with our natural resources. Residents of the San Francisco Bay Area have a tremendous opportunity to use a ridge trail encircling the entire Bay Area, sited along the ridgeline of the hills and mountains surrounding the Bay, providing access to the outstanding views in all directions.

I want to congratulate the Bay Area Ridge Trail Council for its extraordinary leadership and commitment to the project. No other urban trails project in this country has reached this level of complexity—involving over fifty public agencies, one hundred nonprofit organizations, a growing number of corporate supporters, and thousands of trail enthusiasts of all ages and interests. The Bay Area Ridge Trail Council is an outstanding example of volunteerism. The special mix of people—private citizens, park and trails professionals, and nonprofit and corporate leaders—involved in planning, promoting, and developing the Ridge Trail provides an example of people working toward a common vision. It is only with efforts of this magnitude that completion of the 400-mile trail will be realized. Without the leadership and talent of the hundreds of individuals throughout the Bay Area, we would not be where we are today. We are indeed fortunate to have such dedicated volunteers, and I want to offer my personal thanks for their tremendous efforts.

I am pleased that I was able to play a role in this project by assisting in obtaining federal funds in 1987 and in subsequent years to assist in the planning, technical assistance, education, and outreach. Once again, congratulations to all those who are helping to keep the San Francisco Bay Area one of the premier outdoor recreational areas in the United States.

—Congressman George Miller
7th District, California
July 1995

Volunteerism and Community Involvement— the Key to Success

It seems like such a short time ago that the Bay Area Ridge Trail was just an idea in the eyes of our founder, William Penn Mott, Jr. But I look at the Ridge Trail as an example of ideas that can be accomplished.

We had an inspirational leader with a visionary idea and we have a cadre of volunteers and agency partners who are making it a reality. The Bay Area Ridge Trail later took hold because people banded together to create a grassroots movement. These citizens realized the importance of open space, parks, and trails in the Bay Area. Because of their collective commitment, dedication, and perseverance, we have been able to complete some 188 miles of trail.

In these tumultuous times, it's heartening to know that the collective will of the people can succeed.

Many great individuals have had great ideas that never came to fruition. What makes the Bay Area Ridge Trail different? Volunteers. Volunteers made the idea a reality—people who spent hours making phone calls, spent many long evenings in committee meetings, weathered poison oak, heat, and rain to cut new trail, or met with landowners and agency reps to spread the idea.

Because the people involved are committed to land conservation and to proper stewardship of the Bay Area's parks and open space, the Ridge Trail Council's outdoor educational activities reach thousands, offering environmental educational opportunities for people of all ages. Continuing to engage the community each step of the way is the key to transforming a truly bold idea—creating a 400-mile ridgeline trail around San Francisco Bay—into a reality. Our collective efforts will result in providing countless people the opportunity to connect to land in a very special way on one of the most magnificent trails in this country.

It's time to pat ourselves on the back—time to say Thank You to our dedicated volunteers, agency and community partners, and financial contributors.

The Bay Area Ridge Trail Council is proud to present, in partnership with Wilderness Press, this *Official Guide to the Bay Area Ridge Trail.* We are especially indebted to Jean Rusmore, whose contributions as a Council volunteer in the production of our growing series of trail guides has made this book possible. Since 1989 Jean has hiked, researched, and written about each and every leg of the completed Bay Area Ridge Trail. We would be remiss not to thank Frances Spangle also, a Bay Area Ridge Trail Council volunteer who assisted in writing several trail guides on Marin and on the Peninsula.

As you hike, ride, and read about the wonders of the Bay Area Ridge Trail, consider how you might get involved—if you haven't already. To learn more, to volunteer, or to make a contribution in support of the Ridge Trail, contact the Bay Area Ridge Trail Council at 311 California Street, Suite 510, San Francisco, CA 94104. (415) 391-0697.

—Brian O'Neill
Chairman, Board of Directors
Bay Area Ridge Trail Council

THE BAY AREA RIDGE TRAIL

RIDGETOP ADVENTURES ABOVE SAN FRANCISCO BAY

CONTENTS

INTRODUCTION

Bay Area Setting

The San Francisco Bay Area, with its remarkable juxtaposition of bay, mountains, and sea, is one of the premier natural settings of the world. San Francisco Bay, the jewel of this region and one of the largest bays in the United States, forms a unifying feature for nine counties that ring its shores. Cradling the Bay, two arms of the Coast Range run northwest-southeast over the length of the region. Loosely connecting the Inner and Outer Coast ranges are the hills and valleys of the North and South Bay counties.

In the Bay Area's coastal mountains and their rolling foothills is a wealth of natural beauty—redwood forests, wooded streamsides, oak-studded grasslands, rocky peaks, steep mountainsides, lush meadows, and sunny chaparral slopes. During the last seventy years, public agencies, as well as private land trusts, have set aside tracts of land in the mountains and foothills that are now parks, open space preserves, and watersheds. In several Bay Area counties these lands now form a continuous open space corridor—a Bay Area Greenbelt. In city and county parks lying between the Coast Ranges there is a multitude of beautiful public open space—on shady creek banks, in hillside forests, and in greenspaces within residential areas.

All these public open spaces are places for adventure, discovery, recreation, and relaxation. Here is "room to breathe," habitat for diverse plant and animal species, areas for forests to thrive and cleanse our air, and peaceful backdrops to a bustling urban area. Here too, is the route of the Bay Area Ridge Trail—a 400-mile, multi-use trail that, when complete, will link more than 75 public parks and open spaces on the ridgeline surrounding San Francisco Bay.

These public open space lands in the Bay Area lie close to the homes of more than six million residents, most of whom live in the valleys between the hills and mountains of the Coast Range and on the sloping plains that border the Bay. From almost any place in the Bay Area the ridgelands, accented by taller peaks, are visible to Bay Area residents. For them, the sun rises or sets over these mountains, literally and figuratively. Bay Area natives especially, are fiercely proud and protective of their mountains.

The Bay Area's Heritage of Outdoor Enjoyment

The physical grandeur of this setting and its moderate climate, influenced by the Bay and the Pacific Ocean, make the Bay Area ideal for outdoor recreation. It's possible to enjoy hiking, running, bicycling, and horseback riding somewhere in the Bay Area on almost any day of the year. From the earliest inhabitants—the Ohlone, Yurock, Pomo, and other Native American tribes—we know that it was a gentle land. The first explorers marveled at its beauty, its great redwood forests, and its Mediterranean climate. After the Gold Rush, a wave of settlers arrived to farm and work in its salubrious weather. When William H. Brewer traveled in the early 1860s with the first California Geological Survey under the direction of Josiah

D. Whitney, he meticulously recorded his observations in letters to his brother. From these lively records, collected in *Up and Down California, the Journal of William H. Brewer,* we know that he found delight in California's variety of terrain and glowingly praised its marvelous scenery. Some Bay Area sites described in his travels are preserved in today's parklands of our great Bay Area greenbelt.

During the course of Spanish mission and settlement building, the Spanish government gave large land grants to some colonists as rewards for their service. On their vast domains known as "ranchos," these "rancheros" kept thousands of cattle, which they managed by riding well-trained horses. The fine horses and the rancheros' equestrian skills were displayed at rodeos and games that became important social events. The Spaniards established a tradition of skilled horsemanship and love for riding that the Mexican rancheros later carried on.

Anglo cattle ranchers, who blazed trails as they herded their stock, allowed friends—and a relatively small public interested in walking and riding—to cross their lands. Some of these trails are in public use today. These ranchers too, carried on a tradition of fine horsemanship and riding for pleasure.

Europeans who grew up in the mountains of Germany, Austria, and Switzerland recognized the natural beauty of the Bay Area and took pleasure in walking with friends on weekends. They could wander freely through orchards, along farm roads, through friendly neighbors' meadows, and along hillside animal paths. Mt. Tamalpais was a favorite destination after passenger ferry service reached Marin County in the 1920s.

Eventually many hiking and horseback riding groups sprang up to offer trips to the Bay Area's beautiful countryside on trails made by the rancheros, cattle men, early settlers and weekend explorers. Today, trail enthusiasts can find outings geared for a great variety of skills and interest levels. The Bay Area Ridge Trail Council offers trips, led by trained volunteers, to many scenic, historic and cultural sites along the ridges surrounding the Bay. Environmental and natural history groups, as well as many commercial outfitters, offer outings to local, national, and international destinations.

A Land Conservation Ethic

The founding of the Sierra Club in 1892 by John Muir and others who loved the outdoors and its natural wonders, was part of an ethic of land conservation dedicated to preserving areas of natural beauty and unique wilderness quality for posterity. Headquartered in San Francisco, the Sierra Club promoted the establishment of many western national parks and the preservation of Yosemite, and continues today in its conservation mission at the national and international levels.

Many local groups sprang up to lobby for the acquisition of public open space and to support its use. The large Bay Area population of hikers, backpackers, mountain climbers, kayakers, bicyclists, and advocates for all types of trail use became involved in saving land for parks.

Since each of the nine Bay Area counties has an edge along San Francisco Bay, there is an impetus for cooperation and for regional unity. This unity is achieved through governmental organizations—the Association of Bay Area Governments,

the Metropolitan Transportation
Agency, the Regional Air Quality
Control Board, and the Bay Conservation and Development Commission
(BCDC)—that seek to organize and
manage regional affairs. Recent studies, such as Bay Vision 2020, promote
the unification of the area and the need
to preserve its natural resources and to
plan regionally.

Nonprofit grassroots organizations
address current needs or glaring defi-
ciencies in government long-range regional planning and land-use problems. BCDC, for example, brought
about through the Save the Bay cam-
paign, now regulates use and care of

**Congressman George Miller and East Bay
Regional Park Director Ted Radke at dedication of Carquinez Strait to John Muir home
segment of the Ridge Trail, Oct. 12, 1991.**

the Bay and monitors its shores. The Planning and Conservation League, based in
Sacramento, works for good legislation for parks, transportation, and land use.

Recognizing that the Bay Area needed a defining greenbelt of open space for its
cities, far-sighted citizens and committed activists joined the late Dorothy Erskine
to form a group dedicated to achieving this ideal. First known as People for Open
Space, then Greenbelt Congress, and now Greenbelt Alliance, this organization
mobilized the regional fight to achieve a ring of parks, preserves, open space, farms,
and ranches around the Bay Area. As the crusaders grew in numbers, so did the
greenbelt ringing the bay—today a total of 3.8 million acres.

Development of Parks and Open Spaces

With the rapid increase in the Bay Area population after World War II, the
number of people wishing to walk or ride horseback freely in the outlying hills and
valleys grew. Soon outdoor lovers appreciated the importance of obtaining recreation lands for all to enjoy.

Even in the years before World War II, East Bay citizens realized the need for
parks adjacent to their growing cities. Inspired dedicated citizens, aided by civic
leaders, launched the East Bay Regional Park District (EBRPD) by an overwhelm-
ing vote of Alameda County citizens in 1934. Its first acquisition was Tilden
Regional Park. In 1964 most of Contra Costa County joined the district; in 1981
citizens in the remaining area voted to join. Present-day EBRPD's greenbelt of
parks, historic units, and recreation complexes numbers more than 79,000 acres.

Other counties and cities eventually followed suit, setting aside small and large
areas for parks and open space. Most of these parklands lie on the ridges, mountainsides, and foothills of the Coast Range. However, with the recognition that San
Francisco Bay was diminishing in size and purity, agencies around the Bay began
establishing shoreline parks to increase stewardship and appreciation of the Bay.
A notable example is the San Francisco Bay National Wildlife Refuge, a federal

unit under the Fish and Wildlife Service of the Department of the Interior. Its goals are to help preserve the wetlands with their plant and animal life, to aid the cleansing of Bay waters (an unknown or unheeded need until now), and to educate the public about these goals. The California Coastal Commission, set up by a statewide ballot initiative and later resoundingly renewed, has a mandate to protect the entire state's coastal viewshed and to preserve public access to the shoreline.

As the appreciation of our need for breathing space and stretching room grew, other new agencies also took up the cause. Successful examples include the Marin County Open Space District and the Midpeninsula Regional Open Space District in Santa Clara and San Mateo counties. Recently, the Sonoma County Agricultural Preservation and Open Space District was organized, and a ballot measure in southern Santa Clara County to set up an open space authority was passed. Bond measures and initiatives to promote good land use, contain urban sprawl, provide recreational opportunities, and preserve agriculture at city edges were passed. Napa County has adopted land-use regulations designed to protect its world-famous vineyards.

Today, as a result of these many efforts, hundreds of thousands of protected acres in the foothills and mountainsides surround the urbanized Bayside, and more acreage edges the Bay's shores. Coastal counties—particularly Marin, San Francisco, and San Mateo—have thousands of acres in permanent protection under the National Park Service. Local Coastal Plans in Sonoma, Marin, San Francisco, and San Mateo counties afford a measure of protection as well. There is at least one unit of the California State Park System in each Bay Area county. Most Bay Area counties have a county park system; Marin, Sonoma, Alameda, Contra Costa, Santa Clara, and San Mateo counties are blessed with an additional regional park agency.

Many Bay Area parks came into existence through the closing of military bases. Forts Baker, Barry, Cronkite, and Funston, and Milagra and Sweeney ridges were declared surplus in the downsizing of the military following World War II. In 1994, the San Francisco Presidio became a national park under the jurisdiction of the Golden Gate National Recreation Area. A provision of federal law required that these bases be offered to public entities before being offered on the commercial market. Fortunately for the Bay Area, many parks grace our ridgetops and baylands through this provision.

Watersheds, too, are open space. Significant watershed lands preserve open space in Marin, Alameda, Contra Costa, Santa Clara, and San Mateo counties. As the population of San Francisco grew in the mid-1800s, a group of individuals formed the Spring Valley Water Company to assure a steady water supply. From this company evolved the San Francisco Water Department. Eventually SFWD piped water from the Sierra Nevada, and this water department now supplies more than a miilion customers in San Francisco, on the Peninsula, and in the East Bay.

Other jurisdictions began to develop stable water supplies and to store water in reservoirs. Most of these storage areas are in the foothills surrounding the Bay plain. For many years these reservoirs were off-limits to the public. However, when modern purification techniques came into being, some agencies began to open their gates to quiet, passive recreation, such as nature walks and hiking. Today, most water agencies allow some public access, although the SFWD restricts access to groups, which can be no larger than 25 with advance reservations of $5 per person, and they must be led by a responsible person.

The Role of Private, Nonprofit Groups

Private, nonprofit organizations, such as Trust for Public Land, Peninsula Open Space Trust, Marin Conservation League, and Sempervirens Fund, have worked for many years to preserve and protect open space lands for eventual public use. Through gifts, purchases, and easements these organizations can make choice lands available to public agencies. A recent outstanding example is the purchase through POST of 1,227 acres of choice hillside land adjacent to Huddart County Park in San Mateo County. Cooperation among agencies, citizens, large donors, and the federal government brought about this remarkable acquisition. A connector trail through this land will reach the Bay Area Ridge Trail on the crest of the Santa Cruz Mountains.

Here in Bay Area public open spaces is a remarkable network of trails that visitors can explore on foot, by bicycle, or on horseback.

THE BAY AREA RIDGE TRAIL

The unique Bay Area combination of a glorious physical setting, together with avid outdoor enthusiasts, conservationists, and educated, willing volunteers, added to a history of outdoor recreation, a growing greenbelt, and a conservation ethic, was ripe for the establishment of the Bay Area Ridge Trail. Designed as a multi-use ridgeline route, this 400-mile trail proposes to connect public parklands and watersheds of the Bay Area greenbelt circling San Francisco Bay. It will eventually link over 75 parks and public lands that provide magnificent views, offer visits to important historic sites and urban attractions, afford glimpses of the area's cultural heritage, and promote firsthand experience in the Bay Area's diverse ecosystems.

On a network of paths that traverses a broad corridor along the ridgelands, the Bay Area Ridge Trail provides recreational opportunities for hikers, bicyclists, and equestrians. Some segments of the trail are accessible to the physically limited. In less than a half-hour's drive or bus ride from any Bay Area community, at least one segment of the Ridge Trail can be reached. This scenic trail will link communities along the ridgeline and will connect to population centers on the Bayside via feeder trails through existing city, county, regional, and federal parks.

The Bay Area Ridge Trail's Beginnings

When William Penn Mott, Jr. was General Manager of the East Bay Regional Park District in the 1960s, he proposed that a trail be built around the entire ridge of the Bay Area. He also envisioned a trail around the Bay, close to the water, and connector trails to the Sierra Nevada. In the late '80s, he lent his strong support and encouragement to achieving his vision of a ridgeline trail around the Bay.

In 1986, during the review of the Land Use Element of the San Francisco General Plan, language was inserted that promoted public access to the watershed lands of the City and County of San Francisco. The predecessors of Greenbelt Alliance, People for Open Space (POS), began an effort to acquaint the City with the public-access policies of the region's other water departments. At a meeting called on May 17, 1987, the POS group brought together the managers of water departments, county, regional, state, and federal parks departments, trail activists, and leaders of environmental organizations. The purpose of the meeting was to demonstrate to San Francisco that less restrictive public access to other Bay Area water-storage lands does not harm water quality. An interesting, important outgrowth of that meeting was the recognition that the watershed lands, parks, and preserves that surround the Bay could be tied together with a regional trail.

After that meeting a coalition of activists, spurred by the energy and commitment of William Penn Mott, Jr., then Director of the National Park Service, set up the Bay Area Trails Council in September 1987, with Brian O'Neill, Superintendent of the Golden Gate National Recreation Area (GGNRA), as chairman. An informal organization, the Bay Area Ridge Trail Council (established as a project of POS/Greenbelt Alliance), followed in late 1987. Greenbelt Alliance provided office space and administrative support in the early years. From the National Park Service came first-year funding and from GGNRA came staffing. Due to the outpouring of support for the Bay Area Ridge Trail, the informal organization incorporated in 1992 as a private, nonprofit organization. Today, the Council has a membership of 6500 and a growing corps of dedicated, grassroots volunteers.

The Bay Area Ridge Trail Council's Mission

As the Council's mission stated, it "is organized as a partnership of individuals, public agencies, and community groups responsible for facilitating the planning and development of the Bay Area Ridge Trail through community involvement, public-private partnerships, and a commitment to land conservation and resource stewardship. . . ." As "the Council creates links between parks, people, and communities . . . it also fulfills and accomplishes the pioneering vision of William Penn Mott, Jr."

California State Senator Bill Lockyer, Greenbelt Alliance Executive Director Larry Orman, Mrs. William Penn Mott, Jr., and GGNRA Supterindent Brian O'Neill at the announcement of the Bay Ridge Trail plan at Inspiration Point on September 22, 1988.

Bay Area Ridge Trail Accomplishments

As of May 1995, 188 miles of the Ridge Trail have been completed. These miles are dedicated, signed, and in use. An additional 12 miles of trail, scheduled for completion by the end of 1995, also will be dedicated, signed, and ready for use. The total Ridge Trail mileage is calculated along the main route on a single alignment and does not include alternate routes, connector trails to the main route, or side trips. There is at least one Ridge Trail segment in each of the Bay Area counties. Most of these miles traverse trails in public parklands around the Bay Area. However, one 4.5-mile trail is on land leased from the State of California and operated as a park by a private group that offers its use to the public for a nominal fee.

This treasury of public lands unites the nine Bay Area counties that touch San Francisco Bay. The Bay Area Ridge Trail is a composite necklace of trails, made up of diverse jewels, for a variety of users, from hikers, equestrians, and bicyclists, to all who appreciate the beauty of this land. The public spaces it threads offer magnificent views of our Bay Area, places to sit and contemplate and relax, places to restore the spirit, places to test endurance and build stamina. Along these paths an observant user can see many of the area's animal species, countless birds, and hundreds of different wildflowers in season. The parks through which the Bay Area Ridge Trail runs offer a wide variety of trail experiences depending on each trail's exposure to sun, rain, and wind. The presence of animal and plant life will vary according to such exposure, past usage, and present management. Thus a unique experience is to be found on each segment of the Ridge Trail.

The Next Step—Closing the Gaps

Since 1987 the Bay Area Ridge Trail Council, with the full commitment of the public park agencies, has been particularly successful in coordinating the completion of the Ridge Trail on public lands. As of the end of 1995, 200 miles of trail will be complete. Of the 200 miles remaining, about 60 miles are proposed for publicly owned watersheds and relatively short, undeveloped segments in parks and on public road rights-of-way.

The additional 140 miles of the Bay Area Ridge Trail that remain to be completed are proposed for lands in private ownership—ranging from open space and agricultural to suburban and urban uses. The Bay Area Ridge Trail Council is actively involved in reaching out to private landowners, in building sound public policies that support the Ridge Trail, and in assisting our community partners in fund-raising and trail maintenance efforts—critical components necessary to complete the remaining Ridge Trail miles.

To close these gaps in the Bay Area Ridge Trail is an immediate and immense challenge that will take years to fully meet. However, the Council's long-range gap-initiative is designed to complete the remaining 200 miles of the Ridge Trail. Success in this effort relies on the Council's leadership and the on-going involvement and commitment of its members, volunteers, and public agency partners.

The Council's volunteers play a key role in the programs and projects of the Council. From an active corps who serve on the Board of Directors, to others who build trails, who plan and carry out Ridge Trail events, and who raise needed funds, it is the volunteers who are the heart of the Bay Area Ridge Trail Council.

Other Regional Trails

In the Bay Area

After World War II there was a surge of enthusiasm for a round-the-state, border-to-border loop trail, and easements were secured and rights of way developed. However, due to rapid building activity along the route and to lack of legal rights to the trails, most trail segments fell into disrepair and were subsequently closed. Today, the Bay Area Ridge Trail follows some segments of this early trail, the California Riding and Hiking Trail, in Contra Costa and San Mateo counties. See *Carquinez Strait Regional Shoreline to John Muir Historic Site* in Section C, The East Bay, and *Wunderlich County Park to Huddart County Park* in Section D, the South Bay and the Peninsula.

The Anza Trail, a National Historic Trail, follows the path of Captain Juan Bautista de Anza on his quest to find a land route from Mexico to San Francisco. In the Bay Area it traverses Santa Clara, San Mateo, and San Francisco counties. The statewide Coastal Trail hugs the shoreline through San Mateo, San Francisco, Marin, and Sonoma counties. The San Francisco Bay Trail proposes to circle the entire Bay at its edge. Following a plan originally developed and funded by legislation introduced by Senator Bill Lockyer, this trail is now being implemented by the Association of Bay Area Governments, the Metropolitan Transportation Commission, and the nonprofit San Francisco Bay Trail Project. As of 1995, approximately 170 miles of the Bay Trail are complete.

The Skyline to the Sea Trail connects Castle Rock State Park on the crest of the Santa Cruz Mountains with Big Basin State Park on the Pacific Coast at the mouth of Waddell Creek. With support and sponsorship from Sempervirens Fund, the State of California Department of Parks and Recreation, and presently, the California Trails and Greenways Foundation, hundreds of volunteers have built and maintained this 37-mile trail since its inception in 1969.

Two Bay Area trails have been granted national trail status: The Anza Trail is a National Historic Trail and the East Bay's Skyline Trail is designated a National Recreation Trail.

The Bay Area Ridge Trail Council seeks to coordinate planning and accomplish links between the Ridge Trail and these other regional trails and the local trail networks. Proposed as connectors to neighboring communities, these links will become, like the spokes of a bicycle wheel, the trails that bind communities together. The connectors offer local residents the opportunity to reach the long regional trails without ever starting a car.

Long Trails

Long-distance trails connecting several sites, cities, and/or regions, are a challenge to distance hikers and a source of volunteer action and pride in the areas they traverse. The oldest of these trails in the United States is the Appalachian Trail, which stretches from Mt. Katahdin in Maine to Springer Mountain in Georgia. Other well-known trails include the Long Trail in New England, the John Muir Trail in California's Sierra Nevada, and the Pacific Crest Trail from Mexico to

Canada. Around Lake Tahoe, the Tahoe Rim Trail traverses ridgetop lands, and in Southern California, the Santa Ana River Trail offers paved paths on both sides of the river leading to Huntington Beach. Other communities and regions are taking up the long trail idea.

Coordinating California's statewide effort to build trails that link communities and promote stewardship of and appreciation for the wealth of public land at our doorsteps, is the California Recreational Trails Committee. Along with the California Trails and Greenways Foundation, it sponsors the annual spring California Trail Days for building and maintaining trails throughout the state, and it conducts an annual conference for trail advocates.

ABOUT THIS GUIDEBOOK
A Proposal Takes Shape

In late 1989, author Jean Rusmore and Tioga Press publisher Karen Nilsson submitted a proposal to the Bay Area Ridge Trail Council to produce a small guide for each completed Ridge Trail segment. Eventually, these guides were to be assembled in a book. The Council accepted the proposal and agreed to make the maps and print the guides. Frances Spangle, who co-authored other guidebooks with Jean Rusmore, contributed her writing skills and research to the first four Marin County trips and to one in San Mateo County. As of March 1995, 18 guides, each printed in two colors on a folded 11" x 17" sheet, were available for a small price from the Bay Area Ridge Trail Council by calling 415-391-0697. A list of these guides appears in Appendix I.

After Karen Nilsson's untimely death, Thomas Winnett, publisher of Wilderness Press, a premier national guidebook press, graciously took over the project. This volume, dedicated to Karen, is the outgrowth of that proposal.

How To Use This Guidebook

This book includes the completed segments of the Bay Area Ridge Trail, as of press time, in 33 trips, totaling 179 miles, and an additional 9 miles scheduled for dedication in Fall 1995. The trail descriptions here are arranged in clockwise order around San Francisco Bay, beginning in San Francisco. The Marin County segments follow San Francisco, next are the Sonoma County trips, then Napa County, and so on around the Bay. Hence, the Marin County descriptions are written to start at the south end and finish at the north end of each segment. As the route heads across the interior valleys of the North Bay, trail descriptions begin at the west end and finish at the east end. The East Bay descriptions start in the north and end in the south, and across the Santa Clara Valley the trips go from east to west. Heading up the Peninsula and into San Francisco, the route is described from south to north.

The trips are listed in four main sections: San Francisco, the North Bay, the East Bay, and the South Bay plus the Peninsula. Each trip lists the county in which the trip lies, the trip's length, and some brief information about the type of trail surface, elevation gains and losses, access for different user groups, and facilities (amenities) specific to each particular park, preserve, or open space.

In the section entitled **On The Trail** are descriptions of the route giving directions at trail junctions, telling what you may see along the way, mentioning animal and plant life that you may encounter, and sketching some geologic, historic, and cultural features that add to the interest of the trip. Since the author took these trips at different times of the year, and since flowers, shrubs, and trees have their seasons and the presence of animal life varies seasonally, some aspects of the trail's surroundings may have been missed.

Maps

For each trip, the Bay Area Ridge Trail Council has prepared a computer-generated map showing the main Ridge Trail route as a broad, dashed line. This line on the map cannot show as many zigzags as exist on the ground, so the actual length of a trail segment may be greater than the map indicates.

The main Bay Area Ridge Trail route is marked with symbols for hiker, equestrian, and/or bicyclist accessibility on each map. Some trails are marked with the wheelchair symbol. The combination of user group symbols on the map, the Ridge Trail Accessibility information at the beginning of each trip, and the material in the text indicate user access along each segment of the Ridge Trail.

The Bay Area Ridge Trail maps use different line styles for alternate and for connector Ridge Trail routes, and these routes are marked with appropriate user symbols. If an alternate or connector Ridge Trail route is accessible to only one or two user groups, the map designates them with appropriate symbols. However, if a connector route is accessible to all trail user groups, no symbols are shown.

The Map Legend is printed on page of the Introduction. Additional information on the maps includes trailhead parking areas, major roads, and nearby landmarks, which when combined with the text should direct you to the trailhead.

The maps are generally based on the 7.5-minute series of United States Geological Survey topographic maps, which are available from some sporting-goods stores and from the USGS at 345 Middlefield Road, Menlo Park, CA 94025. The current price is $4.00 per map. The two Map Center stores, at 2440 Bancroft Way, Berkeley, CA 94704 and 63 Washington Street, Santa Clara, CA 95050, stock all the 7.5-minute and 1:250,000 USGS topographic maps for the State of California.

Some additional trails in each park are shown on the maps, but for complete information, request a park map from the managing agency. There are maps at some trailheads, but they may not be available when you visit. For other trails in the South Bay and on the Peninsula, useful guides are *Peninsula Trails* and *South Bay Trails*, co-authored by Jean Rusmore and Frances Spangle and published by Wilderness Press, Berkeley, CA. *An Outdoor Guide to the San Francisco Bay Area*, by Dorothy Whitnah and also published by Wilderness Press, is an excellent source for major parklands in the region that the Bay Area Ridge Trail traverses. Additional references and selected readings are in Appendix 4.

Getting There

In this section directions to the trailhead from the nearest major road are given for each end of the trip. In a few instances, the trailhead differs for each class of user. Where there is bus service that reaches a trailhead, or reasonably close to it, that line is named. See Appendix 2 for a list of transportation agencies, their addresses, and phone numbers.

Rules

The hours of operation for many parks and preserves are 8 A.M. to sunset or as posted at the park entrance. However, parks having overnight facilities are open during longer hours. The hours are listed for each park in the trip's tabular material. When in doubt, call the agency that manages the trail section. A list of agency addresses and phone numbers is in Appendix 2.

In general, dogs are not allowed on trails unless on a six-foot leash. In some parks, dogs are required only to be under voice control. Where a trail passes through the jurisdictions of two agencies, the regulations may be different in each, and this fact is noted in the Rules section of that trip.

Many parks charge an entrance fee, some only on weekends, and there may be lower fees for groups. There is usually a fee for special park amenities, such as camping, horse rental, and swimming. Since these fees change every few years, the exact charge is not given in this book. For it, call the agency that manages the park or special facility.

Different agencies' rules vary for bicyclists' use of trails. Some allow bicyclists on fire or service roads; a few allow them on narrow trails. Bicyclists should observe information on the maps, note the routes given in this guide for the Bay Area Ridge Trail, and always observe the icons on trail-head signs.

Sharing the Trails

Many segments of the Bay Area Ridge Trail are shared by hikers, equestrians, and bicyclists. Wherever possible, the Ridge Trail route tries to accommodate all users on a single alignment. If this is not possible, the Bay Area Ridge Trail policy states ". . . due to policy or regulation restrictions, environmental concerns, safety or physical terrain, the Bay Area Ridge Trail Council works cooperatively to secure an additional route that offers an equivalent trail experience." The accompanying chart lists accessibility to Ridge Trail trips by user group.

Variations in speed, height, and power of each type of user require that there be some trail etiquette rules. Some general rules are:
>Observe trail use regulations.
>Be responsible, safe, and considerate.
>Stay on the trail.
>Respect private property.

East Bay Regional Park District signs tell users how to share trails.

Minimize your impact.

Protect plants and wildlife.

Some rules are generally accepted for yielding to other users:

Hikers and bicyclists yield to
equestrians; stop and remain quiet
while an equestrian is passing.

Bicyclists yield to hikers; dismount
and allow the hiker to pass.

A number of agencies have adopted additional rules for bicyclists: Maximum speed is 15 miles per hour; slow to 5 miles per hour when passing or when sight distance is limited. Helmets are a standard requirement of most agencies. Some agencies use radar systems to increase awareness of park speed limits and to help bicyclists know their speed.

Some Hazards for Trail Users

Poison oak is a ubiquitous plant of the Bay Area. It takes different forms, usually seen as a trailside shrub, but mature plants climb trees and occasionally become small trees. It has three-lobed leaves that are shiny green in spring and turn beautiful shades of red and orange in the fall, and it is extremely harmful to those allergic to it. Just to touch its leaves, berries, or leafless twigs can bring on an itchy, blistery rash that takes several weeks to heal. Learn to recognize it and avoid it carefully.

Rattlesnakes are indigenous to this area, but far less widespread than poison oak. They have triangular-shaped heads, diamond markings on their backs, and rattles or segmented sections on their tails. They will try to avoid contact with humans. However, it is well to look down on warm spring days when a rattlesnake may be sunning itself on the trail. Look where you put your hands when climbing on rocks.

Lyme disease is a potentially serious disease caused by the bite of the western black-legged tick. In their active months between December and June, these tiny ticks can brush off trailside grasses and bushes onto your clothes. It is well to wear light-colored clothing so you can see any ticks on it, to keep your arms and legs covered, and to tuck your pant legs into your socks.

Mountain lions are shy, native residents of wildlands in the Bay Area. Sightings of these creatures have become more frequent in recent years due to increased human use of their habitat. A mountain lion is about the size of a small German Shepherd, with a furry tail as long as its body. It is recommended that trail users stand facing any mountain lion they encounter, make loud noises while waving their arms, and not run away.

Feral pigs have spread over many acres of wildlands since their introduction for hunting in the 19th Century. While generally not dangerous to humans, they can be fierce when cornered.

What to Wear and Take Along

Some basic rules for all trail users are to carry plenty of water and some food and snacks, have the appropriate equipment for your mode of travel, take an extra sweater and a windbreaker, wear a hat, and use sunscreen. A small packet of bandaids can be useful. All these items can easily fit in a light day pack. Although many people prefer a small waist pack because it is lighter, it may not have room for all these things.

Specialized equipment for trail users is readily available, but not always needed. Many hikers prefer to wear boots; others find that sturdy shoes with good tread and adequate support are appropriate for most Bay Area trails. Some bicyclists prefer special mountain-biking shoes, and many equestrians like to wear a protective helmet.

Where to Stay

Many Bay Area Ridge Trail travelers will hike or ride one or two segments of the trail on day trips from their Bay Area homes. For those who want to take a longer trip, a weekend or more, there are many miles of continuous Ridge Trail on the ridgelands of Marin, Contra Costa, Alameda, Santa Clara, and San Mateo counties. San Francisco offers a Ridge Trail trip through the city that would fill two hiking days. Hostels, primitive camps and public park campgrounds, located within 2 to 6 miles of the trail, are generally the least expensive places to stay overnight. Where available, these facilities are mentioned in the Amenities section of each trip. Charming bed and breakfast inns, comfortable motels, and some luxurious hotels in towns and tourist areas near the trailheads are listed in local telephone books and with travel agencies. As the public discovers the outstanding scenic and recreation qualities of the Bay Area Ridge Trail, local and national outing companies will undoubtedly offer hiking and riding trips on the Ridge Trail, including transportation to the trailheads and overnight accommodations.

On the following pages are 33 Ridgetop Adventures above San Francisco Bay. To help you choose the right trip for the weather, your abilities, and your interests, see Appendix 3: A Bay Area Ridge Trail Sampler—Trips for Many Reasons.

Welch-hurst, the hostel in Sanborn Park.

TRIP NAME

TRIP NAME	🚶	🐎	🚲	♿
San Francisco				
Fort Funston to Stern Grove	■		■	*
Stern Grove to The Presidio	■		■	
The Presidio	■			
North Bay				
Marin Headlands – Golden Gate Bridge to Tennessee Valley	■			
Marin Headlands – Tennessee Valley to Shoreline Highway	■			
Mount Tamalpais – Shoreline Highway to Pantoll	■		*	
Mount Tamalpais & GGNRA – Pantoll to Bolinas-Fairfax Rd.	■	*		
GGNRA & Samuel P. Taylor State Park	■			
Mt. Burdell Open Space Preserve – Summit trip; Wildlife area	■		*	
McNear Park to Petaluma Adobe	■			
Annadel State Park – Spring Lake County Park to East Gate	■			
Sugarloaf State Park – Visitor Center to Summit	■			
Skyline Wilderness Park – Entrance to South Boundary	■			
Rockville Hills Community Park – N. Entry to Gr. Valley Rd.	■			
Vallejo-Benicia Buffer – Blue Rock Springs to Rose Drive	■			
Benicia Waterfront – Benicia State Rec. Area to Benicia Pt.	■		*	*
East Bay				
Carquinez Reg. Shoreline Park to John Muir Historic Site	■			■
Kennedy Grove to Tilden Regional Park – to Inspiration Point	■		*	*
Tilden Regional Park to Redwood Reg. Park – to Skyline Gate	■		*	
Redwood & Chabot Reg. Parks – Skyline Gate to Bort Mdw.	■			
Anthony Chabot Park – Bort Meadow to Chabot Staging Area	■			
EBMUD Lands to Cull Canyon Rec. Area	■			
Mission Peak Prsrv. & Ed Levin Park – Ohlone Coll. to Wool	■			
South Bay and the Peninsula				
Coyote Hellyer County Park to Metcalf City Park	■			
Santa Teresa Co. Park & Los Alamitos/Calero Creek Park	■			*
Sanborn Co. Park & Castle Rock Park – Saratoga Gap	■			
Saratoga Gap OSP to Skyline Ridge OSP – Horseshoe Lake	■			*
Skyline Ridge & Russian Ridge OSP – Horse. Lk.-Rapley Rd.	■		*	*
Windy Hill OSP – Razorback Ridge-Spring Ridge	■		*	
Wunderlich & Huddart Co. Parks – to Purisima Cr. Rdwd. OSP	■			
Purisima Creek Redwoods OSP – Purisima Trailhd.-N. Entry	■			
Sweeney Ridge to Milagra Ridge	■	*	*	
Mussel Rock to Fort Funston – Daly City & Dunes Trail	■	*	*	

* Parts are accessible; refer to text description.

Map Legend

▪ ▪ ▪ Bay Area Ridge Trail

- - - - Ridge Trail Alternate

—·— Ridge Trail Connector

········ Other Trail

——— Road

—··— Stream

●—● Gate

▨▨▨ Private Property

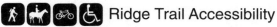 Ridge Trail Accessibility

🅿 Ridge Trail Parking

◭ Camping

$\underset{200}{+}$ Spot Elevation

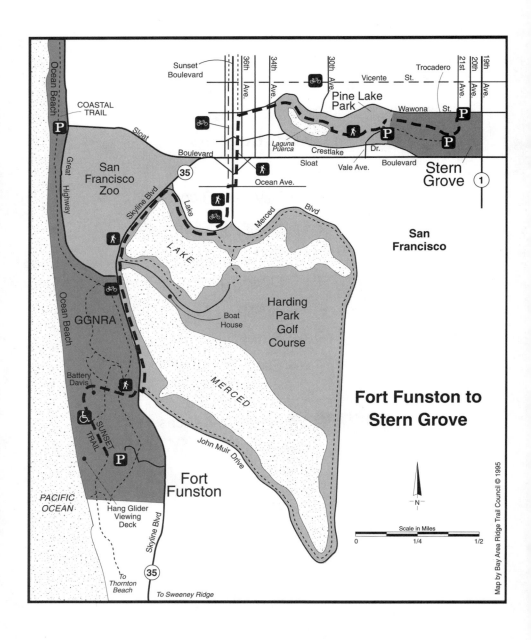

Fort Funston to Stern Grove

Map by Bay Area Ridge Trail Council © 1995

Fort Funston to Stern Grove

From Hang-Glider Viewing Deck to the Trocadero

From bluff-top sand dunes, this segment of the Ridge Trail passes two lakes, a neighborhood of pleasant homes, and then wanders through parkland meadows to reach historic Stern Grove.

Length   3.2 miles.

Location   Southwest corner of San Francisco near Lake Merced.

Trail Characteristics   Mostly paved trail except for short section over dunes. Easy walk except for 115-foot elevation gain in last 0.1 mile; scenery changes from ocean bluffs to protected glens; weather varies from windy and foggy at the coast to warm and sunny in sheltered parks.

Ridge Trail Accessibility
- Hikers—Entire route.
- Bicyclists—Lake Merced path & city streets north to Vicente St. and 20th Ave.
- Wheelchair users—Paved Sunset Trail in Fort Funston.

Trail Management
- Fort Funston—Golden Gate National Recreation Area (GGNRA): 415-556-8642 or 415-239-2366.
- San Francisco streets and sidewalks—San Francisco Department of Public Works: 415-554-5810.
- Pine Lake Park and Stern Grove—San Francisco Recreation and Park Department: 415-666-7200.

Rules
- Fort Funston—Open from sunrise to sunset. Dogs on leash or under voice control. Pick up pet litter.
- Pine Lake Park and Stern Grove—Open from 7 A.M. to 10 P.M. Dogs on leash on park trails and on city streets.

Amenities
- Fort Funston—Visitor center, native plant nursery, hang-glider viewing deck with benches in protected nooks, hang-glider launching site, picnic tables, benches, restrooms, water and telephone.
- Stern Grove—Summer Sunday concerts, tables, benches, restrooms, water, and telephones.

Getting There

By Car

South entrance, Fort Funston—Going south, take Skyline Blvd. (Hwy 35) to Lake Merced, and after passing John Muir Dr., go 0.1 mile and turn right (west) into Fort Funston. At fork in road, bear right and continue to extensive parking area. Sunset Trail entrance on north side of parking area near hang-glider viewing deck on bluff above beach.

Going north, take Skyline Blvd. (Hwy 35) north to John Muir Dr., make a U-turn and go south on Skyline Blvd. 0.1 mile, turn right (west) into Fort Funston, and follow directions in previous sentence.

When leaving Fort Funston, autos and bicycles must turn right. To go north, continue south on Skyline Blvd. to John Daly Blvd. and make a U-turn.

North entrance, Stern Grove—Situated between Sloat Blvd. and Wawona St. just west of 19th Ave. Traveling north on 19th Ave. no left turns are allowed from 19th Ave.; therefore pass Stern Grove, turn right on Ulloa St., turn right at first street, 18th Ave., and then right again on Vicente St. Cross 19th Ave., turn left on 20th Ave. and go to Wawona St. where there is on-street parking. To park in the Grove, go east on Wawona St., turn right on 19th Ave., continue to corner of Sloat Blvd. and 19th Ave., and then turn right down to parking at Stern Grove.

Traveling south on 19th Ave., turn right into Stern Grove parking area from corner of Sloat Blvd. and 19th Ave. Additional parking—turn right off 19th Ave. on Wawona St. for on-street parking, or from 19th Ave. turn right on Sloat Blvd. and turn right on Vale Ave. to park in Pine Lake Park.

By Bus
SF MUNI line 18 daily to Skyline Blvd. at John Muir Dr. Lines 23 and 28 daily to Stern Grove.

On The Trail

As you leave Skyline Boulevard for Fort Funston, consider how "beating swords into ploughshares" benefits the Bay Area and its Ridge Trail. This former military site and several others used in World Wars I and II for coastal defense are now part of the vast Golden Gate National Recreation Area open for public enjoyment. Today Fort Funston's paved parking area covers the site of former Nike silos, and the elevated hang-glider viewing deck and the adjacent hang-glider launching site encompass an earlier military observation point.

Be sure to walk out to the viewing deck for sweeping vistas of the Pacific Ocean from Point San Pedro in the south to Point Reyes in the north. On a clear day the view extends 25 miles offshore to the Farallon Islands. Often seen from this viewing deck is an aerial display by hang-glider flyers soaring on the ocean breezes.

To start the trip from the parking area, **hikers and wheelchair users** take the wide, paved Sunset Trail north along the bluffs. Lining the trail and helping to stabilize the sand dunes are native lavender lupines and coyote bush and exotic acacia and ice plant. After about 200 yards on this trail, there is a junction at which the Ridge Trail goes left, continuing on the Sunset Trail. Soon this trail veers east and passes through the concrete arch of Battery Davis, the site of a World War II gun emplacement.

On the other side of the battery tunnel, at another trail junction, **wheelchair users**

Hang glider floats above surf at Fort Funston.

turn right (south) on a paved trail that rejoins the first segment of the Sunset Trail. From this junction they then return to the parking area.

Hikers continue east, cross an equestrian trail, and after 100 yards take a footpath to the top of a sandy hill. From here hikers descend on a flexible ladder made of wooden cross-bars secured on each side to heavy ropes. The ropes are attached to sturdy posts at the top and bottom of the sand dune. When wet, the wooden cross-bars can be slippery.

At the foot of the dunes, you make a short jog north to the Skyline Boulevard/John Muir Drive intersection. Cross with the signal and go left (north) on the paved path beside fenced, tule-lined Lake Merced in the company of runners, strollers, and bicyclists. As you round the northwest corner of Lake Merced, you may hear the roar of a lion or the piercing scream of a peacock emanating from the forested west side of the street, which bounds one side of the San Francisco Zoo.

The Bay Area Ridge Trail route now turns southeast following the path between Lake Merced and the boulevard of the same name. After passing parcourse stations set in a broad lakeside band, you cross Lake Merced Boulevard to the west side of Sunset Boulevard. This wide avenue, laid out in the tradition of the grand boulevards of Paris and Washington, D.C., has landscaped borders and a parklike center strip, and runs from Lake Merced to Golden Gate Park.

At Ocean Avenue you cross Sunset Boulevard and take the gravelled path on its east side. Follow this path for four blocks, then turn right (east) on Wawona Street, continuing for three blocks to Pine Lake Park at Crestlake Drive and 34th Avenue.

Now you leave city streets to enter a steep-sided, tree-lined canyon. From the entrance the paved path, often strewn with fragrant eucalyptus and cypress seed-pods, goes down rather steeply to marshy Laguna Puerca, then levels off on a dirt footpath hugging the north edge of the lake. (Although early Spanish settlers used this term--translated from the Spanish for "Sow Lake"—no pigs are in sight today; however, you will still see the pine trees that give this park its name.) Blackberry bushes and tall reeds crowd the path, which soon emerges at the first of four narrow meadows filling the rest of the canyon.

Take the asphalt path, heading east up the meadow, until you reach a parking area. On its north edge, beside two large eucalyptus trees, you will find a new trail segment, constructed by volunteers, which joins paths above Stern Grove's West Meadow and Stage Meadow. The paths are edged with handsome, low stone walls which also serve as additional seats for the crowds that come on summer Sundays to enjoy the free concerts held here. This long-standing tradition of fine public performances was started by Mrs. Sigmund Stern in 1931, when she gave the Grove to San Francisco in honor of her husband.

Beyond Stage Meadow on the north hillside sits the charming Trocadero Inn, built in 1892 as a public hotel by George M. Greene, who owned the land for 40 years. The Trocadero Inn, with its deer park, restaurant, dancing pavilion, rowing lake and trout farm, flourished until the Prohibition Amendment to the Constitution took effect in 1920. Refurbished in 1986, the Trocadero appears today much as it did at the turn of the century.

In a dense redwood grove near the yellow-painted Trocadero there are picnic tables beside a small lily pond. When the day is warm, this is a shady place for a backpack lunch after your hike. Then, if you have a shuttle car parked in Stern Grove or at Pine Lake, you can take a short walk to reach it. If you have a shuttle car parked on Wawona Street, climb the steep hillside on a zigzag asphalt path just east of the Trocadero to its end at 21st Avenue and Wawona Street. If you would like to continue on the Bay Area Ridge Trail, see the next segment, *Stern Grove to the Presidio*, for descriptions of attractive parks to visit along that route.

For those who parked at Fort Funston and must return, it will be a 6.4-mile round trip with views from a different perspective. Sunsets over the ocean are particularly dramatic when seen from the hang-glider viewing deck.

To access the Bay Area Ridge Trail from the hang-glider viewing deck, **bicyclists** must travel on the paved road in Fort Funston, return to Skyline Boulevard (Highway 35) and go south to John Daly Boulevard. Make a U-turn and ride north on Skyline Boulevard to John Muir Drive. After you cross this drive, you can join the hikers on the path around Lake Merced, the signed Ridge Trail route. At Sunset Boulevard, cross Lake Merced Boulevard and take the westside path to Vicente Street, a distance of five blocks. Here you cross Sunset Boulevard and continue on Vicente Street to 20th Avenue, where you can ride one block south to a shuttle car parked on Wawona Street or retrace your route to Fort Funston.

Bicyclists may want to continue on the next Bay Area Ridge Trail segment, a 7-mile trip ending at the Presidio, as noted above.   ∎

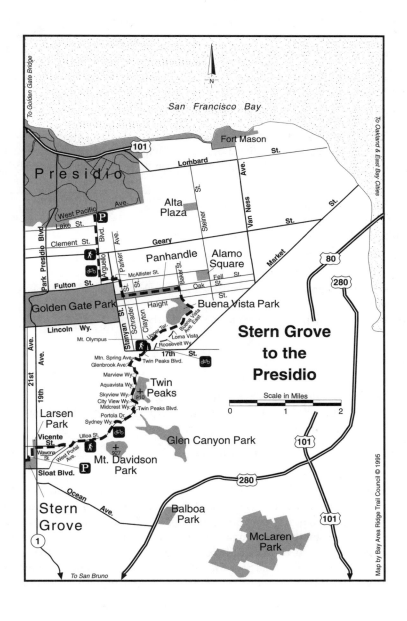

Stern Grove to The Presidio

From Wawona Street at 21st Avenue to Arguello Gate

A gradual climb on city streets through attractive neighborhoods and city parks reaches spectacular bay and ocean views from some of the city's high points.

Length 7 miles.

Location In San Francisco, on the west side of the central city.

Trail Characteristics On city streets and sidewalks, except for short off-street hike to Twin Peaks summit. Elevation gain to Twin Peaks 685 feet, additional gains on stairway walk to Mt. Olympus and on three other climbs to City's hills. Can be foggy and breezy.

Ridge Trail Accessibility
- Hikers—City sidewalks.
- Hikers only—Trail to Twin Peaks.
- Bicyclists—City streets.

Trail Management
- San Francisco streets and sidewalks—San Francisco Dept. of Public Works: 415-554-5810.
- Parks—San Francisco Recreation and Park Department: 415-666-7200.

Rules
- Dogs on leash.

Amenities
- Stern Grove—Telephone, water, and restrooms.
- No public restrooms for rest of trip. Several shopping districts with restaurants, delicatessens, and grocery stores along the route.

Getting There

By Car
South entrance, Stern Grove—Situated between Sloat Blvd. and Wawona St. just west of 19th Ave. Traveling north on 19th Ave. no left turns are allowed from 19th Ave.; therefore pass Stern Grove, turn right on Ulloa St., turn right at first street, 18th Ave., and then right again on Vicente St. Cross 19th Ave., turn left on 20th Ave. and go to Wawona St. where there is on-street parking. To park in the Grove, go east on Wawona St., turn right on 19th Ave., continue to corner of Sloat Blvd. and 19th Ave., and then turn right down to parking at Stern Grove.

Traveling south on 19th Ave., turn right into Stern Grove parking area from corner of Sloat Blvd. and 19th Ave. Additional parking—turn right off 19th Ave. on Wawona St. for on-street parking, or from 19th Ave. turn right on Sloat Blvd. and turn right on Vale Ave. to park in Pine Lake Park.

North entrance, San Francisco Presidio, Arguello Gate—Take Arguello Blvd.
to the Presidio. Limited parking on east side of Arguello Blvd. 100 yards inside
Presidio or at Inspiration Point less than 0.1 mile farther north on Arguello Blvd.
MUNI buses recommended.

By Bus

MUNI lines 23 and 28 serve Stern Grove. MUNI lines 1, 2, 4, 33 and 38 stop on
Arguello Blvd. several blocks south of the Presidio.

On The Trail

Choose a clear day for this trip to take advantage of San Francisco's dramatic
vistas. But even if the day is foggy, visiting seven of San Francisco's many parks
and playgrounds and traversing its distinctive neighborhoods is always rewarding
and best experienced on foot or by bicycle.

This trip begins at Stern Grove in San Francisco's Sunset District in the area of
the former San Miguel Rancho. Originally granted to José Noé in 1839, the rancho
eventually came into Adolph Sutro's hands around 1879. Sutro, a philanthropist
and former mayor of San Francisco, was also the entrepreneur of the former Sutro
Baths, now part of the Golden Gate National Recreation Area. The rancho lands,
mostly shifting sand dunes and beyond the city limits at that time, remained
undeveloped—used only for horse racing and some farming and cattle grazing—for
nearly forty years.

Then, in 1918, when the Twin Peaks Tunnel opened, rapid transportation to
downtown by trolley fostered an era of residential building that culminated in the
feverish expansion of the post-World War II years. Row upon row of houses of
varied façades and trims filled the former sand dunes.

Because the arroyo, given to San Francisco by Mrs. Sigmund Stern in 1931 and
now known as Stern Grove, was continuously occupied from 1847 by the George
M. Greene family, it escaped development. You start your trip where the paved trail
emerges from this wooded glen at 21st Avenue and Wawona Street.

Following the Bay Area Ridge Trail signs, go east one block on Wawona Street,
turn left on 20th Avenue and skirt the Larsen Park greensward. At the turn of the
century, Carl Larsen had a chicken ranch here, which supplied eggs for his Tivoli
restaurant downtown. Today, a swimming pool, tennis courts and children's play
equipment serve neighborhood families.

From the corner of Vicente Street and 20th Avenue, proceed east, cross 19th
Avenue and continue uphill on Vicente to the first of several churches you'll see on
this trip, St. Cecilia's, its façade graced by handsome bronze doors.

Soon the 103-foot concrete cross atop eucalyptus-covered Mt. Davidson in Mt.
Davidson Park looms on your right, and the soaring, spare, rusty-orange frame of
Sutro Tower rises on your left. These will be landmarks for the first half of your
trip. Mt. Davidson, the city's highest peak at 927 feet, commemorates surveyor
George Davidson for exposing a false ownership claim to vast acreages in the
southwest quarter of the city.

Leaving Vicente Street's flowery front gardens, you curve left (northeast) onto

West Portal Avenue. Here is a one-block opportunity to stop at a neighborhood restaurant or buy a deli lunch for a picnic later in Buena Vista Park. Hikers and bicyclists then turn right, uphill, onto Ulloa Street at the point just before the streetcar line disappears into its tunnel. As you progress along Ulloa Street, watch on your left for a steep cliff displaying wavy lines of red rock. This rock is red chert, formed of layers of silica and clay, uplifted from the ocean floor and deposited on the edge of California by movement of the earth's tectonic plates. Red chert is most commonly seen in San Francisco in such layers, or as boulders.

Continuing to the heights of Rockridge Terrace, which is crowned by the colorful, mosaic bell tower of St. Brendan's Church, you reach the intersection of Ulloa and Laguna Honda streets. Here is a sweeping view across the Bay to the Marin Headlands and Mt. Tamalpais.

Now it's a gradual descent and right curve (east) onto Sydney Way before turning left (northeast) on Portola Drive. Across Portola Drive there are more neighborhood shops and restaurants. In just a few blocks you bear left onto Twin Peaks Boulevard. Pause at the Portola Drive–Twin Peaks Boulevard junction to glance southeast across tree-filled Glen Canyon Park and the Bay to see Mt. Diablo rising above the East Bay Hills.

Then, onward and upward, make a quick left turn on Panoramic Drive and in 50 yards a sharp right onto Midcrest Way. After turning left on Cityview Way, make a right

Sutro Tower, San Francisco landmark, is in view on this leg of the trail.

turn (north) on Skyview Way. The street names attest to the remarkable vistas this Bay Area Ridge Trail route offers. In a quick succession of right turns on Aquavista and Marview ways, you skirt the steep sides of Twin Peaks. On windy days you may see people flying kites from the top.

To get the kite-flyer's view from Twin Peaks, turn right onto a foot trail at the junction of Marview and Farview ways. You'll pass a reservoir set aside for fighting fires by this City that remembers the conflagration after the 1906 earthquake. Bicyclists can lock their bikes to the chain-link fence surrounding the reservoir and make the trek to the summit. From the foot trail, you emerge beside Twin Peaks Boulevard and walk south to the summit path that is flanked by boulders of weathered red chert. The windswept, rocky soil beside the path supports one of San Francisco's last remaining habitats of native plants that harbor the endangered Mission Blue butterfly. In spring, indigenous pink checkerblooms, lupines in blue and white, and orange poppies brighten the landscape.

From 910 feet above sea level you have a 360-degree view: the Pacific Ocean, the Golden Gate, and the Coast Range mountains that encircle San Francisco Bay. It is along the ridges of these mountains that other segments of the Bay Area Ridge

Trail lie: Mt. Tamalpais to the north; Vollmer, Mission and Monument peaks to the east; and Kings Mountain to the south. Spread out before you is the magical City of San Francisco. With a good map you can identify its famous hills, its historic buildings, its new skyscrapers, its bracelets of bridges across the Bay, and its many parks.

If you don't make the trek to Twin Peaks' summit, walk past San Francisco's Central Radio Station to the lee of Christmas Tree Point for a more intimate view east, north, and south of city neighborhoods around hilltop parks and landmark public structures, such as the bronze-domed San Francisco City Hall.

When you've had your fill of vistas near and far (on very clear days you can see north to Mt. St. Helena), retrace your steps and bear northwest on Marview Way. On your left at its intersection with Palo Alto Avenue, a path through the trees circumnavigates yet another reservoir.

Past houses with intricate brickwork facing, charming garden gates, and handsome redwood siding, you jog right (northeast) on Glenbrook Avenue for a quick, steady descent to Mountain Spring Avenue, bear right, and then arc sharply left (north) on Twin Peaks Boulevard. Near here in the late 1860s the popular roadhouse, Mountain Spring House, was situated on Corbett Road, a predecessor of present-day Twin Peaks Boulevard. Corbett Road continued past the Trocadero Inn, still standing in Stern Grove, to the now-defunct San Miguel Ocean House and its nearby race track at the beach.

Watch for the Bay Area Ridge Trail signs and stay on Twin Peaks Boulevard as it turns right (east), past a former water tank site, Tank Hill Open Space, pausing to note its exposed, convoluted, layered chert and greenstone rocks. Sighting northwest from here beyond the Golden Gate you see the Point Bonita Lighthouse and farther still, the tip of Point Reyes.

Twin Peaks Boulevard becomes Clayton Street, where another reservoir sits encased in a solid steel tank. Bicyclists and hikers have been following the same route, except for the side trip to Twin Peaks' summit. But now, **bicyclists** turn east on 17th Street and go left (northeast) on Roosevelt Way, which then becomes Loma Vista, and turn right (northeast) on Upper Terrace before rejoining the hikers at Buena Vista Park.

Hikers also turn east on 17th Street, walk a few yards on its north side, and then mount a steep stairway to Upper Terrace. Head left (northeast) at the top, continuing to Mt. Olympus Park, a tiny, circular green space in the geographical center of the city, which surrounds a raised pedestal.

Descend the stairway on the circle's north side to the lower leg of Upper Terrace, and pass well-kept gardens and attractive homes, following a fairly level route to Buena Vista Park. If the day is sunny, you can see the ocean sparkling at the end of intersecting side streets, named for surveyors and developers of this area.

At the entrance to Buena Vista Park your view northwest points to the forested Presidio, where this Bay Area Ridge Trail trip is headed. But before you go there, take a side trip into an early San Francisco green space, Buena Vista Park, a 36-acre hilltop preserved in 1894 for its trees and views. Take the wide, paved path from the end of Upper Terrace and follow it to a grassy, summit knoll with lacy, tree-framed views—a fine lunch stop. It's said that the ornate marble gutters edging the path that circles the knoll are recycled tombstones from relocated cemeteries.

Rejoin the signed Bay Area Ridge Trail route on Buena Vista Avenue East by retracing your steps or by taking one of many paths descending the park's east side. Along Buena Vista Avenue East, you pass refurbished Victorian mansions, lovingly known as "Painted Ladies," and a former hospital converted to residences. Continue downhill on this avenue to Haight Street, which you cross. On the other side of Haight Street, Buena Vista Avenue East changes to Baker Street, which you follow for two blocks north to the Panhandle, a long, tree-canopied, grassy strip that leads to Golden Gate Park.

Hikers bear left (west) on a park path in the Panhandle that parallels Oak Street. **Bicyclists** continue one block on Baker Street, then turn left on the Panhandle's Fell Street path. Rambling under some of the city's oldest trees, these paths replace a boulevard that once cut through the middle of the park, a space now filled with basketball courts, hopscotch games, and children's play equipment.

Just before Golden Gate Park, the Bay Area Ridge Trail route turns right (north) onto Shrader Street and passes St. Mary's Hospital. Shrader Street ends at Fulton Street, and the Ridge Trail continues north on Parker Street after making a very small jog right on Fulton Street.

As fog streams through the Golden Gate, the Ridge Trail route through wooded parks remains in sun.

On the other side of Fulton Street, you go one block on Parker Street past twin-towered St. Ignatius Church on the University of San Francisco campus. At McAllister Street, you turn left (west), pausing in mid-block to admire a tight row of venerable, tiny, stick-style homes, each trimmed in different, but harmonious, dark colors.

Turn right onto Stanyan Street, make a little jog north, and then cross Stanyan to pick up McAllister again. At the corner of Willard North and McAllister, note two small houses on the right, vestiges of pre-1906 San Francisco, tucked in among taller homes and apartments. Growing next to a white picket fence surrounding the corner house is a patriarch among buckeye trees with gnarled, twisted limbs.

A future Bay Area Ridge Trail route, as described in the Golden Gate Park Master Plan, would continue along the Panhandle, cross Stanyan Street, and enter the park. Proceeding west on the north side of John F. Kennedy Drive, **hikers** and **bicyclists** would pass McLaren Lodge, turn right (northeast) on Conservatory Drive West, and follow it past sloping lawns, formal floral displays, and the charming, white, glass-walled Conservatory. They would turn left (north) on Arguello Boulevard, leave the park at Fulton Street, and then continue north on the east side of Arguello Boulevard to McAllister Street.

To complete the last leg of this trip, from the corner of McAllister and Arguello, continue north on Arguello. This route offers more San Franciscana to those who travel it slowly. Just a few blocks north is the playground donated by former mayor Angelo J. Rossi, offering swimming, tennis, and field sports. When you come to a set of concrete steps graced by circular flower-filled planters, you might elect to mount these steps to see the playing fields, tennis courts, and swimming pool in this park. You can continue north about 50 yards and then descend the second set of steps to continue your northward trip.

In the last mile of your trip along this busy boulevard, look for Roosevelt Middle School, an imposing, brick-faced public school, designed by the distinguished architect Timothy Pflueger.

Two houses of worship stand on opposite corners of the intersection of Lake Street and Arguello Boulevard. One, the brown-shingled St. John's Presbyterian Church, dating from 1905, contains stained-glass windows from two churches of the late 1800s. The other, the monumental, neo-Byzantine style Temple Emanu-El, has a fine courtyard and stained-glass windows designed by Mark Adams. (It's possible to enter these churches at posted times to see their windows and to sample the architectural and cultural variety of this City of Saint Francis.)

Climbing a little in the last two blocks, you reach the Arguello Gate of the Presidio of San Francisco. The Spaniards established the Presidio here in 1776 to guard their colony at the edge of the Pacific. Today, Ridge Trail travelers on foot and bike explore a route just west of the Spaniards' path between the military station and the mission settlement.

The next segment of the Bay Area Ridge Trail traverses the Presidio's northwest-trending ridges and continues to the Golden Gate Bridge. See *San Francisco Presidio—From Arguello Gate to the Golden Gate.*   ■

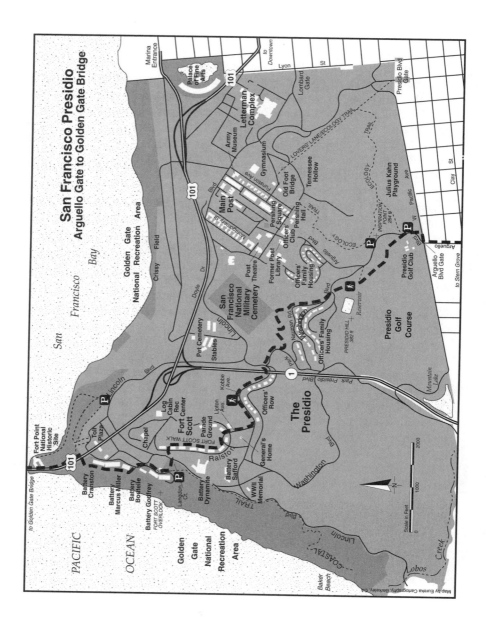

San Francisco Presidio
Arguello Gate to Golden Gate Bridge

San Francisco Presidio

From Arguello Gate to the Golden Gate

On a short trip through forests and grasslands, beside Fort Winfield Scott's historic houses and its Parade Ground, and along the Presidio's coastal bluffs, explore the charm, seclusion, natural wonders, and historic and cultural variety of the nation's newest urban park.

Length 3 miles.

Location In the northwest corner of San Francisco.

Trail Characteristics Trails through forests have minimal elevation change, varying between 2% and 10%. Fort Scott segment is on paved sidewalks. Expect summer coastal fogs, often lingering until afternoon.

Ridge Trail Accessibility
- Hikers—Entire trail.

Trail Management
- National Park Service (NPS), Golden Gate National Recreation Area (GGNRA).

Rules
- Presidio Trails—Open daylight hours. Dogs on leash only; no horses; no bicycles.

Amenities
- No water, restrooms, or phone along the trail route. Water, restrooms, phone, and metered parking at Golden Gate Bridge Plaza. At the Main Post Parade Ground on Montgomery Street in Building 102, is the Presidio project office and visitor information center, 415-561-4323, with water, restrooms, and phone. There is ample free parking.

Getting There

By Car

South entrance, Arguello Gate—Take Arguello Blvd. to the Presidio. Limited parking on east side of Arguello Blvd. 100 yards inside Presidio or at Inspiration Point less than 0.1 mile farther north on Arguello Blvd. MUNI buses recommended.

North entrance, Golden Gate Bridge Toll Plaza—Going south on Hwy 1, turn right immediately after toll booth, turn right again, and turn right yet again; then go under bridge approach, and into toll plaza and metered parking area.

Going north on Hwy 1, turn right into parking plaza immediately before toll booths.

To continue to Lincoln Boulevard free parking area east of plaza, leave plaza on road going downhill (south), and turn left (east) on Lincoln Boulevard. The unpaved parking area is on your left. Look for BATTERY EAST sign.

Alternate North parking, Langdon Court—From Lincoln Blvd. just west of Fort Winfield Scott turn west on Langdon Court to an unpaved parking area near Battery Godfrey beside the Coastal Trail.

By Bus
South entrance, Arguello Gate—MUNI lines 1, 2, 4, 33, and 38 stop on Arguello Boulevard several blocks south of the Presidio.

North entrance, Golden Gate Bridge Toll Plaza—Any Golden Gate Transit bus southbound to San Francisco from Marin and Sonoma counties will stop at the plaza on request .

MUNI lines 28 and 29 daily to the toll plaza.

On The Trail

The Bay Area Ridge Trail runs diagonally across the Presidio from its south--central entrance to its northwest tip, traversing the northeast side of its highest ridge. The general trend of the landscape falls away from this route toward the Bay, so one has stunning views from many points along the way.

As you enter the Presidio through the Arguello Gate, you might note the emblem and insignia on the gate's flanking stone columns. A prominent stars-and-stripes emblem proclaims the founding of the Presidio in 1776, and the insignia of the Infantry, Cavalry, and Artillery decorate the columns. In the more than 200 years since the founding of the Presidio, these gates have been closed only once—at the beginning of World War II.

If you come by car, veer right beyond the gate and go 100 yards on Arguello Boulevard to a parking area at the edge of a rangy eucalyptus forest. If you enter the Presidio on foot, take the trail to your right immediately inside the Arguello Gate and proceed east along West Pacific Avenue. After 100 yards, cross this street and follow the trail north to the parking area on Arguello Boulevard described above.

Across the boulevard on the forested hillside is the entrance to this segment of the Bay Area Ridge Trail route. Before starting up the hill on the Ridge Trail, you might enjoy a visit to Inspiration Point, less than 0.1 mile north on Arguello Boulevard. Spanish soldiers came to this point to scan the Golden Gate for incoming ships carrying supplies from the Old World. Since this military site was, in the early days of the Presidio, Spain's northernmost outpost, the Spaniards undoubtedly scouted the waters for unfriendly ships—British, French, and Russian—which might threaten this tiny toe-hold at the entrance to San Francisco Bay.

From Inspiration Point's wayside exhibits steps lead downhill to a new, unpaved trail which then joins the Presidio's Ecology Trail as it meanders around the southern one-quarter of the Presidio. If you take this trail, you can see a large area of exposed serpentine, California's state rock. Placards there tell how certain plant species thrive on soils composed of this rock to bring luxurious spring-wildflower displays to California's grasslands.

Even if you don't take the Ecology Trail, look on the hillside north of Inspiration Point for a remnant of native serpentine grassland that once stretched across San Francisco. The National Park Service is rehabilitating this area to protect small colonies of two endangered species—the Presidio clarkia and the Marin dwarf flax. If you would like to learn more about the native flora here, you can join a wildflower walk led by a park naturalist. Inquire at the Visitor Center, Building 102, at the Main Post Parade Ground.

After this short side trip from Inspiration Point, wend your way back to the parking area and cross Arguello Boulevard to the Bay Area Ridge Trail route. On it you thread through mature forests of Monterey pine and cypress and a scattering of redwoods. These Presidio forests were planted in 1883 under the direction of Major W. A. Jones, whose objective was to beautify the windswept sand dunes and the coastal scrub landscape, to provide much-needed wind protection, and to camouflage the military fort. He installed plantings on three ridgetops and a circle of trees around the parade ground.

Today, angled sunlight glancing through these trees creates an ethereal, peaceful effect as you walk this trail. Major Jones would be amazed to see the height and proliferation of his forests. The ridgetop trees planted for windshields grew so well that they spread into the valleys, where abundant moisture encouraged vigorous growth. Today's forest is composed of tall, splindly trees, so closely spaced that most of their branches are clustered at the top reaching for sunlight.

The National Park Service plans to do selective removal of some nearly dead trees in the valleys and on the hillsides to afford better Bay views and to introduce sunshine into grasslands, valleys, and riparian corridors.

As you continue up a gentle rise, you see the fence that surrounds the post reservoir in a eucalyptus grove uphill on your left. Through the trees on your right are glimpses of San Francisco's famous skyline and of Alcatraz Island, a former fortress and then a federal prison.

If you hear shrill shrieks of birds in this forest, a red-shouldered or a red-tailed hawk is probably the source. These birds are often seen and heard here. Sharp-shinned hawks, much smaller birds with long tails and rounded wings, have been sighted also. Since hawks don't like to cross open waters, these raptors often use the Presidio for food, shelter, and a staging area and rest zone on their annual migration flights across the Golden Gate.

You make a gradual descent to Washington Boulevard, cross it, turn left, staying on the road's edge for a short distance, and then turn right on Nauman Road. Skirting the back side of former Army officers' housing, you see below the road a huge blackberry bramble, perfect cover for quail and rabbits. If you come to this unique, urban wildlife habitat in early morning or at dusk, you may see quail at the bramble's edge or even on the road. At most any time of day, you can hear the quail's distinctive call, "Be careful, be careful."

Halfway around curving Nauman Road, look on your right in the eucalyptus

The National Cemetery in the Presidio overlooks San Francisco Bay.

forest for a trail surfaced with decomposed granite which leads downhill to a corner of the San Francisco National Cemetery. Built in the 1850s, this was the Presidio's first post cemetery. It was converted to a National Cemetery in the 1880s. Robert Todd Lincoln, son of Abe, is buried here. General Funston, who commanded the rebuilding of the Presidio after the 1906 quake and for whom the southernmost coastal fort of the GGNRA is named, also rests here.

Among the many famous people interred here are the relatively unknown Native American scout "2 Bits" and Pauline Cushman Fryer, a Union spy in the Civil War. Phillip and Sala Burton, heroes today for preserving the Marin Headlands and the San Francisco oceanside beaches and Bay fronts in the GGNRA, are also buried here. Here too, lie the remains of 400 "Buffalo Soldiers," outstanding African-American Indian War soldiers, many of them Medal-of-Honor winners. You can walk through a wide opening in the cemetery wall to find grave markers for these people.

At the corner of the cemetery wall is a United States Geological Survey marker, where a wayside exhibit will commemorate those buried here. From this vantage point you can look beyond the cemetery's white markers, arranged in symmetrical rows on a gentle slope, to the opposite side of the Golden Gate. Here lie more recent military installations, among them the World War II bunkers of Fort Barry and the Coast Guard installations at East Fort Baker.

Also at this corner is a sign that directs you west to a trail that eventually terminates at the Park Boulevard/Kobbe Avenue intersection across from the arched entrance to Fort Winfield Scott. Built in 1882 and named for a commanding general of the U.S. Army during the Mexican-American War, this fort became the headquarters for the coastal defenses of San Francisco in 1913.

Cross Park Boulevard and go under the arch and the elevated lanes of Highway 1 to the sidewalk on Kobbe Avenue's east side. A leisurely stroll beside splendid, hand-laid stone walls takes you past the fort's spacious officers' houses fronted with sloping lawns and gardens of old-fashioned flowers. Bright orange and yellow nasturtiums still flourish here in the coastal fog belt.

At the corner of Kobbe and Upton avenues, turn right on Upton to see the General's mansion, set on a grassy knoll. Its gracious Georgian entry is flanked by double columns on each side of the portico. Where Upton Avenue veers right, continue north on Kinzey Street to an elongated, open greensward—the Post Parade Ground—partially surrounded by former Army buildings. Veer left (west) on the broad Fort Scott walk in front of the buildings for a stroll around the parade ground.

When this fort was built, this extensive open space commanded an uninterrupted view of the Marin Headlands, the Golden Gate, and Richardson Bay. Now trees block some of the near view, but you can still see these landmarks and the Golden Gate Bridge's dramatic, rust-colored towers, which clearly define the entrance to the Bay. Even on foggy days, the towers' tops can be visible, swept clear of fog by fresh ocean winds.

As you amble around the parade ground on a clear day, look out at the blue Bay waters filled with sailboats heeling in the wind, windsurfers skimming across the waves, and great ships, mostly ocean-going freighters, cruising to or from distant ports. Alcatraz Island sits in a swirl of swift Bay currents, now part of the GGNRA, and a National Park you can reach by ferry from San Francisco.

East beyond the heights of this grassy prominence lie Coit Tower, the Transamerica Pyramid, other downtown skyscrapers, and the Bay Bridge leading to the populous East Bay cities. There the Campanile's tall shaft rises on the UC Berkeley campus, and forested public parklands crown the surrounding hills. Topping the distant view are two East Bay landmarks—triangular-shaped Mt. Diablo and half-spherical Round Top, both within public parklands.

Continuing north along the west side of the Fort Scott parade ground, you pass buildings constructed in Mission Revival style, popular in the early 20th century. If you notice a square, two-story building, the northernmost one on the far side, it is the former Fort Scott stockade, now devoid of inmates.

When you arrive at a passageway between Buildings 1207 and 1208, swing left and proceed to Lincoln Boulevard. Carefully cross this busy street and continue on Langdon Court, go through a parking lot, and then pass Building 1648, the former Nike Missile Building. Here you pick up the Coastal Trail for a walk north past four coastal defense batteries built from 1891 to 1900. Along this trail are plaques that tell the story of these coastal defenses, the earliest of which had a one-mile range. (Later Nike missiles had a 75-mile range.)

Just seaward from the missile building is Battery Godfrey. On its landward side you see a ramp used to transport ammunition stored below ground to guns behind low walls on upper concrete platforms. Its rifles were mounted on disappearing carriages and retracted below the battery's walls after firing so the soldiers could safely load the guns.

Just beyond the following battery, Battery Boutelle, you reach an opening with a fabulous view of Land's End, the Point Bonita Lighthouse, and the Marin Headlands. Seaward past the Golden Gate's high cliffs, indented by small, crescent-shaped beaches, lie the Farallons—small, rocky islands 25 miles offshore. On a very clear day, these picturesque cliffs and rocky shores seem quite benign. But when it's foggy, the many-voiced warning horns, now computer-driven, announce the imminent danger of rocky points, small islets, and treacherous tides to ship traffic navigating the hazardous waters at the entrance to San Francisco Bay.

The next battery, Marcus Miller, retains a small square, concrete lookout, known as a base-end station, which in conjunction with another such station, could triangulate the position of its targets or the site of its shell landing.

To continue toward the Golden Gate Bridge, bear left on the Coastal Trail, a top-of-the-cliff path where you hear the surf crashing and the seagulls screeching

Although close to urban areas, the Ridge Trail traverses wild and scenic terrain.

as they battle the winds. From this trail, too, you can get a slight approximation of a ship's view as it enters the Bay. After traversing the wild and scenic coastal bluffs west of Battery Marcus Miller and Battery Cranston, the Coastal Trail dips under the bridge and reaches a trail on the right that goes uphill (south) to the Golden Gate Bridge Plaza. Tourists and locals alike flock here on clear days to enjoy the world-class views of Gate, Bridge, City, Bay, and enclosing hills. Here too, are restrooms, metered parking and a visitor/gift center.

If the weather is too windy and foggy, take the trail on the east side of Battery Marcus Miller, follow it through the bridge-maintenance yard, cross to the sidewalk of the road under the bridge's south portal, and emerge at the Golden Gate Bridge Plaza.

From the north side of the Golden Gate, five completed segments of the Bay Area Ridge Trail lead 35 miles north without interruption through the Marin Headlands, along the flanks of Mt. Tamalpais, and then down Bolinas Ridge to Samuel P. Taylor State Park. For the first of these segments see the description of

Fort Point was constructed in 1861 to guard the entrance to San Francisco Bay.

the *Marin Headlands—GGNRA, From Golden Gate Bridge North to Tennessee Valley.*

But before you go to Marin County, you might take a short, 0.4-mile walk from the toll plaza to Fort Point. You can reach this trail from the plaza by returning to the Coastal Trail and descending north toward the Bay at the Golden Gate Bridge. Fort Point was one of three forts planned in the 1850 to defend the Bay and Gate from attack. The second fort was to be directly across the Gate at Lime Point, but was never completed. A third fortification of about 109 cannon batteries and two mortars was built on Alcatraz Island.

When the Golden Gate Bridge was built, Fort Point was preserved. Now directly beneath the bridge, it stands to remind us of over 200 years of Golden Gate defenses. The Spaniards established a small bastion of 13 guns here at White Cliff Point, naming it Castillo de San Joaquin. After falling into disrepair during the Spanish and Mexican periods, it was claimed by Army Lt. John C. Fremont in 1846. In the late 1850s the United States Army built this massive three-story brick fortress, which was first occupied in 1861 and intermittently used through World War II. Now a National Historic Site, it is open for conducted day tours and special evening programs by the National Park Service.

To reach the Lincoln Boulevard parking area on the east side of the bridge plaza, return to the Coastal Trail and follow it east through a short tunnel built of brick, part of the original Battery East (1876). Beyond the tunnel you can climb to an observation deck to look down at the top of the fortifications, the Bay, and Fort

Point. As you continue east on the Coastal Trail, look for a path that bears right (south) to the alternate parking area on Lincoln Boulevard, where you could have a shuttle car waiting. From this parking area you drive along Lincoln Boulevard southeast under Highway 101, pass the National Military Cemetery, and reach the Main Post Parade Ground and Visitor Information Center.

This trip only samples the remarkable story of the San Francisco Presidio—from establishment of the first Spanish military outpost in 1776 through Spanish and Mexican settlements, the Gold Rush, and the early California statehood period to its present National Park status. Although the military presence is diminished, its influence will stay on with an outstanding military museum, the 19th and 20th century coastal defenses, and the intact, historic Civil War building, Fort Point. Many interesting tours led by experienced volunteers and National Park Service staff offer more detailed information about this historic site. Inquire at the Visitor Information Center, Building 102, a former enlisted men's barracks, situated in the row of historic brick buildings on Montgomery Street facing the Main Post Parade Ground.   ■

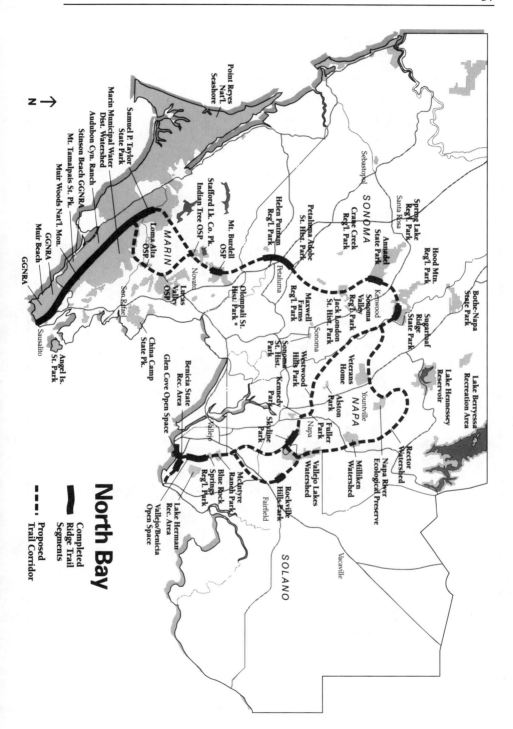

North Bay

— Completed Ridge Trail Segments

╍ ╍ Proposed Trail Corridor

N →

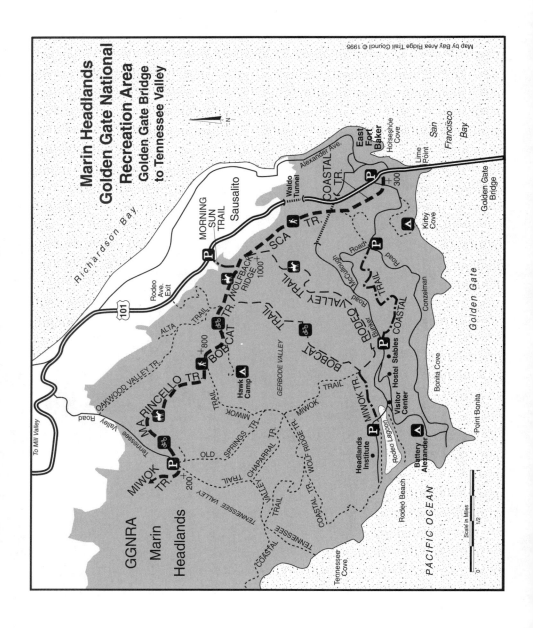

Marin Headlands
Golden Gate National
Recreation Area
Golden Gate Bridge
to Tennessee Valley

Map by Bay Area Ridge Trail Council © 1995

Marin Headlands—Golden Gate National Recreation Area

From Golden Gate Bridge North to Tennessee Valley

A dramatic trip from the Golden Gate Bridge to ridgetops above Sausalito, with views over San Francisco Bay, the coastal hills, and the Pacific Ocean.

Length 4.6 miles.

Location In Marin County, north of the Golden Gate Bridge and west of Sausalito.

Trail Characteristics Width varies from narrow path to wide service road. Often windy and sometimes foggy. Elevation gain of 600 feet from bridge to ridgetop, through open grassland and chaparral. From Bunker Rd. to Five Corners, 700-foot elevation gain. Open grasslands from Five Corners to Tennessee Valley with elevation loss of 600 feet.

Ridge Trail Accessibility
- Hikers—Entire route, as well as bicycle and equestrian trails to Ridge Trail route.
- Hikers only—Coastal Trail and SCA Trail from north end of bridge to junction with the Rodeo Valley Trail.
- Equestrians—From Bunker Rd. trailhead northeast on Rodeo Valley Trail and Ridge Trail north.
- Bicyclists—Connector trail from Conzelman/McCullough rds. junction west to Bunker Rd. trailhead, northwest on Rodeo Valley Trail, northeast on Bobcat Trail to Five Corners, and on Ridge Trail route north.
- Hikers, bicyclists, and equestrians—Five Corners to Tennessee Valley.

Trail Management
- Golden Gate National Recreation Area (GGNRA): 415-331-1540.

Rules
- No park closing hours. No dogs allowed on Ridge Trail route. For information regarding pet regulations on other trails in Marin Headlands, see Trail Management.

Amenities
- North end of Golden Gate Bridge—Ample parking for hikers and bicyclists.
- Conzelman/McCullough roads junction—Limited parking for all trail users.
- Bunker Road trailhead—Ample parking for horse trailers and all trail users.
- Miwok trailhead at east end of Rodeo Lagoon near Headlands Institute—Additional parking for all trail users.
- Marin Headlands visitor center—Water, telephone, and restrooms; open daily 8:30 A.M. to 4:30 P.M.

- Headlands Institute (415-332-5771) offers environmental education programs and conference facilities.
- Hawk Camp—Overnight camping and restrooms; Kirby Cove and Battery Alexander—Group camping; reservations required: 415-331-1540.
- Golden Gate Hostel—Open daily all year from 4:30 P.M. to 9:30 A.M.; reservations advisable: 415-331-2777.

Getting There

By Car
South entrance, Golden Gate Bridge northwest parking—Going north on Hwy 101, take Alexander Ave. exit and turn left to go under highway. Go right up Conzelman Rd. and make an immediate left turn onto road down to parking lot. Or, continue on Conzelman Rd. to parking at junction with McCullough Rd.

Going south on Hwy 101, take the Sausalito exit, bear left, go right up Conzelman Rd., and then immediately turn left onto road down to parking lot.

Bunker Road trailhead—With the re-opening of Fort Baker-Fort Barry Tunnel in 1995, autos and bicyclists may now travel through tunnel to Bunker Rd. trailhead. To reach tunnel traveling north on Hwy 101, take the Alexander Ave. exit and turn right toward Sausalito. The tunnel entrance is the first road on your left (west). Signals regulate one-way auto traffic. Bicycle traffic in both directions; watch for flashing yellow light.

Traveling south on Hwy 101, take the Sausalito exit, turn right and go under the highway toward Sausalito. Entrance to tunnel is on your left..

North entrance, Tennessee Valley—From Hwy 101 near Mill Valley take Stinson Beach–Mt. Tamalpais exit and go west on Hwy 1 (Shoreline Hwy.) for about 0.4 mile. Turn south on Tennessee Valley Rd. and continue to parking at end of road.

By Bus
Golden Gate Transit buses 20, 60, 70, and 80 stop at Spencer Ave. on Hwy 101 daily for access to the Morning Sun Connector Trail. MUNI bus 76 to Marin Headlands on Sundays only.

On The Trail
Hikers, equestrians, and bicyclists take different trails to reach the Bay Area Ridge Trail route and then they travel the same route from a junction often called Five Corners. Each user's route to this junction is described separately below. Trails in Marin County have a long history, and some trails retain their historic names. This narrative and the maps use the long-established names, although some of these do not appear on trail signs. However, the Ridge Trail route is clearly marked on signposts with the blue, white, and red logo .

Hikers start at the trailhead parking near the northwest portal of the Golden Gate Bridge. From the west corner of the parking lot, cross the road that goes under the

A lone toyon tree stands at a switchback on the Coast Trail through endangered species habitat.

bridge and pick up the Bay Area Ridge Trail, also the Coastal Trail, which goes up through a Monterey cypress forest and continues 0.2 mile to Conzelman Road. Cross Conzelman Road and start up railroad-tie steps to begin a 600-foot climb up an open hillside. You zigzag along this narrow trail through coastal scrub, seemingly nondescript, but as the signs warn, habitat for the endangered species, the Mission Blue butterfly. The signs also say stay on the trail.

From a switchback partway up the hill, you can look back over the waters of the Golden Gate past Lime Point. In 1775 Juan Ayala, the first European to enter San Francisco Bay, saw this "white island rock" as he anchored his ship, the *San Carlos,* nearby. Later, it was called Lime Point for its covering of bird lime. Today, the Golden Gate Bridge, completed in 1937, spans the narrow entrance to the Bay that Ayala navigated two centuries earlier.

The trail climbs steeply northwest above Highway 101. At your feet blooms a bright variety of yellow daisies, blue lupines, pearly everlastings, and brilliant red

Indian paintbrush, all of them growing amid bracken fern and the ubiquitous poison oak. As the trail rises, the traffic sounds fade and the view northeast widens to include Richardson Bay and the Belvedere Peninsula.

A small footbridge crosses seeping springs where moisture-loving yellow mimulus thrives. Turn around here and enjoy magnificent views of San Francisco's skyline, Alcatraz and Angel islands, and the East Bay Hills beyond. Northeast at the foot of this hill you are climbing, you can see East Fort Baker's historic buildings, with red-tiled roofs, that ring Horseshoe Cove. This old fort is soon to become part of the Golden Gate National Recreation Area, and it is hoped that the Bay Area Discovery Museum, which is presently housed there, will remain. Beyond Horseshoe Cove, the view of the Bay is enlivened by the sight of yachts heeling over in the brisk winds coming through the Gate.

At the ridgecrest, you come to a trail junction where Ridge Trail hikers should take the right fork (northwest) on the 0.8-mile SCA Trail, built by the Student Conservation Association. The left fork is the Coastal Trail, which goes up over Slacker Hill, then descends west to Rodeo Lagoon. If the day is clear, the views around the compass from this ridge are dramatic. It is here that you first see west across the Marin Headlands to the Pacific Ocean and northwest over the vast expanse of open land that comprises the 12,000-acre Marin Headlands.

Hikers follow trail across Wolf Ridge past white rock outcrops.

These lands were once part of the 20,000-acre Rancho Saucelito, granted by the Mexican Governor of California to the Englishman William Antonio Richardson in 1841. Richardson was forced to sell his land to Samuel Throckmorton in 1860 to cover his debts. In 1855 the U.S. Army bought the tract that now serves the north end of the Golden Gate Bridge, and in 1873 the Army began installing fortifications there, the last of which was a Nike missile site dismantled in 1974.

Continuing northwest on the SCA Trail, climb up a slope where rattlesnake grass and oats blow in the wind, and you come to a sign that states, HIKERS, PRIVATE PROPERTY, TURN WEST HERE. The Ridge Trail turns farther west here as a single-track trail contouring the hillside at the head of a canyon below a row of houses. From this trail you can look 600 feet down into Rodeo Valley and see the west entrance of the tunnel that cuts under the ridge you have just walked along.

Along a grassy slope, accented by jagged outcrops of white rock and flowery in spring, the narrow trail climbs gently, passes through a small eucalyptus grove, and continues for a half mile before turning up to the ridgetop. Here, high above

Sausalito, it meets the Rodeo Valley Trail, the Bay Area Ridge Trail equestrian route, which has climbed northeast from the Bunker Road trailhead.

Now **hikers** and **equestrians** continue past a private road on the right, go left around a white metal, fire-protection gate onto the Alta Trail, and then round the east side of a wooded, antenna-crowned hill. Here the trail passes the half-mile Morning Sun Trail, a connector trail that rises on 300 feet of railroad-tie steps from the Spencer Avenue exit off of Highway 101 in Sausalito. At this exit there is trailhead parking, a telephone, and Golden Gate Transit bus connections.

Hikers and equestrians on the Bay Area Ridge Trail continue northwest from the Morning Sun Trail intersection along an oak-shaded hillside, where there are occasional views of the Bay, and patches of apricot-colored sticky monkey flowers grow on the banks. In about a half mile, you near the convergence of five trails known as "Five Corners" to fans of the Marin Headlands trails, although no sign identifies it as such. Watch carefully for this junction—on foggy days it may be hard to see. Do not continue straight ahead at this junction. Instead, jog about 30 feet left (west) to meet the Bobcat Trail, the Bay Area Ridge Trail route for bicyclists, which comes up from Gerbode Valley. A sign BOBCAT TRAIL identifies this trail, on which you turn right (northwest) and then continue toward Tennessee Valley.

Equestrians begin at a trailhead off Bunker Road at the junction of the Coastal and Rodeo Valley trails in the Marin Headlands. At this trailhead there is ample parking for horse trailers and water for horses. Start your trip by crossing the *ridge trail*-signed wooden bridge over willow-bordered Rodeo Creek and head north along the lower slope of the hill between Rodeo and Gerbode valleys. In spring, the field above the creek is bright with yellow mustard and the air is filled with the calls of red-wing blackbirds.

Head east along the Rodeo Valley Trail and continue along the edge of the valley past rock outcrops for about a mile. In some steep pitches and gentle grades, the trail continues for another mile, winding up to the ridgetop to meet the north end of the SCA Trail, where equestrians join hikers to share the trail to Five Corners.

Bicyclists begin at the same trailhead that equestrians use (above) off Bunker Road. You ride west on the Rodeo Valley Trail (multi-use going west only) to the Bobcat Trail junction and turn northeast here. (Bicyclists can also park at the Miwok trailhead at the east end of Rodeo Lagoon near the Headlands Institute.)

As you start your 2-mile trip up Gerbode Valley, blue bush lupines bloom by the trailside in spring. Ahead is the site of the old Sam Silva dairy, one of the many dairies along this coast owned by Portuguese who came to these shores in the mid-1800s. Now, all that remains is the groves of eucalyptus and Monterey cypress and a few persistent fruit trees and rose bushes. You can make out the cistern that supplied water to the dairy, high on the hill above.

Past the ranch the trail begins its climb up a hillside that looks out over the floor of the valley, where you'd see the City of Marincello, had it not been for the efforts of Martha Gerbode and other staunch conservationists who succeeded in turning

From Hawk Hill, just west of the Ridge Trail, observers track raptors crossing the Golden Gate.

the Headlands over to the Nature Conservancy and then to the Golden Gate National Recreation Area, thus preventing the building of the planned city.

For about a mile the Bobcat Trail winds in and out of canyons to finally reach the ridge above at what is known as Five Corners, where hikers, equestrians, and bicyclists meet to share the Bobcat and Marincello trails to Tennessee Valley.

From Five Corners, **all trail users** follow the Bobcat Trail due west up a slight incline to a spectacular view: Mt. Tamalpais to the northwest, Richardson Bay to the east, and the Pacific Ocean to the west. At the top of the incline you pass a little meadow fenced for "Resource Protection" against footsteps, hoof prints, and wheel tracks, where buttercups, poppies, brodiaea, scarlet Indian paintbrush, and native grasses now flourish. After a small dip and rise, you see the trail that goes southwest a half mile downhill to primitive Hawk Camp. Pause here to look back for a last glimpse of San Francisco's skyline and the tip of the Golden Gate Bridge tower. Above these heights hawks soar watching for field mice and voles in open grasslands and wary rabbits as they hurry across the road to the cover of chaparral.

Continuing on the Bobcat Trail, bear right along the rocky, rutted, main fire road. In less than 1/4 mile you reach the Marincello/Bobcat trails junction. The Bobcat Trail veers left (southwest) uphill, and the wide, signed, Marincello Trail, the Bay Area Ridge Trail route to Tennessee Valley, stays right (east of the Bobcat Trail) in the lee of the hills. It winds 1.7 miles down the road laid out in the 1960s to that once-proposed city, Marincello. At the top of the steep road banks, there are modest stands of Monterey pines, cypresses, and a few eucalyptus, that were planted by the would-be developers of this city. Here and there by the roadside are clumps of willows and tall woodwardia ferns watered by seeping springs.

The hillside falls off steeply east into Oakwood Valley, beyond which lie Richardson Bay and Belvedere. As you drop down into Tennessee Valley, the trail makes a wide curve west. The Miwok stables and corrals, part of an old dairy ranch, are in sight as you near the trailhead at the road below.

At the Tennessee Valley trailhead you will find pleasant picnic tables under a grove of pines. The next segment of the Ridge Trail route continues north from here on the Miwok Trail to Shoreline Highway and Mount Tamalpais State Park beyond. See *Marin Headlands, Golden Gate National Recreation Area—Tennessee Valley to Shoreline Highway.*

For an easy 4-mile side trip from Tennessee Valley, follow a 2-mile trail that leads down to Tennessee Cove.   ■

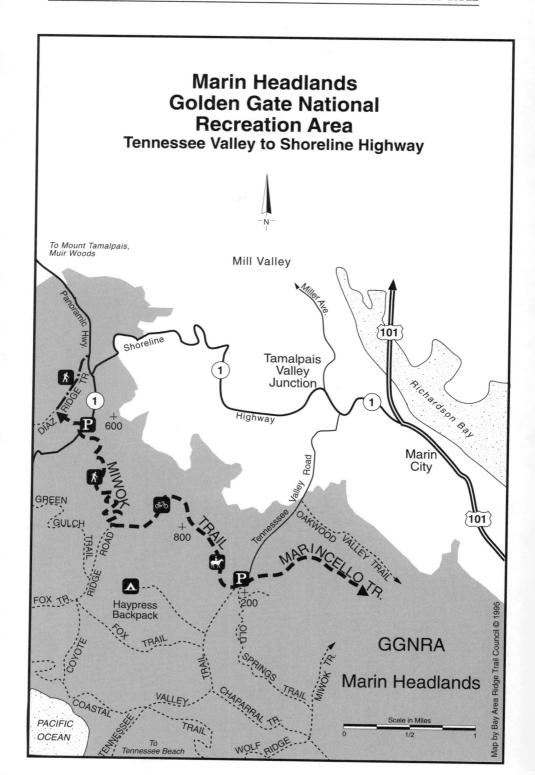

Marin Headlands
Golden Gate National
Recreation Area
Tennessee Valley to Shoreline Highway

—N—

To Mount Tamalpais,
Muir Woods

Mill Valley

Miller Ave.

Shoreline

Panoramic Hwy.

RIDGE TR.

1

101

Tamalpais
Valley
Junction

1

Richardson Bay

DIAZ

1

P
+ 600

Highway

1

Marin
City

MIWOK

GREEN

GULCH

+ 800

TRAIL

Tennessee Valley Road

OAKWOOD VALLEY TRAIL

MARINCELLO TR.

101

RIDGE ROAD

FOX TR.

P
+ 200

Haypress
Backpack

COYOTE

FOX   TRAIL

OLD   SPRINGS   TRAIL

MIWOK TR.

GGNRA

Marin Headlands

COASTAL

VALLEY   TRAIL

CHAPARRAL TR.

PACIFIC
OCEAN

TENNESSEE

To
Tennessee Beach

WOLF   RIDGE

Scale in Miles

0   1/2   1

Map by Bay Area Ridge Trail Council © 1995

Marin Headlands—Golden Gate National Recreation Area

From Tennessee Valley to Shoreline Highway

A trip over coastal hillsides offers sweeping views of San Francisco Bay, with ocean breezes, and flowers in spring.

Length 3.4 miles.

Location In Marin County, west of Hwy 101 and northwest of Sausalito.

Trail Characteristics From Tennessee Valley to trail fork below Coyote Ridge, a climb of 800 feet over a sometimes steep valley trail. From trail fork to Hwy 1, a gentle grade on a service road. Often windy, sometimes foggy.

Ridge Trail Accessibility
- Hikers, equestrians, and bicyclists.

Trail Management
- Golden Gate National Recreation Area (GGNRA): 415-331-1540.

Rules
- No park closing hours. Dogs allowed on the Bay Area Ridge Trail only; must be on leash at all times.

Amenities
- Tennessee Valley–Parking for cars and horse trailers, portable toilets, telephone, stables with water and boarding for horses, conducted rides, riding lessons.
- No amenities along trail.
- Hwy 1 (Shoreline Hwy)—Limited parking.

Getting There

By Car
South entrance, Tennessee Valley—From Hwy 101 in Mill Valley take Stinson Beach–Mt. Tamalpais exit and go west on Hwy 1 (Shoreline Hwy.) for about 0.4 mile. Turn south on Tennessee Valley Rd. and continue to parking at end of road.

North entrance, Shoreline Hwy.—From Hwy 101 in Mill Valley take Stinson Beach–Mt. Tamalpais exit and go 2.7 miles west on Hwy 1 (Shoreline Hwy.). After passing Panoramic Hwy. turnoff north, go 0.4 mile more to roadside parking. There is room for 4 cars on north side and for 6 cars on south side of highway. Do not block fire road gate.

On The Trail

The trailhead in narrow Tennessee Valley lies at a low divide from where creeks flow east to Richardson Bay and west to the ocean. In addition to the Bay Area

Ridge Trail route climbing northwest along the Miwok Trail, a network of trails fans out from the valley for either short, easy trips into the hills and canyons or long expeditions—south into Gerbode and Rodeo valleys or north to Muir Beach and Green Gulch. These trails are popular and very busy on weekends. One such popular trail whose trailhead also lies in the valley extends two miles down to Tennessee Cove, well-known for its powerful surf. It was here in 1853 that the three-masted sidewheel steamship *Tennessee*, on a voyage from Panama, ran aground in a fog. All aboard were saved.

To begin your trip on the Bay Area Ridge Trail to Shoreline Highway, find the Ridge Trail sign and the Miwok Trail sign on the north side of the parking area at the end of Tennessee Valley Road. Cross a bridge over a small creek, and follow its course upstream through a grove of native scrub oaks and non-native eucalyptus, so often imported and planted as windbreaks for dairy ranches in this coastside country.

After ¼ mile, the Ridge Trail/Miwok Trail turns uphill out of the canyon on switchbacks. Looking across the stream you see a scattering of oaks and madrones on the grassy hillside. By the trail are apricot-colored blossoms of sticky monkey flower. In spring, open grasslands are bright with flowers—pink mallow, blue brodiaea, golden poppy, and blue ground iris.

Up several flights of innovative hard rubber water bars—alternatives to railroad ties designed to prevent erosion and to allow both bicyclists and equestrians to maneuver—the trail rises quickly toward the ridge ahead. At the ridgecrest look right to see the Pacific Ocean through a notch in the hills at the west end of

Well-marked trails guide Ridge Trail users.

Tennessee Valley. Soon you see east across Richardson Bay to Belvedere Island and Angel Island, and beyond to the East Bay. Such vistas are surely what were envisioned for the Bay Area Ridge Trail.

Open grassy patches amid chaparral and rock outcrops bloom with pink mallow, silver-leaved lupine, and blue-eyed grass. Along a section of trail ahead is a patch of lupines on which the endangered Mission Blue butterfly depends. The trail had to be re-routed here, on a rather steep grade, to avoid obliterating the lupines.

Looking back across Tennessee Valley, you see the dark bay-tree-covered hill along which the Marincello Trail descends from the south. Above the trail to the north is a grove of tall eucalyptus crowning the hill ahead. Your route circles east of the grove.

As the Miwok Trail approaches the grove, a narrow path marked for hikers only turns left (west) a shortcut to Coyote Ridge ahead. Hikers who choose to travel along this steep, grassy hillside will discover an extravagant display of wildflowers in spring.

However, staying on the Miwok Trail, you will continue north, then west, beside the edge of a forest—a sheltered, shady stretch where wood ferns carpet the ground. As you round the hilltop, you catch sight of the Miwok Trail as it extends north from Coyote Ridge, winding in and out of deep canyons and crossing chaparral-covered hills that plunge steeply into Tamalpais Valley below.

Nearing the ridgetop, you meet the Coyote Ridge Trail, which heads southwest to meet the Green Gulch and Fox trails, and continues then to drop down to the Coastal Trail.

The open hills before you were once part of the vast Rancho Saucelito—extending from the Marin Headlands to Stinson Beach—granted to William Richardson. This enterprising Englishman left his ship in San Francisco in 1822; two years later he married the daughter of the Mexican Commandante of the Presidio. In 1838 he was granted the 20,000-acre Rancho Saucelito by the Mexican governor of California. Because of the failure of other ventures, he soon lost most of the rancho to the even more enterprising Samuel Throckmorton. These lands were subdivided; many ranches were bought for use as dairies by Portuguese immigrants from the Azores. Hay to feed the dairy cows did not thrive along this foggy coast, however, and by the mid-1890s the Portuguese had abandoned their dairies.

Today most of Richardson's Rancho Saucelito remains as open land and is now part of the Golden Gate National Recreation Area. Long gone are the grizzlies and elk hunted by vaqueros and early settlers, but bobcat, deer, fox, and an occasional mountain lion still range over these hills.

From Coyote Ridge, the Ridge Trail/Miwok Trail continues along the hillside and affords views of houses nestled on the hills above Tamalpais Valley Junction. Nearing the highway, you pass through woods of eucalyptus and oak. Ferns line the trail; toyons and elderberry flourish.

Just before reaching the end of this Bay Area Ridge Trail segment, a recently built, short section of trail, buttressed with railroad ties and flanked by round, pressure-treated posts of a greenish tinge, directs you to a point where there is enough sight distance for hikers, equestrians, and bicyclists to safely cross Shoreline Highway. As you head toward the highway, you look west to Muir Beach and the Pacific Ocean. Ahead, across the road, is Diaz Ridge, on which the Miwok Trail continues toward Mount Tamalpais State Park.

From a small parking area on the far side, the Bay Area Ridge Trail sign marks the continuation of the Ridge Trail northward over Diaz Ridge. See *Mount Tamalpais State Park—From Shoreline Highway to Pantoll*. ∎

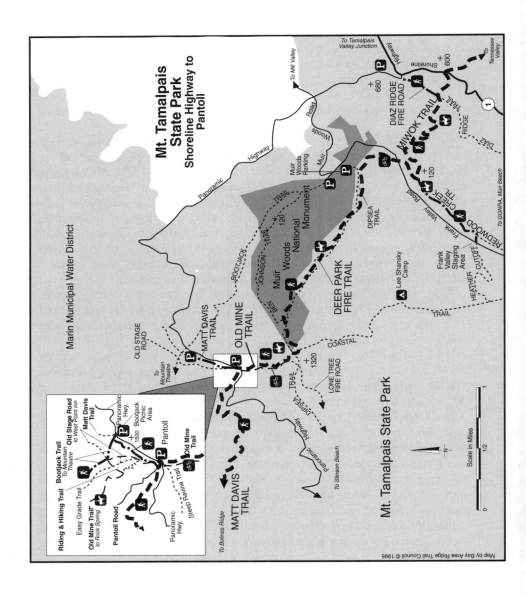

Mt. Tamalpais
State Park
Shoreline Highway to
Pantoll

Mt. Tamalpais State Park

Map by Bay Area Ridge Trail Council © 1996

Mount Tamalpais State Park

From Shoreline Highway to Pantoll

Follow the Miwok Trail down grassy slopes and through oak woodlands, then climb along the Deer Park Fire Trail at the edge of Muir Woods to reach Pantoll Ranger Station.

Length 5.4 miles.

Location In Marin County, west of Mill Valley, in Mount Tamalpais State Park.

Trail Characteristics Miwok Trail descends 2.1 miles on an easy grade losing 500 feet in elevation to Redwood Creek Trail. The Deer Park Fire Trail and Old Mine Trail climb steadily to Pantoll Ranger Station, a gain of 1,400 feet through forests and meadows.

Ridge Trail Accessibility
Hikers and equestrians—Miwok and Redwood Creek trails.
- Hikers, equestrians, and bicyclists—Deer Park Fire Trail and Old Mine Trail/Service Rd.

Trail Management
- Mount Tamalpais State Park: 415-388-2070.

Rules
- Open 7 A.M. to ½ hour past sunset. No dogs allowed. Bicycles limited to fire trails.

Amenities
- No water or restrooms along trail.
- Pantoll Ranger Station—Walk-in campground, restrooms, water, phone, and parking (fee).

Getting There

By Car

South entrance, Shoreline Hwy.—From Hwy 101 in Mill Valley take Stinson Beach/Mt. Tamalpais exit and go 2.7 miles west on Hwy 1 (Shoreline Hwy.). After passing Panoramic Hwy. turnoff north, go 0.4 mile more to roadside parking. There is room for 4 cars on north side and for 6 cars on south side of highway. Do not block fire road gate.

Alternate parking on Panoramic Hwy.—Follow directions above, but turn north on Panoramic Hwy, continuing north around the first sharp bend to roadside parking. Pass through gate on west side of road to well-signed Diaz Ridge Fire Trail and continue ¼ mile to the Miwok Trail.

Equestrians—A staging area off Frank Valley Rd. provides access to the Redwood Creek Trail and the Deer Park Fire Trail.

Bicyclists—Deer Park Fire Trail access off Frank Valley Rd.

North entrance, Pantoll Ranger Station—From Hwy 101 in Mill Valley follow directions above, but turn north on Panoramic Hwy. and continue approximately 6 miles northwest to parking at ranger station. Parking fee at Pantoll and at Bootjack Picnic Area.

By Bus
Golden Gate Transit bus 63 to Pantoll weekends and holidays.

On The Trail

To begin this Bay Area Ridge Trail trip through the southeast section of 6,000-acre Mount Tamalpais State Park, **hikers** and **equestrians** start at the Miwok Trail roadside parking area on Shoreline Highway. (Or, from roadside parking on Panoramic Highway, hikers can take the gated, signed Diaz Ridge Fire Trail west for ¼ mile to pick up the Miwok Trail.)

The Miwok Trail starts on switchbacks up a greasewood-covered hillside enlivened with purple iris and lavender bush lupine in season. A twenty-minute walk up a gentle grade brings you to the ridgetop. Here you meet the Diaz Fire Trail coming from Panoramic Highway and heading southwest down to Muir Beach.

From broad, grassy Diaz Ridge, views open up to San Francisco Bay, Richardson Bay, Belvedere, Angel Island, and across to the East Bay Hills. On clear days, you glimpse the Pacific Ocean to the west.

Straight ahead rises Mt. Tamalpais. Its 2,571-foot peak, upthrust by fault movement over millions of years, now towers over the Bay Area. The mountain was revered by Coast Miwoks who settled by its streams and along its coast and bay waters more than 7,000 years ago. Newcomers from Europe were drawn to its peaks and slopes, and by the late 1800s thousands of hikers thronged its trails on weekends. The Mt. Tamalpais Railroad reached the summit in 1896. Hiking clubs and the Tamalpais Conservation Club, formed in the early 1900s, helped construct and maintain trails. In 1928, Mount Tamalpais State Park was created. From Diaz Ridge you can see many of the trails and fire roads on the mountain.

After crossing the Diaz Ridge Fire Trail, the Miwok Trail heads down into Frank Valley, a drop of 500 feet. This pleasant trail, with alternating clearings of tall grass and groves of oaks, descends on a comfortable grade of many switchbacks. From the first traverse over grasslands you look down into the dark redwood canyon of Muir Woods. Northwest, across Frank Valley, is the ridge followed by the Deer Park Fire Trail. Halfway down into the valley a bench by a meadow offers a chance to pause.

The Miwok Trail follows a tributary to Redwood Creek, passing a handsomely turned signpost which notes that the Miwok Trail was built by the Youth Conservation Corps in 1981. Go upstream from here on the Redwood Creek Trail for 0.3 mile.

**The Bay Area Ridge Trail route crosses Redwood Creek,
a free-flowing, trout-filled stream.**

Where the creek and the trail bend around a jumble of rocks, giant bay laurels spread a wide canopy and a pool reflects the sky and overhanging branches of alders, making this an inviting place to stop for a snack before the long climb to Pantoll. Redwood Creek rises high in the canyons above Muir Woods and flows to the ocean at Muir Beach. Steelhead trout swim up the creek to spawn (no fishing is allowed). The trail follows the creek, crossing a footbridge, then turning up to Muir Woods Road.

The entrance to Muir Woods National Monument is 0.75 mile up the road. However, continue directly across the road to the gated, signed Deer Park Fire Trail. Here, **bicyclists** join **hikers** and **equestrians** on this broad fire road, which swings up through scanty chaparral into oak woodland above. For 2.8 miles it climbs steadily up the ridge to the Pantoll Ranger Station, a gain of 1,400 feet.

At times the trail is in a fir forest, then it crosses meadows and ducks back into the forest again, where the shade is welcome on sunny days. In about a half mile, the fire trail crosses the Dipsea Trail, the route of the 7-mile foot race from Mill Valley to Stinson Beach, run each June since 1905. The Dipsea Trail affords an alternate route for hikers, crossing the fire trail several times, more or less paralleling it to the ridgetop. In another half mile the fire trail emerges on a stretch of meadow from which you can see the domes of a military installation on Mount Tamalpais' west peak.

Red-tailed hawks and turkey vultures with wingspreads of nearly six feet are often seen above the meadow scanning it for hapless field mice or carrion. In spring, these meadows are bright with flowers. You may not see any black-tailed deer, but you can be sure they are nearby from their tracks along the trail.

As the trail enters the forest again, tall redwoods remind us that we are on the edge of Muir Woods. Farther up the fire trail in a forest of Douglas firs, we pass through a corner of Muir Woods National Monument. The trail steepens, veering left to emerge onto broad grasslands below Pantoll.

Westward is a view of the Pacific Ocean, or as is often the case, the fog bank covering it. South and east are the Bay and San Francisco's skyline.

The Dipsea Trail veers west on its way to Stinson Beach and you cross it to continue north on the Old Mine Trail for 0.5 mile to the Pantoll Ranger Station. **Hikers** and **equestrians** can keep somewhat to the right, just above the trail junction, on an alternate path of the Old Mine Trail through a Douglas fir forest. **Bicyclists** use the adjacent service road.

From Pantoll, **hikers** can continue north on the next segment of the Bay Area Ridge Trail, beginning on the existing Matt Davis Trail just across Panoramic Highway. **Bicyclists** do not have a signed, designated Ridge Trail route north from Pantoll; **equestrians** take the Old Stage Road to begin the next trip. See *Mount Tamalpais State Park and Golden Gate National Recreation Area—From Pantoll to Bolinas-Fairfax Road.* If you are not continuing north, you could arrange to meet friends at the Pantoll Ranger Station and go for lunch at nearby Rock Spring or Bootjack picnic areas.   ■

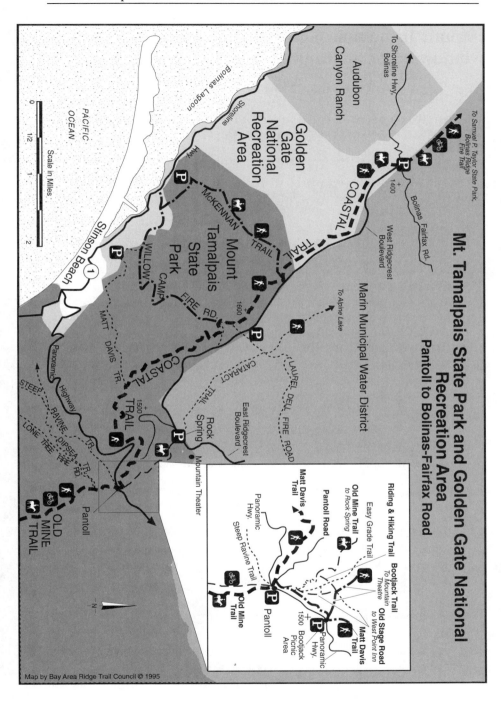

Mt. Tamalpais State Park and Golden Gate National Recreation Area
Pantoll to Bolinas-Fairfax Road

Mount Tamalpais State Park and Golden Gate National Recreation Area

From Pantoll Ranger Station to Bolinas-Fairfax Road

Staying high on the steep Bolinas Ridge for most of its way, this route offers exhilarating views of the Pacific Ocean, Bolinas Lagoon, San Francisco Bay, and Mt. Tamalpais.

Length 6.4 miles.

Location In Marin County on west shoulder of Mt. Tamalpais north of Panoramic Hwy.

Trail Characteristics Often foggy in mornings and late afternoons. For hikers there are a number of gains and losses of several hundred feet. Equestrians gain 470 feet in elevation from Pantoll to Rock Spring.

Ridge Trail Accessibility
- Hikers only—Matt Davis and Coastal trails.
- Equestrians—Old Stage and Old Mine trails to Rock Spring. Coastal Trail from "Apple Orchard" to Bolinas-Fairfax Rd.
- Hikers and equestrians—McKennan Gulch Trail connector trail west to Stinson Beach.
- Hikers and equestrians—Willow Camp Fire Road connector trail west to Stinson Beach.

Trail Management
- Mount Tamalpais State Park—State of California, Department of Parks and Recreation: 415-388-2070.
- North of Mount Tamalpais State Park—Golden Gate National Recreation Area (GGNRA): 415-331-1540, and Marin Municipal Water District (MMWD): 415-924-4600.

Rules
- Pantoll Rd. and Ridgecrest Blvd.—Open from 7 A.M. to sunset; may be closed in times of high fire danger or hazardous road conditions.
- Mount Tamalpais State Park—Trails open daylight hours. No dogs.
- GGNRA and MMWD—Dogs on leash only.

Amenities
- Pantoll Ranger Station—Walk-in campground, restrooms, water, phone, and parking (fee).
- Rock Spring—Picnic area, restrooms, water, restrooms, and hitching rack for horses. Water and restrooms also at nearby Mountain Theatre.
- Along Bolinas Ridge—No amenities. At junction of Laurel Dell Fire Road and east side of Ridgecrest Blvd.—Hitching rack and parking.

Getting There

By Car

South entrance, Mount Tamalpais Pantoll Ranger Station—From Hwy 101 in Mill Valley take the Stinson Beach/Mt. Tamalpais exit, go 2.7 miles west on Hwy 1 (Shoreline Hwy.) to the Panoramic Hwy. turnoff (north), and take it approximately 6 miles northwest to parking at ranger station in Mount Tamalpais State Park. Parking fee at Pantoll and at Bootjack Picnic Area.

North entrance, Bolinas-Fairfax Rd.—From Pantoll Ranger Station in Mt. Tamalpais State Park, take signed road to Mt. Tamalpais. At the Ridgecrest Blvd. intersection, turn left and continue northwest to Bolinas-Fairfax Rd. junction. Park on south side of road. Trail entrance across the road. Or, take Bolinas-Fairfax Rd. west from Fairfax or east from Hwy 1 to junction of Ridgecrest Blvd.; parking on south side of road. Road subject to closure.

By Bus

Golden Gate Transit bus 63 to Pantoll, weekends and holidays only; continues to Stinson Beach to serve the McKennan Gulch, Willow Camp, and Matt Davis trails.

On The Trail

For over a century, Mt. Tamalpais has drawn visitors to its heights for breathtaking views, forest glades, flowery slopes, and challenging trails. The Bay Area Ridge Trail route takes full advantage of these features as it traverses the west side of Bolinas Ridge in Mount Tamalpais State Park and the GGNRA.

Hikers begin the Bay Area Ridge Trail route along the Matt Davis Trail at the stone steps across Panoramic Highway from the Pantoll parking lot. Named after Matt Davis, the "dean of Mt. Tamalpais trail builders," this well-kept old trail from Stinson Beach across the mountain, built and rebuilt over the years, is a hiker's favorite.

Keep left around a serpentine rock outcrop. For the next half mile, the trail contours through a forest of oaks and firs. Soon it enters a ravine where a stream splashes over moss-covered rocks, and giant ferns stand 6 feet tall. Around the next bend, a grassy spot above the trail is blue with hound's tongue blossoms in March. Douglas irises bloom by the trail's edge in April.

As the trail rounds a south-facing slope, it emerges from the woods to cross a steep, grassy hillside and climb over a saddle. From this vantage point, you see Bolinas Lagoon ahead (west) in the distance and, looking back (southeast), the San Francisco skyline. After going in and out of a tree-filled gully, the trail–again in grasslands—reaches the junction with the Coastal Trail, on which hikers head north. From this junction the Matt Davis Trail continues down to Stinson Beach.

The Coastal Trail, now a narrow path—the Bob Cook Memorial segment—turns upward to round a steep slope. From these heights you look down on the town of Stinson Beach, and on a still day you can hear the roar of the surf. As the trail enters a forested ravine, the sounds of surf fade and the splashing of a creek is heard. From

Volunteers help to maintain the Ridge Trail on its route along Bay Area ridgetops.

the far side of the ravine, in the open, the long curve of Stinson Beach is in sight—beyond, Bolinas Lagoon and the white line of waves breaking on Duxbury Reef can be seen.

The trail next crosses steep hillsides punctuated by great serpentine outcrops. In gullies, spreading bay trees, their roots buttressed by these rocks, cling to the hillside. Networks of deer tracks crisscross open meadows above dark, forested ravines. At the forest's edge far below, hikers often see grazing does and their fawns. They raise their heads as they sense intruders.

In the sky, vultures with wingspans of six feet circle in strong updrafts from the steep slopes. On fine days, bright-winged hang gliders share the skies, born aloft by the same updrafts. Taking off from launch sites by Ridgecrest Boulevard, they slowly wheel their way down to their landing site on Stinson Beach.

By March, buttercups and California poppies begin to appear in the grass, soon followed by a colorful array of spring wildflowers.

The Coastal Trail continues in and out of folds on the ever-steeper hillside, climbing toward a spur of Bolinas Ridge. Here you meet the Willow Camp Fire Road, which descends to Stinson Beach from Ridgecrest Boulevard, and the Coastal Trail crosses a saddle in this spur and enters a ravine. On the other side of the ravine beside the trail, a stone bench overlooking the sea honors Bob Cook, the Eagle Scout who conceived this trail and persisted in its completion by volunteers.

Around another open slope, the trail enters woods of bay trees where a lively creek rushes down Stinson Gulch. A bridge takes hikers to the far side where ferns, mossy rocks, and a grove of moisture-seeking maples are a damp contrast to these exposed hillsides.

From the creek you climb up the hillside to Ridgecrest Boulevard. From this point you follow the road's edge around a bend for about 500 feet to the McKennan Gulch Trail gate. From the boulevard, you see for the first time on this trip the Marin hills and mountain peaks to the northeast. On clear days, you can see Mt. St. Helena in the distance.

The Coastal Trail resumes beyond the McKennan Gulch Trail gate and drops down into a tight gully. Railroad-tie steps lead to a rivulet where a Bay Area Ridge Trail sign marks the route. At this point you leave Mount Tamalpais State Park and enter GGNRA lands for the last 2 miles of the trip.

The trail continues around the hill, keeping above the woods of McKennan Gulch and below a small knoll. After crossing a little flat dotted with great boulders and edged by a fence to keep out the feral pigs, the trail follows close to Ridgecrest Boulevard. Below is a green, spring-fed meadow where an old apple orchard marks the site of a mountain cabin. Here the unsigned equestrian trail from the east side of Ridgecrest Boulevard joins the Coastal Trail.

Ahead, a tall fir forest extends over the ridgetop. The Bay Area Ridge Trail, accessible at this point to both hikers and equestrians, bears west under the trees to cross a broad chaparral-covered hillside. The trail then drops down on switchbacks through scrub oaks to cross a dry stream bed before climbing steeply into a forest.

The trail levels off here, and $\frac{1}{4}$ mile farther enters a ridgetop redwood forest. This was the site of heavy logging in the 1850s when majestic trees, some as much as 50 feet in circumference, were cut to build Gold Rush San Francisco. Today, a grove of stately second-growth redwoods shades the summit of Bolinas-Fairfax Road at the end of Ridgecrest Boulevard. Here the Ridge Trail crosses to the Bolinas Ridge Trail, the next leg of the Bay Area Ridge Trail, which is open to hikers, bicyclists, and equestrians. See *Golden Gate National Recreation and Samuel P. Taylor State Park,*

Equestrians leave Pantoll Ranger Station, cautiously cross Panoramic Highway, and take the paved Old Stage Road past three uphill hiking trails. Continue to the junction of the California Riding and Hiking Trail, marked by a water trough, and follow this steep, shaded trail to open grasslands above which are spectacular panoramic views of San Francisco, the ocean, and the multiple peaks of Mt. Tamalpais. After negotiating railroad-tie steps, take a short stretch of the Old Mine Trail, and then cross Ridgecrest Boulevard to Rock Spring parking lot.

There is currently no signed equestrian trail northwest from Rock Spring parking lot for a distance of about 3 miles, until the crossing of West Ridgecrest Boulevard at the "Apple Orchard."* Therefore, from the Rock Spring parking lot riders head northwest along the east shoulder of the boulevard to the Laurel Dell Fire Road, where there is parking also. Continuing on the east shoulder, equestrians cross the boulevard beyond the McKennan Gulch Trail gate and join hikers at the "Apple Orchard" on the Coastal Trail through the GGNRA-managed western slope of Bolinas Ridge to Bolinas-Fairfax Road.   ■

---

* Although an authorized equestrian route does not exist on the east side of Ridgecrest Boulevard, the Bay Area Ridge Trail Council will continue to pursue viable alternatives. For current information regarding both the bicycle and equestrian alignments please contact the Bay Area Ridge Trail Council.

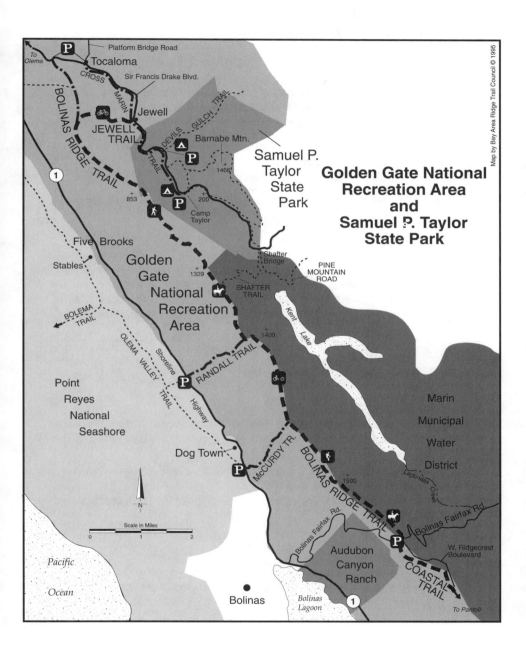

Map by Bay Area Ridge Trail Council © 1995

Golden Gate National Recreation Area and Samuel P. Taylor State Park

To Olema

Platform Bridge Road

Tocaloma

CROSS MARIN

Sir Francis Drake Blvd.

Jewell

BOLINAS RIDGE TRAIL

JEWELL TRAIL

DEVILS GULCH TRAIL

Barnabe Mtn.

1466'

Samuel P. Taylor State Park

1

853

200

Camp Taylor

Five Brooks

Stables

Golden Gate National Recreation Area

Shafter Bridge

1329

SHAFTER TRAIL

PINE MOUNTAIN ROAD

1400

Kent Lake

BOLEMA TRAIL

OLEMA VALLEY TRAIL

Shoreline Highway

P

RANDALL TRAIL

Point Reyes National Seashore

Marin Municipal Water District

Laguanitas Creek

Dog Town

P

McCURDY TR.

BOLINAS RIDGE TRAIL

1500

N

Scale in Miles

0   1   2

Bolinas Fairfax Rd.

Bolinas Fairfax Rd.

W. Ridgecrest Boulevard

P

Pacific Ocean

Bolinas

Audubon Canyon Ranch

Bolinas Lagoon

1

COASTAL TRAIL

To Pantoll

Golden Gate National Recreation Area and Samuel P. Taylor State Park

From Bolinas-Fairfax Road to State Park Entrance

Take these trails into damp forests, through tall chaparral and over broad, cattle-grazing lands for sweeping views of Marin County.

Length

To Samuel P. Taylor State Park—12.8 miles.

To parking at Platform Bridge at Tocaloma—11.4 miles.

To alternate trailhead at Olema Hill on Sir Francis Drake Boulevard—11.3 miles.

Location In Marin County on the ridge between Olema Valley and the Lagunitas Creek/Kent Lake canyon east of Bolinas and west of Fairfax.

Trail Characteristics This wide, unpaved, service road on the crest of Bolinas Ridge descends northwest with elevation loss of 1300 feet. In forested areas trail surface is soft and springy; through chaparral section surface is bare, rocky sandstone. Long stretches of trail on open ridge offer little shade, can be windy, and sometimes foggy in summer. Cows graze on or near trail. The Cross Marin Trail is paved from Platform Bridge south through Samuel P. Taylor State Park, mostly in shade.

Ridge Trail Accessibility

- Hikers, equestrians, and bicyclists—Entire route.
- Wheelchair users—Cross Marin Trail.

Trail Management

- Bolinas Ridge and Jewell trails—Golden Gate National Recreation Area (GGNRA) with operational assistance from Point Reyes National Seashore: 415-663-1092.
- Lands east of Bolinas Ridge Trail and south of Shafter Trail—Marin Municipal Water District (MMWD): 415-924-4600.
- Cross Marin Trail—GGNRA, as above, and Samuel P. Taylor State Park: 415-488-9887.

Rules

- Bolinas Ridge Trail and Cross Marin Trail—Open during daylight hours. Subject to closure in times of high fire danger. Dogs on leash on fire road only. Leave gates to cattle-grazing lands as you find them. When in doubt, close gate.
- Pantoll Rd. and Ridgecrest Blvd.—Open from 7 A.M. to sunset; may be closed in times of high fire danger or hazardous road conditions.

Amenities

- Bolinas Ridge and Cross Marin trails—No water, restrooms or telephone.

- Samuel P. Taylor State Park—Water, restrooms, picnicking, camping, and parking. Current State Park fee schedule applies. For camping reservations call Mistix: 1-800-444-7275.
- Water trough for horses (nonpotable for humans) on Shafter Trail.
- Devils Gulch Horse Camp reservations: 415-456-5218.
- American Youth Hostel reservations at Point Reyes: 415-663-8811.
- Point Reyes National Seashore backpack camp reservations: 415-663-1092.
- Commercial campgrounds and inns at Olema.

Getting There

By Car

South entrance, Bolinas–Fairfax Rd./Ridgecrest Blvd. junction—From Pantoll Ranger Station in Mount Tamalpais State Park, take signed road for Mt. Tamalpais. At the Ridgecrest Blvd. intersection, turn left and continue northwest to Bolinas-Fairfax Rd. junction. Park on south side of Bolinas–Fairfax Rd. Trail entrance across the road. Or, take Bolinas-Fairfax Rd. west from Fairfax or east from Hwy 1 to junction of Ridgecrest Blvd.; park on south side of road. Road subject to closure.

North entrance, (1) The Jewell Trail—Take Sir Francis Drake Blvd. to parking at Samuel P. Taylor State Park, then go northwest 2.1 miles on Cross Marin Trail to junction with Jewell Trail. No off-road parking and no bridge across creek at Jewell Trail. Limited additional parking at Tocaloma at Sir Francis Drake Blvd./Platform Bridge Rd. junction, 3.5 miles north of S.P. Taylor Park, and 1.5 miles northwest on Cross Marin Trail from Jewell Trail junction.

Equestrian parking—Beside Sir Francis Drake Blvd. across from Devils Gulch entrance. If camping, check in at Devils Gulch campground.

(2) Alternate trailhead, north terminus of Bolinas Ridge Trail at Olema Hill—On Sir Francis Drake Blvd. go 4.1 miles northwest of Samuel P. Taylor State Park or 0.6 mile west of Tocaloma (Sir Frances Drake Blvd./Platform Bridge Rd. junction) to parking area on south side of road.

By Bus

Golden Gate Transit bus 65 to Samuel P. Taylor State Park weekends and holidays.

On The Trail

From the heights of Bolinas Ridge there are magnificent views of sparkling ocean, tree-covered ridges, deep canyons, oak-dotted hills, and distant peaks. From Bolinas Ridge, too, are glimpses of Marin County history as you pass trails named for early landholders and tread the paths of Mexican ranchers, Anglo settlers, rugged loggers, and prosperous dairymen of later years. In the Olema Valley west of the trail lies the San Andreas Fault, which made history in 1906 by giving Marin County a violent shake. Just northwest in the sheltering arm of Point Reyes is the bay named for Sir Francis Drake, who is said to have anchored there in 1579.

The Ridge Trail route descends through forests and rolling grassland on Bolinas Ridge.

To start your trip at the Bolinas–Fairfax Road summit, walk or ride into the cool, dark Douglas fir and redwood forest. As you wind along the wide service road, notice on your left the low, wire-mesh fence designed to exclude feral pigs from the Audubon Canyon Ranch west of the ridge. These pigs, once imported for sport hunting, have proliferated and are now a menace to wild plants and animals and are to be avoided by humans.

Before long you emerge from the conifer forest to pass through a dense growth of chaparral and coastal scrub, which makes a low, prickly border on both sides of the trail. From occasional openings in the chaparral you can see down to the coast, and even hear the breakers crashing on Duxbury Reef. Look south behind you to see Mt. Tamalpais, Marin County's most prominent landmark.

This part of the ridge and the lands on either side were once clothed with a majestic redwood forest. With the Gold Rush came a demand for lumber, which in a few years obliterated this magnificent forest. Even some loggers expressed dismay at the devastation. Oxen dragged cut logs down to Bolinas Bay, which was deep enough for ships until erosion-born silt filled it. Today, some second-growth trees have attained splendid heights, and salal, Oregon grape, and huckleberry form a shiny undergrowth.

Just 3.4 miles from your trip's start, the McCurdy Trail begins a 1.7-mile descent west to Highway 1 at Woodville, also known as Dogtown, which once boasted a number of flourishing lumber mills during the logging period. Continuing along the ridge for another 2 miles, you travel through a luxuriant second-growth forest to reach the Randall Trail junction, from which the Randall Trail descends 1.7 miles to Highway 1 in the Olema Valley. The widowed Sarah Seaver Randall, a pioneer of the valley, raised a large family and operated a successful dairy. She held ranch properties here, and her home, awaiting historic designation, still stands nearby.

Beyond the Randall Trail, the forest thins and pastures edge the trail. Turkey vultures wheel through the skies, and a cacophony of bird song comes from the trees. Seeing the cows graze here, you may remember pictures of Mexican ranchers,

Cattle grazing beside the trail remind Ridge Trail users of former Mexican ranching days.

who raised cattle for their hides and hunted the once-numerous elk. After the coming of the Anglos, dairy herds grazed these fields, supplying milk for dairies famous for their products. The cows you see today are mostly beef cattle.

You pass the Shafter Trail, named for the Shafter brothers, astute lawyers from Vermont, who became rich landowners in the county. James McMillan Shafter's house, "The Oaks," now a retreat center for the Vedanta Society, still stands on private property near the Bear Valley Trail in Point Reyes National Seashore. According to legend, one of the Shafter cows fell into a large fissure created by the 1906 earthquake.

Although the Shafter Trail, open to hikers, equestrians and bicyclists, descends east to the Shafter Bridge over Lagunitas Creek on Sir Francis Drake Boulevard, using this trail to reach Samuel P. Taylor State Park is not recommended. No bridge crosses the creek to access the Cross Marin Trail going northwest to the state park, and fording the creek can be hazardous at high water. In addition, lack of adequate shoulders on Sir Frances Drake Boulevard makes its use unsafe.

Beyond the Shafter Trail junction, the Bolinas Ridge Trail, your Bay Area Ridge Trail route, now completely out in the open, drops into little ravines and then climbs up rounded knolls for views west to wooded Inverness Ridge and north to Tomales Bay. On clear days the blue waters of Tomales Bay shimmer in the sunshine, carrying the eye to the bay's outlet on the coast. This long finger of water is on the northward continuation of the San Andreas Fault into the Pacific Ocean.

Beside a spring-fed pond you come upon evidence of past habitation—a depression for house foundations and five eucalyptus trees planted in a tight row. The Longley family occupied a house here until 1888, where Thomas Longley reportedly operated a roadhouse. The house was later moved several miles downhill and eventually destroyed. Today the eucalyptus trees, called "The Five Sisters," can be seen from Tomales Bay. Nothing else remains to tell the settler's tale, but today's cows still come to drink from the pond.

For 4 miles past the Shafter Trail turnoff, the pastoral scene extends up to the forested ridgeline and down to the barns nestled in Olema Valley. When the Bolinas

Ridge Trail curves east around cattle chutes and corrals, you reach a junction from where the Bolinas Ridge Trail goes 1.3 miles north to Sir Francis Drake Boulevard. However, the designated Bay Area Ridge Trail route, the 0.9-mile Jewell Trail, descends east from this junction, following the ridgecrest through steep grasslands punctuated by white, lichen-covered outcrops. Clumps of wind-sculpted oaks frame dramatic views of Barnabe Mountain in the east and Pine Mountain farther south. In spring this spare landscape is brightened by wildflowers of many hues. Rounding a curve at the former Omar Jewell ranch homesite, you pass another line of eucalyptus and a few fruit trees.

Now you drop down rapidly to a gate at the Cross Marin Trail on the edge of Lagunitas Creek. Samuel P. Taylor's mill on this stream, formerly called Papermill Creek, once produced paper bags and newsprint for San Francisco. Today, the 2,700-acre Samuel P. Taylor State Park occupies his mill site. You can reach the park by traveling southeast on the Cross Marin Trail. This trail is laid out along Lagunitas Creek on the historic North Pacific Coast Railroad* right-of-way, bankrolled by the Shafter brothers and other financiers in the 1870s. The railroad extended from Sausalito to Samuel P. Taylor's mill and continued on to logging camps in Cazadero.

This segment of the Bay Area Ridge Trail ends at the Jewell/Cross Marin trails junction. If you are planning to camp or pick up a car shuttle at Samuel P. Taylor State Park, from the Jewell Trail junction travel 2.1 miles southeast on the Cross Marin Trail to the park headquarters. However, if you parked at Platform Bridge or have a shuttle car waiting there, from the Jewell Trail junction go northwest 1.5 miles on the Cross Marin Trail and cross to roadside parking at the Sir Francis Drake Boulevard/Platform Bridge Road junction or at off-road parking behind the Platform Bridge, accessible from Platform Bridge Road. Sturdy mountain bicyclists could reverse direction and make the 1,300-foot ascent to cars at the Bolinas-Fairfax Road summit.

Equestrians with reservations at Devils Gulch Camp can follow the Cross Marin Trail southeast to the first bridge (closed to autos) over Lagunitas Creek, then proceed across Sir Francis Drake Boulevard to the camp's entrance road.

The next leg of the Bay Area Ridge Trail starts in Novato in Mt. Burdell Open Space Preserve. The exact route of the trail between Samuel P. Taylor State Park and Mt. Burdell has not been determined.   ∎

---

* Later the North Shore and then the Northwestern Pacific Railroad.

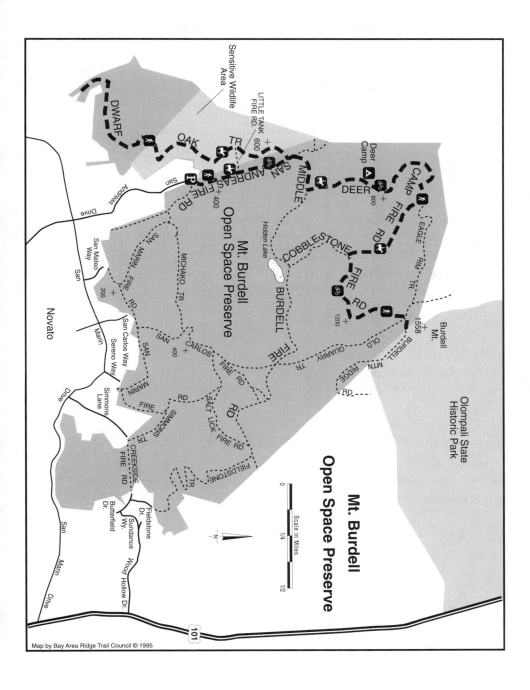

Mt. Burdell
Open Space Preserve

Scale in Miles
0   1/4   1/2

Map by Bay Area Ridge Trail Council © 1995

Mt. Burdell Open Space Preserve

From San Andreas Gate to Olompali State Park

Climb through grasslands dotted with ancient oaks to a spectacular vista of North Bay ridges accented by prominent peaks. A round trip on the Dwarf Oak Trail traverses the Sensitive Wildlife Area.

Length Mt. Burdell—5.2 miles round trip. Add 1 mile for round trip to quarries and overlook. Add 2.6 miles for round trip on Dwarf Oak Trail.

Location In Marin County north of Novato and west of Hwy 101.

Trail Characteristics Trip to Burdell Mountain is entirely on fire protection roads, often rocky and steep, with intermittent shade and an elevation gain of 1160 feet. West- and south-facing slopes can be very hot in summer. Dwarf Oak Trail generally faces east and offers more shade.

Ridge Trail Accessibility
- Hikers, equestrians, and bicyclists—Fire roads on Ridge Trail trip to Burdell Mountain and alternate return.
- Hikers and equestrians—Dwarf Oak Trail.
- On this preserve, fire roads are multi-use; narrow trails are open to hikers and equestrians.

Trail Management
- Marin County Open Space District (MCOSD), Novato Area: 415-499-6387.

Rules
- Open year-round. Dogs allowed on leash, except in Sensitive Wildlife Area. Group and overnight use require permit available through district staff.

Amenities
- No water, restrooms, telephone, or trash receptacles. Please pack out trash.
- Deer Camp—Hitching racks, horse water trough (nonpotable), portable toilet (seasonal).

Getting There

By Car
From Hwy 101 (Redwood Hwy.) in Novato, turn west on San Marin Dr. At San Andreas Dr., turn right and continue about ½ mile to open area on right where green gate and Marin County Open Space District (MCOSD) signs mark preserve entrance. Park on public street. Do not block driveways.

By Bus
Golden Gate Transit bus 50 to Novato at San Marin/San Andreas intersection daily.

On The Trail

This preserve, the largest of the Marin County Open Space District's holdings, takes its name from 1,558-foot Burdell Mountain on the preserve's east boundary. The preserve encompasses almost 1,600 acres of predominantly oak savanna and grasslands interspersed with dense woodlands in protected areas.

The Coast Miwoks lived in this area since 1300, where they subsisted on shellfish collected in the marshes and on acorns and wild game taken from the oak-studded hills to the west. When Camilo Ynitia, the Miwoks' last chief, received a Spanish land grant in 1834, he named his village and the lands surrounding his village Rancho Olompali. He later sold part of the rancho to James Black.

Burdell Mountain was named for Galen Burdell, the first San Francisco dentist. Burdell married Mary Black, who received a large part of the Rancho Olompali from her father as a wedding present. The Burdells built a fine house on the east side of the mountain and developed orchards and gardens on the site of the large Miwok village, Olompali.

Part of the southwest corner of Mt. Burdell Open Space Preserve is set aside as a Sensitive Wildlife Area, and the trail through it, the Bay Area Ridge Trail route, is open to hikers and equestrians only. Since parking and access to the west entrance to the wildlife area are limited, and since there is no outlet through Olompali State Historic Park, all trail users should enter through the gate at the end of San Andreas Drive.

Beginning at the San Andreas Drive gate, **hikers, equestrians, and bicyclists** go north on a wide park patrol road, the San Andreas Fire Road, the marked Bay Area Ridge Trail route, which hugs the wooded east side of the Sensitive Wildlife Area. You ascend gradually for $\frac{1}{2}$ mile through a canyon that terminates in the preserve's central valley. Lying northwest of this valley, there are 1,200-foot ridges fringed with dark tree silhouettes. To the east rises Burdell Mountain and to the west is the low hill of the Wildlife Area. In the near foreground a corral or cattle pen north of the open space preserve boundary sets a pastoral tone for this trip.

Passing the Dwarf Oak Trail junction on the west, you veer east from the valley through sloping grasslands on the Middle Burdell Fire Road to a grove of ancient, deciduous white oaks. One old giant's diameter measures close to 5 feet. In late winter, the great limbs of these trees, gnarled, twisted and wide-spreading, present striking, gaunt silhouettes against the greening fields. In their summer dress these oaks cast welcome shade for human visitors and seasonal bovine residents. The fallen oak limbs are large enough to serve as convenient resting places. It was in this handsome grove that the Ridge Trail's Mt. Burdell segment was dedicated in October 1990.

Just across from this majestic grove the marked Bay Area Ridge Trail route goes left (north) on the Deer Camp Fire Road. Contouring below the steepest part of the mountain, this 1.5-mile trail heads due north, then swings around east and south to join the Cobblestone Fire Road.

After rambling along through the grasslands for the first $\frac{1}{4}$ mile of this trail, you then make a short steep climb, and come to a broad, wooded plateau. Here shady

Deer Camp, a 25-acre picnic and camping site fenced against cattle intrusion, invites you to pause for a snack or lunch. Organized groups can get permission for overnight camping, but they must carry their own water, and no fires are allowed. A portable toilet, hitch racks and a circle of log benches are situated under a canopy of fine Kellogg (black) oaks, large live oaks, and many bay trees.

Resuming your upward way, make a long, steep curve around an isolated clump of buckeye trees on your right. The buckeyes' bare limbs shine silvery in winter, but burst with new growth as early as February to herald spring. By May, the fragrant spikes of white flowers tinged with pink fill the air. By summer, especially in dry years, you will see only dry branches because the buckeye trees' leaves shrivel and drop.

Burdell Mountain dominates the west side of Petaluma Valley.

After ascending steadily for the next ½ mile, the trail levels off, and you can look for the biggest elderberry tree on the preserve. It's on your left, standing leafless in winter, but covered in summer with branchlets of fine leaves and clusters of cream-colored flowers, which produce a fall crop of edible, blue-gray berries.

Shortly after the trail levels off beside a luxurious woods, you reach the Cobblestone Fire Road junction, where you turn left. As you start your climb, the relay tower appears above the forested ridgetop near the west shoulder of Burdell Mountain. But your destination is still 400 vertical feet and about one mile away.

To reach the summit and the boundary of the preserve, begin climbing along wide but rocky Cobblestone Fire Road. This road takes its name from the basalt rock that was quarried here to pave San Francisco streets in the 1860s and 70s. Basalt, a dark igneous stone, is readily split, chipped and made into cobbles. From pits on the west side of Burdell Mountain, Chinese laborers dug out and chipped rectangular 4-inch-thick stone blocks. After loading the cobbles onto wooden sleds, the workers slid them down the steep western face of the mountain. Scars of the sleds' descent are still visible from this trail.

Continuing uphill, you pass lush clumps of California bay trees growing among boulders on north-facing slopes. It's said that the Olompali Miwoks used these boulders as hunting blinds, or perhaps set traps for game near them. As your very rocky road approaches the summit, you see to the left a private road to the relay tower, a telephone company repeater station. Here also, you pass on your right the Old Quarry Trail, for hikers and equestrians only, which drops 800 feet in elevation down the steep canyon between Burdell Mountain and the ridge you just conquered.

The Burdell Mountain summit is just a few feet beyond the preserve boundary, but the trail to it is not open. You bear right onto paved Burdell Mountain Ridge Road, leading to the rock quarries. The main quarry is on your left, well-worth a short walk to see the exposed, layered rock walls of the pits where cobbles were removed. Although small trees and shrubs have gained toeholds in the crevices and masked some of the walls, the size of the pit helps you empathize with the Chinese laborers who excavated it by hand. Just beyond the main pit are smaller diggings, even more overgrown.

On the other side of the road is an overlook that presents a hawk's eye view of the preserve and a series of distant, high ridges almost circling northern Marin County. If the day is bright, you can make out Hicks Mountain in the northwest, Mt. Tamalpais south, and the shoulder of Burdell Mountain curving around to the west. But when fog lies in the valleys, only the ridgetops are visible.

After enjoying the vistas and the red-tailed hawks and turkey vultures that often soar aloft, return past the quarries to a short trail on your right that leads to a very old rock wall, hand-built by Chinese laborers. It marks the boundary of Olompali State Historic Park. Since the trail through this park is not complete at this writing, return downhill on the Cobblestone Fire Road to the Deer Camp Fire Road junction. For different views, a bit steeper route and a rainy-winter surprise, veer left here, continuing on the Cobblestone Fire Road. Curving southwest, this road enters a beautiful, mature oak-and-bay woods. The soft duff under the great tree branches erupts with mushrooms in spring and nurtures ferns year-round. In early spring white milkmaids and blue hound's tongue greet observant trail users.

Follow the trail along a high, open, west-facing shoulder and then turn southeast descending beside a bare, steep mountainside on your left. At the Middle Burdell Fire Road junction lies a great meadow nestled in a high valley, surprisingly inundated in wet winters by storm waters washed from the surrounding slopes. The fenced, flooded meadow, called Hidden Lake, is said to have been deep enough for swimming 40 years ago. Today, when dry, it provides seasonal cattle-grazing.

From the junction bear right on the Middle Burdell Fire Road and go around the meadow/lake under a lush forest canopy. At the crest of a west-facing, precipitous hillside, you descend rapidly, bending northwest through the grasslands, ablaze with brilliantly colored wildflowers in spring.

Soon you reach the Deer Camp Fire Road junction in the grove of ancient white oaks. Continue ¼ mile downhill on the Middle Burdell Fire Road to the preserve's central valley. If you return to this valley at sunset, you will be rewarded with a spectacular view of the northwest ridges outlined against a glowing red-orange sky.

Here, **hikers** and **equestrians** can veer right into the Sensitive Wildlife Area for an interesting 2.6-mile round trip on the Dwarf Oak Trail. **Bicyclists** continue downhill on the San Andreas Fire Road to the preserve gate.

To take the trip on the Dwarf Oak Trail through the Sensitive Wildlife Area, **hikers** and **equestrians** go through a gate marked NO DOGS, NO BICYCLES on the west side of San Andreas Fire Road. Then traverse a grassy hillside where bird lovers have placed several western bluebird nesting boxes. Although these lovely, blue-winged, rusty-red-breasted birds have lost nesting trees and grasslands habitat, they will nest in specially constructed boxes. Their swooping flight, bright plumage, and lilting song bring delight to those fortunate enough to encounter them in the wilds.

Bird flight is darting and quick, but the lovely flowers at your feet hold still, giving more time to appreciate them. Especially beautiful in spring and early summer are the deep yellow suncups and bright yellow buttercups found in the moist, sunny meadows beside this trail.

Continuing west, you climb gradually up and around the mountain that forms

The rare white fritillary can be found on moist hillsides

the southwestern flank of the preserve. You thread through a dense oak-and-bay forest where the stream banks are draped with ferns and honeysuckle. When you come out of the forest canopy, you reach a mossy rock garden and a mound with seemingly stunted oak trees growing from cracks in the rock— probably the trees that give their name to the Dwarf Oak Trail.

Then you return to an evergreen oak-and-bay forest, punctuated in fall by the golden leaves of a few Kellogg oaks. Soon you head west along the grassy slopes just above the neighboring subdivision. At this writing the southwestern leg of the Bay Area Ridge Trail route ends at a gate leading to a path between private homes. It is hoped that someday the trail will extend west to O'Hair Park. But for now, the intervening land is privately owned, so retrace your steps on the Dwarf Oak Trail through the rolling oak savanna and cool forest back to the San Andreas Fire Road.

The next segment of the Bay Area Ridge Trail is in Petaluma in Sonoma County (see *McNear Park to Petaluma Adobe State Historic Park*). Although this destination is about 7 miles away as the crow flies, the exact alignment of the route to that park has not been determined.   ■

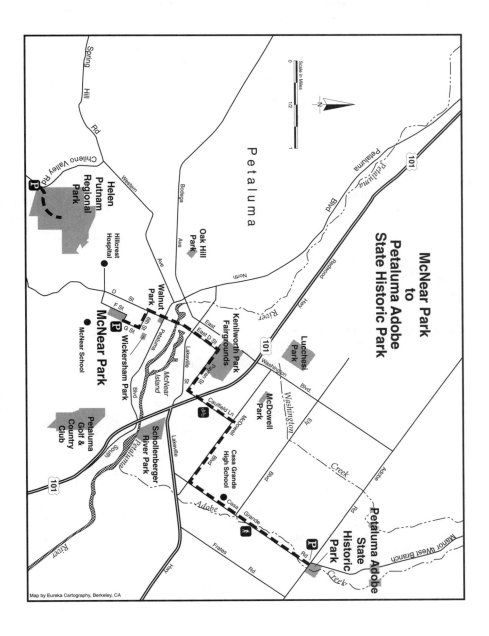

Map by Eureka Cartography, Berkeley, CA

McNear Park To Petaluma Adobe State Historic Park

From 11th & G Streets to Casa Grande/Adobe Roads

Stroll past restored Victorian houses and cross Petaluma River on a historic drawbridge enroute to a foothill eucalyptus grove near General Vallejo's Adobe.

Length 5.2 miles.

Location In Sonoma County in the city of Petaluma and on unincorporated lands east of Hwy 101.

Trail Characteristics In city limits the relatively level route is on paved sidewalks and bike lanes. Mature trees offer shade in McNear and Walnut parks and in older neighborhoods. Neither bike lanes nor sidewalks exist beyond city limits, although the 2-3-foot road shoulder is paved. No shade along this section, except for a large, state-owned eucalyptus grove on northwest corner of Casa Grande and Adobe roads, opposite Petaluma Adobe.

Ridge Trail Accessibility
- Hikers and bicyclists.

Trail Management
- McNear Park; sidewalks and bike lanes—City of Petaluma: Parks Dept: 707-778-4380; Public Works: 707-778-4303.
- Petaluma Adobe State Historic Park—State of California, Department of Parks and Recreation: 707-762-4871.

Rules
- McNear and Walnut parks—Open daylight hours.
- Petaluma Adobe State Historic Park—Open 8 A.M. to 5 P.M., entrance fee.

Amenities
- McNear Park—Picnic tables, horseshoe pits, tennis courts, baseball fields and children's play equipment, restrooms and water. Boys and Girls Clubhouse adjacent.
- Petaluma Adobe—Historic adobe with furnishings of the period, water, restrooms, picnic tables, ample parking, bicycle racks, guided group tours by arrangement.

Getting There

By Car
West entrance, McNear Park—From Hwy 101 take East Washington Blvd. exit, go west on it to Payran St. and turn left (south), then turn right (west) on East D St. Turn left (south) on 6th St. and right (west) on G St. to parking along this street or on 11th and F streets.

East entrance, Eucalyptus Grove, at Adobe Rd./Casa Grande Ave. intersection—From Hwy 101 take East Washington Blvd. exit and go east on it to Adobe Rd. Turn right (south) and proceed to off-road parking at edge of a large eucalyptus forest on west side of road.

By Bus
Golden Gate Transit bus 80 to 4th and C streets daily.

On The Trail

In late Fall 1995, the Bay Area Ridge Trail Council dedicated a trail in Helen Putnam Regional Park and the route from McNear Park to Petaluma Adobe State Park as an official segment of the Bay Area Ridge Trail. The half-mile Helen Putnam Regional Park trail rises to the top of a little knoll (480 feet) and offers views of the surrounding hills and the town of Petaluma. It is hoped that someday the short gap between these two hiking and bicycling trails will be closed.

To begin your walk or bicycle ride at pretty McNear Park on the corner of 11th and G streets, start where a small grove of redwoods casts shadows on the picnic tables, benches, and horseshoe pits set in acres of lush green lawns. Nearby are tennis courts and brightly colored slides, swings, and climbing apparatus for young children, with plenty of benches from which parents can supervise the juvenile scene.

Longtime Petaluma residents may remember McNear Park's benefactor, George P. McNear, who was born in this town in 1857. It was he who gave the land for this park, as well as a handsome sum to maintain it. In addition, he gave land for McNear School, just east of the park, and for a local golf course. Prominent in many civic affairs, George McNear also played an important part in the poultry industry here, which earned Petaluma the name "Egg Basket of the World."

Leaving the park, choose the side of G Street that fits the day's weather—sun or shade—and follow this street east to 6th Street. Here turn left (north) and see several large and handsome Victorian houses. Mature trees in well-kept gardens, surrounded by picket fences, cast welcome summer shade over the sidewalk.

At East D Street you go right (east) and pass more Victorians and the historic city post office. In Walnut Park on your right at the East D Street/South Petaluma Boulevard intersection, a few black walnut trees remain to give credence to the park's name. In this city of many parks, again you will find green lawns, benches, and picnic tables. From each of the park's four corners, a broad walk leads to the charming, round bandstand in its center.

On South Petaluma Boulevard, which fronts the park's east side, you could take a two-block detour north to see the McNear building in the city's 99-building district recorded in the National Register of Historic Places. The McNear building's graceful iron front is typical of the sheet- or cast-iron facades popular here in the 1880s and 1890s. Prefabricated in San Francisco and shipped by boat to Petaluma, these iron fronts were only one item of commerce that travelled on the Petaluma River. In fact, boats on the Petaluma River carried supplies for the 49ers, and then consistently carried grain and farm products downriver to San Pablo Bay and on to San Francisco from the Gold Rush days till 1950.

Returning to East D Street and going just three blocks from Walnut Park, you will cross this river on the historic D Street drawbridge. One of the oldest drawbridges still in use in California, its steel roadbed lifts for water craft too tall to pass under it. Upstream is a mooring and landing facility often used by vacationing boaters from San Francisco Bay. As you cross this bridge, look downstream to McNear Island, for yet another reminder of the "first citizen of Petaluma," as declared by a 1937 historian when George was an active 80 years old. According to the town's General Plan, McNear Island is zoned for eventual park use.

In the next half mile, your way is through a mixed commercial and residential neighborhood on East D Street. At the Sonoma Marin Fairgrounds and Kenilworth Park on Payran Street, turn right (south), continuing for 0.5 mile to a shopping center on the corner of Caulfield Lane. After turning left (east) on Caulfield Lane, you will find sidewalks on the north side of the street and bike lanes on both sides. New subdivisions fill the land on either side of the street and the sidewalks are edged by tall fences and graced with flowering plum trees. Then, making a right turn (south) on McDowell Boulevard, you find ranch style housing, wide bike lanes, and only a little shade.

At Casa Grande Road you turn left, continuing east past even newer subdivisions and the playing fields and sprawling buildings of Casa Grande High School. A planted median strip and new trees bordering the sidewalks continue until Ely Boulevard. You are now on the route to General Mariano Vallejo's partially restored, fine adobe ranch headquarters building, La Casa Grande, although it is

The Petaluma Adobe, headquarters of General Mariano Vallejo, depicts life in Mexican ranching days.

still one mile away. The terrain you travelled on this trip from the Petaluma River was once part of Vallejo's vast holdings during the Mexican period of California.

On your way along Casa Grande Road, you cross Adobe Creek twice and continue toward Vallejo's historic ranch house. Northeast lie the foothills and higher ridges of the Sonoma Mountains, creased by gentle folds filled with California oaks, sycamores, and bay trees. These mountains and all the land east to Sonoma Creek and thousands of acres from the shores of San Pablo Bay north almost to Glen Ellen were part of Vallejo's huge Rancho Petaluma. On his extensive acreage, Vallejo grazed Mexican longhorn cattle, raised sheep and goats, and grew a great variety of crops to supply the ranch's needs. Today, some of the land beside Casa Grande Road still remains in agricultural use.

As you rise into the foothills you come to the state-owned eucalyptus grove on your left at the southwest corner of Adobe and Casa Grande roads. This Bay Area Ridge Trail trip ends at the eucalyptus grove, where you may have left a shuttle car at off-road parking on Adobe Road. Hikers and bicyclists returning to McNear Park may enjoy a visit to Petaluma's riverside shops and restaurants on 2nd Street, just two blocks north of the Ridge Trail route on D Street.

The next leg of the Bay Area Ridge Trail starts in Spring Lake Park in Santa Rosa (see *Annadel State Park)* on the other side of the Sonoma Mountains from here. As yet, the route to this park has not been designated.

Although your Petaluma trip ends here, you will traverse other lands in Vallejo's holdings as you circumnavigate the Bay Area on its ridgelines. See Ridge Trail trips *Vallejo-Benicia Buffer* and *Benicia Waterfront.*   ■

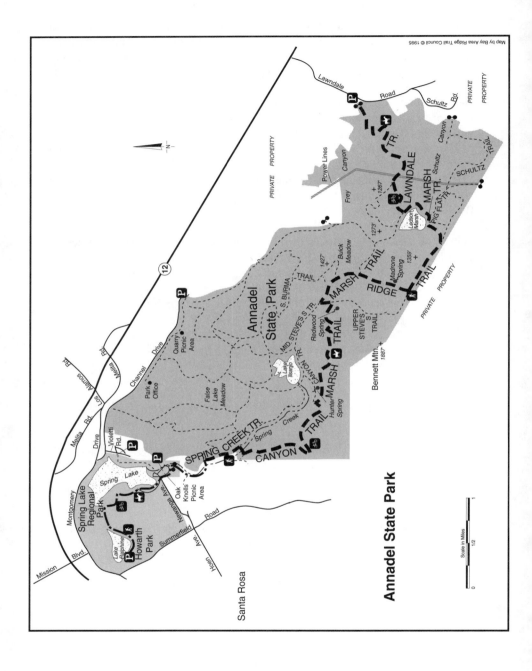

Annadel State Park

Annadel State Park

From Spring Lake Park to Annadel Park East Gate

Gradually climb the west side of Bennett Mountain along rock-strewn, grassy hillsides, through oak woodlands and conifer forests, and then descend past spring-fed meadows to the park's east side.

Length 9 miles.

Location In Sonoma County east of Santa Rosa.

Trail Characteristics Wide, unpaved, rocky park roads. Some trails on west and south-facing slopes can be hot in summer. Elevation gain of 1,100 feet to Bennett Mountain's east side, then subsequent loss of 1,000 feet.

Ridge Trail Accessibility
- Hikers, equestrians, and bicyclists.

Trail Management
- Spring Lake Park—Sonoma County Parks Department: 707-527-2041.
- Annadel State Park—State of California, Department of Parks and Recreation: 707-539-3911.

Rules
- Spring Lake Park—Open from 8 A.M. to sunset, entrance fee.
- Annadel State Park—Open sunrise to sunset, no dogs on trails, bicyclists must observe 15-mile-per-hour speed limit, slow to 5 mph when passing or when visibility is poor, and stay on authorized trails. Trails not suitable for road bicycles nor for inexperienced riders. Current State Park fee schedule applies.

Amenities
- Spring Lake Park, Oak Knolls Picnic Area—Water, restrooms, picnic tables, telephone, swimming lagoon, and camping.
- Annadel State Park—Occasional picnic tables on Marsh Trail, bench and hitch rack at Marsh Trail/Burma Trail junction. No water, restrooms, or telephone on entire Ridge Trail route. Park office, picnic area, water and restrooms at Channel Dr. parking lot. Restrooms at Lake Ilsanjo and at Marsh/Two Quarry trails intersection. No camping facilities, but campsites available at Spring Lake Park and Sugarloaf Ridge State Park nearby.

Getting There

West entrance, Spring Lake Park—From Hwy 101 in Santa Rosa, take Hwy 12 east. At Farmers Lane (marked Hwy 12), continue straight onto Hoen Ave. and pass Summerfield Rd. Turn onto first street on left (Newanga Dr.), and after 1 block follow Newanga Dr. as it veers right. Continue to Spring Lake Park entrance and go right to parking at Oak Knolls Picnic Area.

East entrance, Lawndale Rd.—In Santa Rosa take Hwy 12 east about 9 miles, then turn south on Lawndale Rd. and continue about 1 ½ miles to a small parking area on right side of road.

On The Trail

Two local parks are connected by trail to Annadel State Park—Howarth City Park and Spring Lake County Park. This trip begins at the Oak Knolls Picnic Area in Spring Lake Park and follows a gravelled road on the levee beside Spring Creek. In summer the creek is dry, but in winter water flows from the northwest side of Bennett Mountain through Annadel State Park to the flood-control basin of Spring Lake. The gravelled trail, much favored by local bicyclists, hikers, and equestrians, leads due south along the base of a west-facing hillside, just outside Annadel State Park's boundary.

After ½ mile the levee trail crosses the creek and then continues outside the park boundary for another ½ mile. Where the trail crosses a concrete weir for Spring Creek flood control, you go straight ahead to enter Annadel State Park's 5,000 wilderness acres. Immediately you step into an oak-and-buckeye woodland on the Canyon Trail. The stone foundations on your right are all that remain of a cabin built by one Dr. Summerfield, a former owner of this land. However, all the land in this park had been part of Rancho Los Guilicos, granted in 1839 to a Scottish sea captain, John Wilson, a Mexican sympathizer, who was married to Ramona Carrillo de Pacheco. Since Wilson was away at sea most of the time, his nearly 19,000 acres remained relatively untouched.

Long before Mexican expansion, local Native Americans inhabited this land for generations. They were a southern group of Pomos, described as The Bitakomtara. It is thought that there were about 20 tribelets, each speaking a slightly different dialect and occupying its own land. The Bitakomtara territory encompassed approximately 200 square miles in the Santa Rosa area, from Laguna de Santa Rosa

Moss-covered Sonoma Volcanic rocks and native grasses cover hillsides on the Marsh Trail.

east to Sonoma Creek, and south from Mark West Creek nearly to Cotati.

The Native Americans lived well on this land, harvesting acorns from several species of oaks, fishing the creeks and hunting or trapping game, especially deer, squirrels, and rabbits. On this trip over former Native American lands you will see many oak trees, find their acorns on the trail, pass springs that feed the creeks, and traverse the meadows where these native people could dig bulbs and harvest berries, seeds, and grains. In spite of many changes of ownership, little has changed this land's meadows and woods. Today's visitors can find a near-wilderness here, especially on the more remote Bay Area Ridge Trail route.

Continuing on the Canyon Trail, you emerge from the shady forest into a gentle valley, and see ahead the low, rounded ridge of Taylor Mountain, and in the foreground large homes of a nearby subdivision. After you make a hairpin turn to the left, your uphill way begins in earnest. From this open hillside you can look down to Spring Lake in the north and beyond to Rincon Valley. On clear days Mt. St. Helena's long shoulder, with its taller, prominent left hump, is visible in the distance. Looking south from this trail at 1,000 feet, you see Bennett Mountain's 1,887-foot summit just outside the park.

If you come here in late March or early April, you may find the rare white fritillary blooming on a moist hillside in the grasslands. Soon the wide but rocky road (your trail) comes to an intersection, where you leave the Canyon Trail and take a 1.6-mile segment of the Marsh Trail, still climbing. Along this trail are splendid examples of northern oak woodlands made up of Oregon white oaks, black oaks, buckeyes, and occasional manzanitas. Beautiful, lush stands of California fescue, a native gray-green bunchgrass with tall, graceful stalks and feathery flower heads, fill the spaces between rounded, moss-covered boulders on the forest floor. The Pomo people collected fescue seeds for food.

In the shade of redwoods and Douglas firs, with soft duff underfoot, you cross the headwaters of Spring Creek. Here where the road banks are draped with ferns and redwoods tower overhead, a quiet serenity seems to prevail. You continue in forest past the foot trails, Upper Steve's S Trail on the right and his Middle S Trail on the left.

In another half mile you come out of the woods at the edge of a great, grassy field, Buick Meadow. At a junction with the Burma Trail, a bench and hitchrack invite you to rest and enjoy the grass-lands, golden in summer, velvety green in winter and spring. You take the Marsh Trail, which goes right past a magnificent stand of Oregon white and California black oaks that graces the slopes above the meadow. Some are over 200 years old. Biologists tell us that these oaks are not regener-ating, although the trees are setting seed. Appar-ently there are not enough predators to keep the

Emerging from the woodlands, hikers step into Buick Meadow.

rodents—mice, voles, and squirrels who eat the acorns—under control. Hawks and owls, as well as coyotes, are the rodent's natural predators.

After 0.3 mile the Marsh Trail swings left (east) and you take the Ridge Trail right (south) through a 100-acre controlled burn that took place in 1994. The oaks, manzanita, and coyote bush will survive fire very well, but Douglas firs and invasive eucalyptus do not. The more desirable trees and shrubs are already root-sprouting and looking very healthy. The meadows will be filled with flowers and the bunchgrass will be lush after winter rains.

Beyond Madrone Spring, nonpotable and dry most of the year, you reach the 150-year-old rock wall marking the southern boundary of the park and of Rancho Los Guilicos. Here at the 1,400-foot high point of your trip, look north across the meadows and Ledson Marsh to Hood Mountain and Sugarloaf Ridge State Park. Hood Mountain is named in honor of William Hood, who owned Rancho Los Guilicos for almost 30 years. Just east of Hood Mountain lie Bald Mountain and Red Mountain, both on the Bay Area Ridge Trail route through Sugarloaf Ridge State Park. The rocks in the fence here and those strewn about the hillsides and grasslands are mostly basalt, an igneous rock of the Pliocene Age Sonoma Volcanics formation that is found throughout the Sonoma and Mayacmas Mountains.

If you have a knapsack lunch, start looking for a picnic table under a lovely oak after the Ridge Trail turns north toward Ledson Marsh. If you pass the Pig Flat Trail going right, you've missed the table, but it is just a short distance back to it.

When you feel refreshed, rejoin the Marsh Trail on the east side of the marsh. A low dam contains the natural winter run-off from the hillsides until summer's heat prevails. In fall, the reeds' gold and brown tones present a subdued contrast to the dark green woods.

At a trail junction on the north side of the marsh, swing right on the Lawndale Trail to begin your descent to the park's east entrance. In the next 1/3 mile look for piles of chips and dark basalt rock, remains of cobblestone quarrying that occurred in the late 19th century. Basalt rocks like those you have stepped on and walked around on the trail, and those you've seen lying on the hillsides, were chipped and shaped into paving stones by European immigrants, then sent by barge and train to San Francisco. It was a thriving industry until modern auto users preferred smoother rides.

At the park office is an exhibit of previous quarrying done by the Pomo people, who shaped obsidian into arrowheads, knives, scrapers, and spearheads. Since these artifacts are significant clues to the Native American culture, visitors are asked to leave them intact wherever they are seen.

Now on your final 1.6-mile descent, you cross under powerlines and weave in and out of ravines in a last redwood-and-fir forest. Restored in mind and spirit after this trip on the park's remote trails, you traverse a south-facing hillside in a grassy canyon and go through a gate at the Lawndale Road parking area.

The next leg of the Bay Area Ridge Trail begins in Sugarloaf Ridge State Park, which is about 5 miles northeast of this parking area. See *Sugarloaf Ridge State Park.*   ■

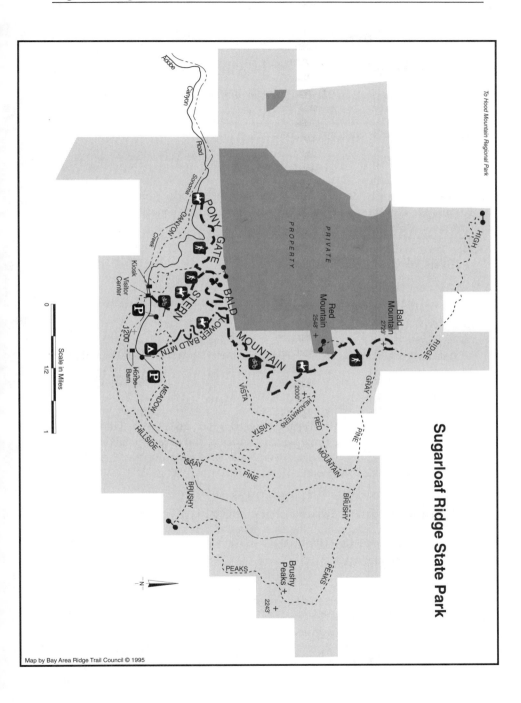

Sugarloaf Ridge State Park

Scale in Miles
0   1/2   1

Map by Bay Area Ridge Trail Council © 1995

Sugarloaf Ridge State Park

From Visitor Center to Bald Mountain Summit

This trip takes you from an enclosed, remote valley to a mountaintop with unobstructed, far-flung views of Northern California.

Length   5.4 miles round trip; 6.7 miles using hikers' alternate return.

Location   In Sonoma County east of Santa Rosa in the Mayacmas Mountains.

Trail Characteristics   Most of route is on service roads that traverse grasslands, oak-fir-madrone woodlands and chaparral-covered slopes. One section of road is paved. Elevation gain of 1,500 feet from visitor center to top of Bald Mountain. Summer temperatures can be very high.

Ridge Trail Accessibility
- Hikers, bicyclists, and equestrians.

Trail Management
- State of California, Department of Parks and Recreation: 707-833-5712.

Rules
- Park open daily. Fee for day use, car camping and group camping. Current State Park fee schedule applies. Dogs must be on leash at all times, not allowed on trails.

Amenities
- Water, restrooms, and parking near picnic areas with barbecues and tables. Campsites with tables, fire rings, restrooms, water, no showers. Group campsite with barbecues, fire rings, water, pit toilets, and several small corrals for horses. Visitor center with deck, telephone. Concession-operated stables for horse rental, guided rides only.

Getting There
- From Hwy 12 east of Santa Rosa or northwest of Kenwood, turn north on Adobe Canyon Rd., continuing to road's end. Parking area is on left after passing park entrance kiosk and visitor center. Horse trailers park just past barn 0.5 mile beyond kiosk.

On The Trail
Hikers and bicyclists start this trip on the Stern Trail, just across the entrance road from the visitor center. The center is a convenient meeting place for groups, and its displays provide a background to the park's natural and cultural history. The wide Stern Trail heads uphill, northwest, through grasslands and past scattered clumps of scrub oak. **Equestrians** ride from the barn to the group campsite parking area, then go west on the Lower Bald Mountain Trail, which turns uphill to join the Bald Mountain Trail.

At the Stern/Bald Mountain Trail junction you might pause to look west over the Sonoma Creek canyon to ridge after ridge of coastal mountains between here and the sea. If early morning fog lies in the interior valleys, the ridgetops peek out, giving the effect of islands rising from misty inland seas. Conical Hood Mountain is on your right, the highest point in neighboring Hood Mountain Regional Park. Due south beyond the park's boundary is the rugged linear ridge from which Sugarloaf Ridge State Park takes its name. The bare rock columns on its north face are remnants of nearby Mt. St. Helena's volcanic activity some seven million years ago. Look for that sleeping giant when you reach the end of this trip.

Now take the Bald Mountain Trail on your right (northwest), pass around a metal gate across the paved road and begin your ascent in earnest. The cuts on this road, built for service vehicles enroute to the microwave station on Red Mountain, reveal large veins of bluish-green serpentine, our California State rock and an indicator of fault zones. The St. John's Mountain Fault crosses this mountain.

If you take this trail early in the day in summer, the high road banks and modest oak-fir-madrone woodlands offer much-needed shade. In spring, clumps of iris edge the road, brightening your way with lavender or cream blossoms. Even in summer, apricot-colored sticky monkey flowers, purple asters, and the tawny, two-foot flower stalks of native bunchgrass grace the road's edge.

In less than ½ mile you reach the junction with the Lower Bald Mountain Trail, an equestrian connector to the Ridge Trail. If the day is clear, you can see south to Mt. Tamalpais in Marin County. In almost any weather, you can look down on the park's meadows, barns, and visitor center.

Then continuing steadily uphill, you pass the Vista Trail. A short detour on this trail will take you to a lovely vernal pool. This depression, filled with winter rains, contains a unique community of springtime plants that bloom and die in concentric rings as the waters recede. Enjoy it from the trail and respect its fragile environment.

Black oaks grow beside trail on upper slopes of Bald Mountain.

Return to the Bald Mountain Trail, where the vegetation alternates between woodland and chaparral, depending on soil and exposure. On stretches of trail facing due south, chaparral covers the slopes. Then farther uphill, oaks and madrones fill little ravines, often in the company of bay trees. These oaks and madrones are old-growth trees, but in the valleys below, an 1880s settler stripped the hardwood forest. He burned the wood for charcoal, which he then sold to heat homes and run steam engines in nearby communities.

There is evidence of early Native American habitation here since about 5000 B.C. The last group were the Wappos, whose village was called Wilikos. The natives' firm resistance to the intruding Spaniards earned them the name Wappo, a derivative of the Spanish word for brave, *guapo*. However, weakened by cholera and smallpox, their numbers diminished and they were eventually relocated to a Pomo reservation. The last full-blooded Wappo died in 1909.

The Spaniards ran cattle on these hills before the arrival of the first settlers, in 1867. But farming was never very successful here, and in 1920 the State of California purchased these lands for a reservoir, which never materialized. Later, Sonoma State Hospital ran a summer camp program with swimming pool and cookhouse. In 1964 the area became part of the California State Park System.

Now, as you climb to the heights of this 2,700-acre park, you can turn back often to look over the steep, rugged terrain that previous peoples struggled with. Except for a large vineyard just outside the southern boundary of the park and a few large ranches on the west, little agricultural activity remains in the mountains. Instead, many acres north of Adobe Canyon Road are in public open space—Sugarloaf Ridge State Park and Hood Mountain Regional Park.

Resuming the upward climb, you round bends and curve into heads of small ravines, still on the paved road. Past the Red Mountain Trail cut-off at about 2,200 feet, you begin to see black oaks and bigleaf maple trees on the east-facing slopes that drain into Sonoma Creek's headwaters. Then, off to the northeast and across a steep ravine, you see the grass and brush-covered slopes of the park's northern ridge, along which the Gray Pine Trail extends to meet the Brushy Peaks Trail. When the paved road turns sharply left to ascend private Red Mountain, the Bald Mountain Trail goes right and then immediately left on a very steep dirt road. Now you traverse open, sloping grasslands dotted with bright wildflowers in spring and glowing, rosy-red buckwheat in fall.

In about 0.4 mile from the turnoff you veer around the north side of the summit and reach the junction with the High Ridge and Gray Pine trails. The former heads downhill, a tempting direction after the last upward pitch, but instead, take the Gray Pine Trail right for about 100 yards. Then go right to reach the summit—a rounded, bare mountaintop. An exhilarating 360-degree sweep around the compass greets you. Identified on two vista displays are (clockwise from San Francisco): the towers of the Golden Gate Bridge, Mt. Tamalpais, the Sonoma hills, Mt. St. Helena, the long Blue Ridge separating Napa County from the Central Valley, Mt. Diablo and then back to San Francisco. Even Snow Mountain to the north and the Sierra Nevada to the east are visible on a clear winter day. With Northern California at your feet, here's the place for a pleasant picnic. Or you can find a protected shelf just below the summit for the view north to Mt. St. Helena.

Since the Bay Area Ridge Trail route between this park and the next completed segment in Napa County (see *Skyline Wilderness Park*) is not determined, you must return downhill—a faster trip than your upward trek. **Hikers:** on your return from the mountaintop, combining the Gray Pine and Meadow trails makes an interesting and extended loop trip.

■

View east-northeast from Bald Mountain (Sierra Nevada on horizon.)

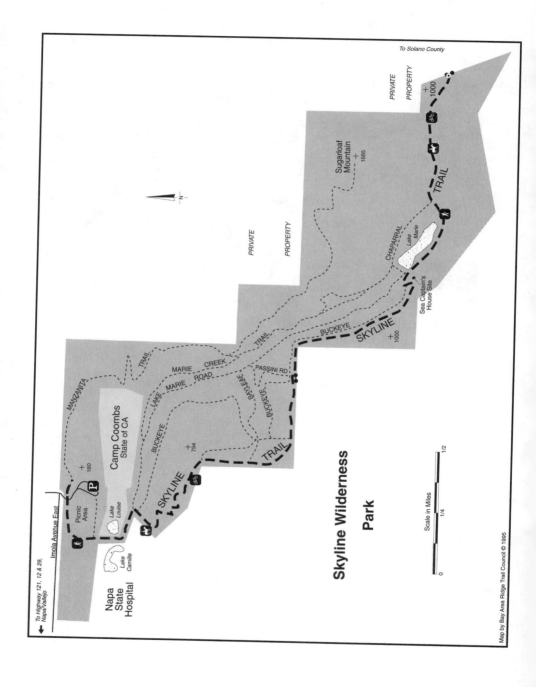

To Solano County

PRIVATE PROPERTY

+ 1000

TRAIL

Sugarloaf Mountain
+ 1685

PRIVATE PROPERTY

CHAPARRAL

Lake Marie

Sea Captain's House Site

BUCKEYE   SKYLINE

TRAIL   + 1000

MARIE   CREEK

TRAIL

LAKE   MARIE   ROAD   PASSINI RD.

BAYLEAF

MANZANITA   TRAIL   BUCKEYE   BUCKEYE

Camp Coombs
State of CA   + 794   TRAIL

SKYLINE   SKYLINE

P   TRAIL

Lake Louise

Picnic Area   + 160

Imola Avenue East

To Highway 121, 12 & 29,
Napa/Vallejo

Napa State Hospital

Lake Camille

N

Skyline Wilderness

Park

Scale in Miles

0   1/4   1/2

Map by Bay Area Ridge Trail Council © 1995

Skyline Wilderness Park

From Park Entrance to South Boundary

After a steep climb in the first mile, this trail ambles through oak forests and high grasslands to views of North Bay marshes and mountains, then continues beside a perennial stream to the far reaches of the park.

Length 8.8 miles round trip; no exit at southeast end.

Location In Napa County near Napa State Hospital in southern foothills of Napa Valley.

Trail Characteristics This trail is for hardy hikers and careful equestrians and bicyclists. It is a narrow, often rocky trail with limited visibility.

Ridge Trail Accessibility
- Hikers, equestrians, and bicyclists—Entire route.

Trail Management
- Skyline Park Citizens Association: 707-252-0481.

Rules
- Park open from 9 A.M. to sunset. Skyline Park's current day-use fees apply, varying in amount for different conveyances and different trail users. No swimming in lake. No dogs on trails or in picnic area.

Amenities
- Parking, restrooms, and water at picnic area near park entrance. Several picnic tables near Lake Marie, approximately 3 miles up the trail. Horse arena, archery range, overnight RV facilities available.

Getting There
- From Hwy 29 south of Napa, turn east on Imola Ave. After passing Napa State Hospital, look for the park entrance on the right (south).

On The Trail

Skyline Wilderness Park was established in 1983 when 850 acres of Napa State Hospital grounds were declared surplus by the State of California. A dedicated local group, wishing to preserve the beautiful Marie Creek Canyon and its surrounding watershed, formed the nonprofit Skyline Park Citizens Association. It leases the land from the state and manages these foothill forests and grasslands for public enjoyment. Today, many trails thread through the park, and others are planned to reach its highest point, Sugarloaf Mountain. The Skyline Trail, designated as a section of the Ridge Trail, is the most westerly and longest route, reaching the southeastern park boundary near the Solano county line. Plan for a round trip of at least 8+ miles, start early, especially on warm days, and take plenty of water.

To begin this trip, leave the picnic area near the park entrance and bear right to gravelled Lake Marie Road, which crosses a fenced causeway between two ponds, Lake Louise and Lake Camille, still part of the State Hospital grounds. Lake Marie Road bends left (east), and in about 600 feet, you turn right (southeast) off it onto the Skyline Trail and, in a few yards, pass the Buckeye Trail.

The Skyline Trail zigzags up a steep hill studded with volcanic rock outcrops. At each bend west, the trail comes close to a low wall, built of these rocks gathered in early ranching days. In spring, native wildflowers—bright orange, yellow and blue—accent the green grasslands; in summer, golden oats contrast with the dark lichen-covered rocks.

You now enter an oak-and-buckeye woods where the trail straightens and levels off a bit, having gained almost 600 feet in elevation in less than a mile. As the trail heads south, lovely views open to the Napa marshlands edging San Francisco Bay. On beyond lies majestic Mt. Tamalpais. Not so attractive is the open jaw of an immense rock quarry, gnawing close to the park boundary.

At a trail junction the Bayleaf Trail arcs left (east), but the Skyline Trail keeps to the right here and at all trail junctions on the outward-bound trip, most of which are well-marked. Now you are on a high grassy meadow, where the light-pink blooms of bitterroot are found in spring. Although bitterroot implies an unpleasant taste, Native Americans considered it a delicacy when peeled and cooked.

Then the trail veers east through chaparral shrubs and ubiquitous poison oak, contours along the hillside and heads down to a crossroads. Here a spur road from Lake Marie Road enters a private holding outside the park through the "Passini Gate."

Pink checker blooms dot grasslands in spring.

Just across this road in an oak woodland, you start climbing to the high grasslands at the western edge of the park. When it's clear, you can see chaparral-covered Mt. George due north and Mt. Tamalpais southwest. Seen too, are hawks and scrub jays, woodpeckers and towhees, just a few of the many birds that the quiet hiker can observe in this wilderness park. In the soft dirt of the path, you will see the prints of many animals—deer, raccoons, bobcats, and even feral pigs.

Now 2.3 miles from the park entrance, you traverse a steep hillside where perennial Marie Creek cuts a deep cleft between this hillside and 1,630-foot Sugarloaf Mountain. Here in a dense forest, the trailside is festooned with ferns.

Then in a small clearing, you come upon the skeleton of a house—a tall chimney and stonework foundations. Although known as the Sea Captain's House, local historians say that it was originally built for the gatekeeper who tended the dam at Lake Marie, just a few hundred feet below. When the state decided it no longer needed the gatekeeper, it took down his house. A trail turnoff nearby goes down to the lake, but the Skyline Trail continues above.

From here the trail follows an old, rocky roadbed through a mature oak-and-fir forest. It then descends to cross the creek upstream from the lake. Now on the north side of Marie Creek, look for some boulders to perch on while eating your knapsack lunch. This beautiful, remote wilderness truly befits the park's name.

Note a left turnoff (northwest) for the Chaparral Trail, an alternate route for your return trip. However, continuing on the Skyline Trail for the next 1.1 miles, you follow the meandering creek, leaving it only to skirt a sloping meadow. Then you cross to the south side of Marie Creek where a tributary joins it. On a gentle forest path, you soon reach a locked gate, the trail's end.

It is planned that someday this trail will continue south into Solano County to join other Bay Area Ridge Trail segments in Fairfield, Vallejo, and Benicia. In the meantime, retrace your steps along the route you just followed or return by any of several other trails that lead to the park entrance. The Chaparral and Marie Creek trails, for hikers only, and Lake Marie Road, multi-use, return through the valley.

The next segment of the Bay Area Ridge Trail begins in the hills west of Fairfield. See *Rockville Hills Community Park*.   ■

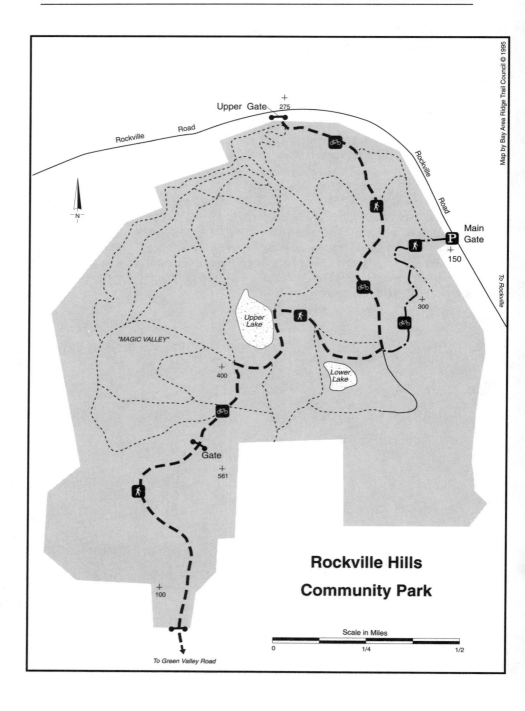

Upper Gate
+ 275

Rockville   Road

-N-

Rockville
Road

Main
Gate
P
+ 150

To Rockville

Upper
Lake

"MAGIC VALLEY"

+ 300

+ 400

Lower
Lake

Gate
+ 561

+ 100

**Rockville Hills
Community Park**

Scale in Miles

0   1/4   1/2

To Green Valley Road

Map by Bay Area Ridge Trail Council © 1995

Rockville Hills Community Park

From North Entrance to Green Valley Road

A gentle climb from the park's north entrance leads past cliffs of volcanic rock to a large blue-oak forest in a remote, grassy valley and then descends to a paved trail through a private subdivision.

Length   3 miles plus 0.5 mile on urban trail; 7 miles round trip.

Location   In Solano County between Suisun and Green valleys about 5 miles west of Fairfield.

Trail Characteristics   The first third of trip follows a paved road, after which park trail is on wide, unsurfaced service roads; trail through private subdivision is paved. Since most trees in park are deciduous, the trail on a winter day can be comfortably sunny, yet in summer, the predominant blue-oak forest offers welcome shade.

Ridge Trail Accessibility
- Hikers and bicyclists.
- Horses not allowed in park.

Trail Management
- The Solano County Farmlands and Open Space Foundation—707-428-7580—manages the park for the City of Fairfield: 707-428-7435.

Rules
- Open from 8 A.M. to dusk. No swimming in lakes. Bicyclists must wear helmets, stay on trails, and yield to hikers.

Amenities
- Picnic tables set beside two lakes and on scenic knolls. No water, telephone, or restrooms at park or nearby. Volunteer Park Ambassadors offer nature programs and provide trail maintenance.

Getting There

From I-80 take Suisun Valley exit and go north on Suisun Valley Rd. After passing Solano Community College, turn left on Rockville Rd. Rockville Hills parking area is on left 0.8 miles from turn. The north trail entrance is 0.6 mile farther up the road; off-road parking on either side.

On The Trail

The city of Fairfield bought these rocky, wooded highlands in the 1970s from a local ranching family—the Masons. The park site was once part of a large cattle ranch, originally purchased by the city for a golf course. After golf-course proponents improved existing stock ponds for irrigation and laid out golf-cart paths on the hills and in the interior valley, the Fairfield citizens defeated a bond issue to fund further golf-course development. Instead, the area became a city park. In 1991 the Solano County Farmlands and Open Space Foundation took over the management of this 600-acre park and installed picnic tables on shaded knolls and beside level, lakeside lookouts.

The crossroads settlement of Rockville on Suisun Valley Road once lay on the old stage route between Benicia and Sacramento. In the early 1850s it was the site of summer encampments where settlers attended prayer meetings. Seeking a permanent structure, the locals contributed money and volunteer labor to erect a church on land given by an early pioneer family. The stone walls, quarried in the Rockville Hills, withstood the 1906 earthquake, but fell into disrepair in the 1920s. In 1940 the church was restored as a pioneer monument and it stands today just north of the Rockville crossroads in the shade of ancient oaks in the Rockville Public Cemetery.

To begin your trip from the fenced parking area of Rockville Hills Community Park, take the half-mile connector trail that rises to an intersection with the main Bay Area Ridge Trail route in the valley, shaded by blue oaks, that surrounds the lakes. However, to experience the entire Ridge Trail route from the north end of the park, continue driving north on Rockville Road for 0.6 mile to roadside parking and a gated entrance on the south side of the road.

Blue oaks cast welcome shade for hikers and bicyclists.

Three trails branch out from this north entrance. To take the main Bay Area Ridge Trail route, follow the wide, paved road on the left, which ascends through trailside cover of red-berried toyon, shiny-leaved, mahogany-trunked manzanita, and shrubby coyote bush. Live oaks cling to the steep hillsides above and below the trail, offering welcome shade on warm days. In late spring, blue Douglas iris and light-orange sticky monkey flower fill the banks with color.

Climbing around a northeast-facing hillside, you pass a couple of trails on your left, routes to the main parking area, which could serve as alternate connectors to the main Ridge Trail. But staying on the paved trail, you soon look south across the farmlands to Suisun Bay and its fleet of unused, decommissioned Navy vessels moored there—the mothball fleet. Northeast of the Suisun Bay marshes lie the low Potrero Hills, partially surrounded by the Rush Ranch, a 2,000-acre estuarine nature preserve of the Solano County Farmlands and Open Space Foundation. In addition to protecting and restoring marshland and riparian habitats, this foundation strives to conserve agricultural lands and preserve key open space lands between Solano County's established communities.

Continuing on the paved road past a trail on your right, you pass under sizable deciduous white oaks, their great branches arching over the trail to provide filtered shade. At the crest of the hill, look west to see a high, rocky ridge topped by tall towers supporting ribbons of electric transmission lines. The park's central valley lies between this ridge and the trail you are following.

Now descending past some very large specimens of manzanita, you look down at the lakes nestled among stands of mature blue oaks. These oaks, first identified by David Douglas, a botanist in the early days of western-states plant collecting, can withstand the high summer temperatures and scant rainfall of these Inner Coast Range foothills. When the blue oaks begin to leaf out in late spring, their thick, slightly lobed leaves take on the characteristic blue-gray color of their name.

About one mile from the start, the Bay Area Ridge Trail swings right (west) at the junction where the connector trail to the main parking area goes left (east). High on a knoll to the left in a grove of blue oaks is a picnic site offering vistas over the surrounding plain. However, to continue your trip through Rockville Hills Park from the junction, arc right into the grasslands on an unpaved trail which passes

Upper Lake draws picnickers and waterfowl to its shores.

close to Lower Lake and then heads for larger Upper Lake. In spring, your way will be brightened by masses of wildflowers, including low-growing daisy-like gold-fields, bright yellow johnny-jumpups, and tall blue brodiaea.

As you rise to the top of Upper Lake's low dam, you may find tame, year-round resident ducks and geese which swim and waddle toward any hapless visitor who spreads out lunch at lakeside tables. Migratory water birds, winter visitors only, are less sociable. Birds of the surrounding blue-oak woodland—acorn woodpeckers, flickers, and western bluebirds—are even less interested in visitors, but their bright plumage will reward you with quick displays of color.

From the dam you can look across the lake to the rocky cliffs that form the backbone of the park. This rock formation, known as Sonoma Volcanics, is made up of undifferentiated volcanic and sedimentary rocks, ash, basalt and andesite, dating from the late Miocene and Pliocene epochs, some two to ten million years ago. Rockville Hills Park marks the southern limit of a 40-mile-long band of Sonoma Volcanics.

Bear left at Upper Lake to follow the trail along the east side of the lake and veer right around its south end. At the second trail intersection, a Green Valley trailhead and Bay Area Ridge Trail sign points left. But before you make this turn, you might want to take the trail straight ahead for a short side trip into delightful, cool "Magic Valley." Immense live oaks grow at the base of north-facing slopes here, co-existing with valley and blue oaks. If you continue on this trail, you pass a trail turnoff on the left, but continuing farther, you veer south and reach a picnic table on a knoll overlooking Green Valley. The trail then turns east to rejoin the Ridge Trail, about 1 mile from the beginning of the "Magic Valley" side trip.

However, to continue on the main Bay Area Ridge Trail route from the Green Valley trailhead intersection by the lake, turn left (south) to make a short ascent along a steep-sided ridge. At the crest of the hill the trail levels off in a saddle and then drops down to the Green Valley gate, which marks the entrance to a one-hun-dred-acre donation from the adjoining subdivision developer. Go through the gate and step or ride onto a narrow trail on a thickly wooded, steep side-slope. Shiny-faced buttercups on tall stems herald spring here, and poppies last into summer.

Then, emerging onto a high, treeless plateau, you look due south to that northern California landmark—Mt. Diablo, its 3,849-foot summit rising prominently above the surrounding plain. Overhead, you may see hawks lazily circling and searching the grasslands for their prey of mice, voles, and gophers. With luck, you may spot a pair of black-shouldered kites, identified by their long white tails and sharply pointed wings, known to frequent this area.

The trail veers right, and shortly bends left (south). If you continue straight (west) at this bend and go to the edge of the plateau, you can get an uninterrupted view of the lush fields of Green Valley set against a backdrop of the mountains that serve as a natural boundary between Napa and Solano counties. Twin-topped, 1,330-foot Elkhorn Peak, fringed with a thatch of trees, stands due west. If you visually follow this line of mountains north along undulating, tree-cloaked slopes, you will see the Twin Sisters in Solano County, each reaching over 2,000 feet in elevation.

Now return to the bend where you left the main trail and head south across this plateau into a grove of ancient evergreen oaks, their branches sculpted by the prevailing northwest winds and their trunks 4 to 6 feet in diameter. Following the path through these widely spaced, venerable trees can give the impression of walking down a *grande allée* of some fabled estate of yesteryear. A pause here will give you time to bask in their shady grandeur and enjoy wildflowers in spring or the soap plant's tall, wavy stalks bearing bluish-white blossoms on summer evenings.

Then, continue across the ridgetop and follow the wide trail that descends on a steep, eastern hillside dotted with California buckeye trees. These gnarled, white-barked trees stand out against the dry grass in winter, and their long, erect spikes of dense, pinkish-white blossoms scent the air in spring. From this hillside you see across a small valley to the park's eastern wooded ridge.

From here a short descent on a south-facing hillside takes you under transmission lines to a wide, fenced corridor and a gate to a private housing development. Signs remind trail users to stay on the 0.5-mile paved urban trail that winds under the powerlines through this private community. Do not stray onto the private streets or lawns, but continue on the paved path to Green Valley Road.

Since there is no designated southern staging area and no parking on Green Valley Road, retrace your steps through Rockville Hills Park on one of many alternate routes and stop for a picnic enroute. In the late afternoon, red-wing blackbirds calling from the reeds in Lower Lake and swallows snatching insects in mid-air will provide aerial entertainment.

The next segment of the Bay Area Ridge Trail begins at Blue Rock Springs Park in Vallejo. See *Vallejo-Benicia Buffer*. ∎

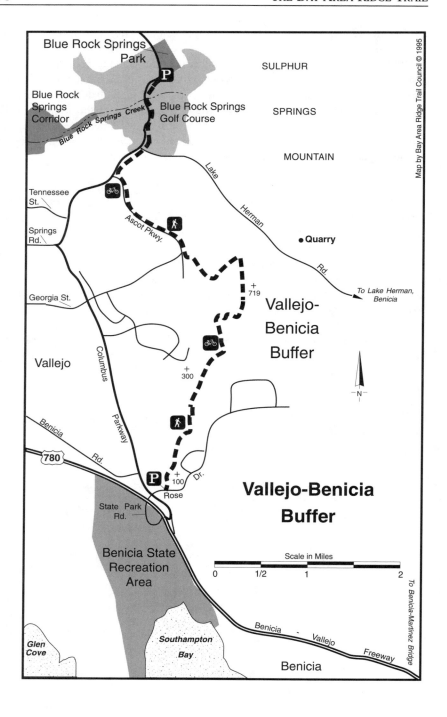

Vallejo-Benicia Buffer

From Blue Rock Springs Park to Rose Drive

From the rolling green lawns and shady picnic areas of Blue Rock Springs Park, a paved streetside path joins an off-road trail that meanders down a hilly open space easement, almost reaching Benicia State Recreation Area.

Length 4.9 miles. Sidewalks and bike lanes—1.9 miles; Buffer Trail—3 miles.

Location In Solano County hills between eastern Vallejo and western Benicia.

Trail Characteristics Paved sidewalks with landscaped borders and bike lanes stretch from Blue Rock Springs Park to beginning of Buffer. Buffer Trail unpaved, of varying width, and with no shade through hilly grasslands. Initial elevation gain of 300 feet followed by several ups and downs with eventual 300-foot loss. Can be windy and foggy, but may be hot and dry in summer.

Ridge Trail Accessibility
- Hikers—Sidewalks and Buffer Trail.
- Bicyclists—Bike lanes and Buffer Trail.

Trail Management
- Sidewalks and bike lanes—City of Vallejo: 707-648-4285.
- Blue Rock Springs Park and upper Buffer Trail—Greater Vallejo Recreation District: 707-648-4600.
- Lower Buffer Trail—Benicia Recreation Department: 707-746-4285.

Rules
- Blue Rock Springs Park—Open 8 A.M. to dusk. No dogs. Parking fee.
- Buffer Trail—Open dawn to dusk.

Amenities
- Blue Rock Springs Park—Picnic tables, children's play equipment, small lake, lawns, restrooms, water, telephone, and adjacent golf course and driving range.
- Buffer Trail—No water, restrooms or telephone.

Getting There

North entrance, Blue Rock Springs Park—From I-80 take Columbus Pkwy. east for 2.5 miles, turn left (east) into park. Ample parking.

South entrance, Rose Drive—Going east on I-780 (Vallejo-Benicia Fwy.), take Benicia State Park Rd. exit, bear right, and circle around to cross over the freeway. Continue to Columbus Pkwy., cross it onto Rose Dr. and park in first block on west side of street only. Trail entrance on north side of day-care center.

Going west on I-780 (Vallejo-Benicia Fwy.), take Columbus Pkwy. exit, and turn right (northeast) on Rose Dr. Find parking and trail entrance as above.

On The Trail

As you begin your trip over the lands north of Carquinez Strait, consider that they were once part of a vast, eleven-square-league land grant encompassing most of present-day Vallejo, Benicia, and Cordelia, approximately 99 square miles. Known as Rancho Soscol, the grant was awarded in 1844 by Governor Micheltorena to General Mariano Vallejo for his military service and generous loans to the Mexican government.

In 1847 the present-day city of Benicia was named Francesca after General Vallejo's wife. However, since the older settlement of Yerba Buena was renamed San Francisco, the town by the Carquinez Strait selected Benicia, another of Señora Vallejo's names.

Although today's thriving city of Vallejo was named for the general, he never resided there. Instead, he lived comfortably and well in Sonoma, protected by his own army of Mexican soldiers. Nevertheless, General Vallejo worked hard to place the second California state capital in Vallejo, and he contributed land and a building to house the state legislature.

On January 5, 1852 the legislature met in the new Vallejo capitol building, but their stay was short. By January 12 of that year, the dissatisfied legislature moved to Sacramento, returning to Vallejo only for a brief stay in 1853 due to floods in Sacramento. However, the legislature did compliment Vallejo for his generosity by naming today's city after him, even though Vallejo himself had suggested "Eureka."

Vallejo and many subsequent landowners ran cattle over these hills and shipped hides through the Strait to San Francisco and on to world ports. Today, the cattle are gone and houses cover the hillsides. But a 500-foot-wide easement on the boundary between the cities of Vallejo and Benicia creates a ridgeline greenbelt. Although the easement is called a Buffer, it really serves as open space joining the two cities bearing the Vallejo family names.

This trip over General Vallejo's former lands begins in Blue Rock Springs Park. Once the site of an elegant home and lavish gardens built by General Frisbie, son-in-law of General Vallejo, it later became a popular picnic place. Now managed by the Greater Vallejo Recreation District, its green lawns, spring-fed pond, picnic tables and big trees attract many visitors year-round.

West lies Blue Rock Springs Corridor, where a connector trail following Blue Rock Springs Creek leads to the park. East of the park on Sulphur Springs Mountain are three sites known to have been occupied by Native Americans.

To begin this segment of the Bay Area Ridge Trail, head south from Blue Rock Springs Park on the bike lanes or on a paved sidewalk along the east side of Columbus Parkway. Following along the municipal golf course's fence, you pass Lake Herman Road on your left and come to a signalled crossing at Ascot Parkway, where you turn left. Well-landscaped banks dotted with young trees or clipped green lawns edging the trail make a pleasant 1.9-mile trip between the park and the Buffer Trail entrance.

In less than a mile along Ascot Parkway, and just past Georgia Street, look for a landscaped entry in front of a weathered-gray fence on the east side of the street. A

Toddlers enjoy a snack in the shade of Blue Rock Springs Park.

few steps lead to an opening where the signed Bay Area Ridge Trail takes off.
Manzanita, toyon, coffeeberry, and springtime blue lupine, all native California
plants installed by volunteers, fill the space beside the trail for the first 50 feet.

Zigzag along the single-track trail to the 640-foot summit of the first of this trip's
many hilltops. Before you lies the long sweep of the greenway's undulating terrain
that stretches almost to the shores of Southampton Bay on Carquinez Strait. Seeing
that homes are built right up to both sides of the Buffer, you can appreciate the
persistent efforts of activists who convinced the Vallejo and Benicia councils to
create this linear open space, now a trail and a wildlife corridor.

Behind you, across Lake Herman Road, lies an active quarry. Although there are
few rocks visible along this trail, you can see in the exposed rock of the quarry's
terraces some examples of the Buffer's ancient underlying rocks. East of the quarry,
Sulphur Springs Creek drains the rugged slopes of Sulphur Springs Mountain and
eventually flows into Lake Herman. Solano County's 1994 Trails Plan shows a
County Feeder Trail along Sulphur Springs Creek.

The trail from this first hilltop heads north into a swale before it makes a long
traverse and a switchback to reach the highest point on the trip—an altitude of 719
feet. From this vantage place you can see impressive bodies of water: Lake Herman,
the local water supply, lies due east; beyond the lake on Suisun Bay, the Navy's
mothball fleet floats on relatively quiet waters; just south below you, one-third of
California's water, drained from the Sierra Nevada into the San Joaquin and
Sacramento rivers, surges through Carquinez Strait. Beyond the strait, San Francisco Bay spreads out over a vast expanse of tidelands, marshes, sloughs, and open
waters. On a clear day you can see the towers of the Golden Gate Bridge under
which these waters flow to the Pacific.

South across the strait rise the Contra Costa Hills, where another segment of the Bay Area Ridge Trail courses along the ridgeline. Here on this Solano County hilltop, as from many viewpoints along the route circling San Francisco Bay, Ridge Trail travelers have a great opportunity to orient themselves to Bay Area geography. In fact, when visibility is good here, you can see five of the nine Bay Area counties that the Ridge Trail traverses.

For the next ½ mile you follow a wide track over the hilltops south until a Bay Area Ridge Trail sign points right (west), downhill. This narrower trail, built on a gentle grade by a team of volunteers, contours along the west-facing hillside. When you meet a concrete-sided drainage ditch with a V-cross section, again head south, paralleling the ditch.

In spring, the rolling grasslands of the open space are ablaze with orange poppies and blue lupines. As the season progresses, yellow-flowered mule ears on strong, erect stems add their color to the hillsides. Special floral treats peeking through the grasses in early June are heavenly blue brodiaea and lemon-yellow mariposa lilies. The bulbs of these plants, when roasted, were favorite foods of Native Americans.

Joining the wider track again, follow the fence line undulating up and downhill, until another single-track trail veers right (south), thus avoiding a very steep hill. After contouring along the hillside and rounding a couple of switchbacks, you dip into a little valley and trend left. Here, on the Benicia side of the easement, pretty gardens and colorful children's play equipment hug the fence line.

Then three switchbacks carry you to the crest of the last hilltop, bringing good views of Southampton Bay and the Benicia State Recreation Area, which this trail will someday reach. If the day is clear, ships on the fast-flowing waters of Carquinez Strait are visible and sometimes even audible from here. A ramble along the fence line, with a few zigzags and moderate undulations over the last hilltops, takes you to the final abrupt, steep descent to trail's end at Rose Drive in Benicia.

There is a short gap between Rose Drive and the beginning of the next segment of the Bay Area Ridge Trail. See *Benicia Waterfront*. If you are returning to Blue Rock Springs Park, allow plenty of time for the uphill trip, especially on hot summer days.   ■

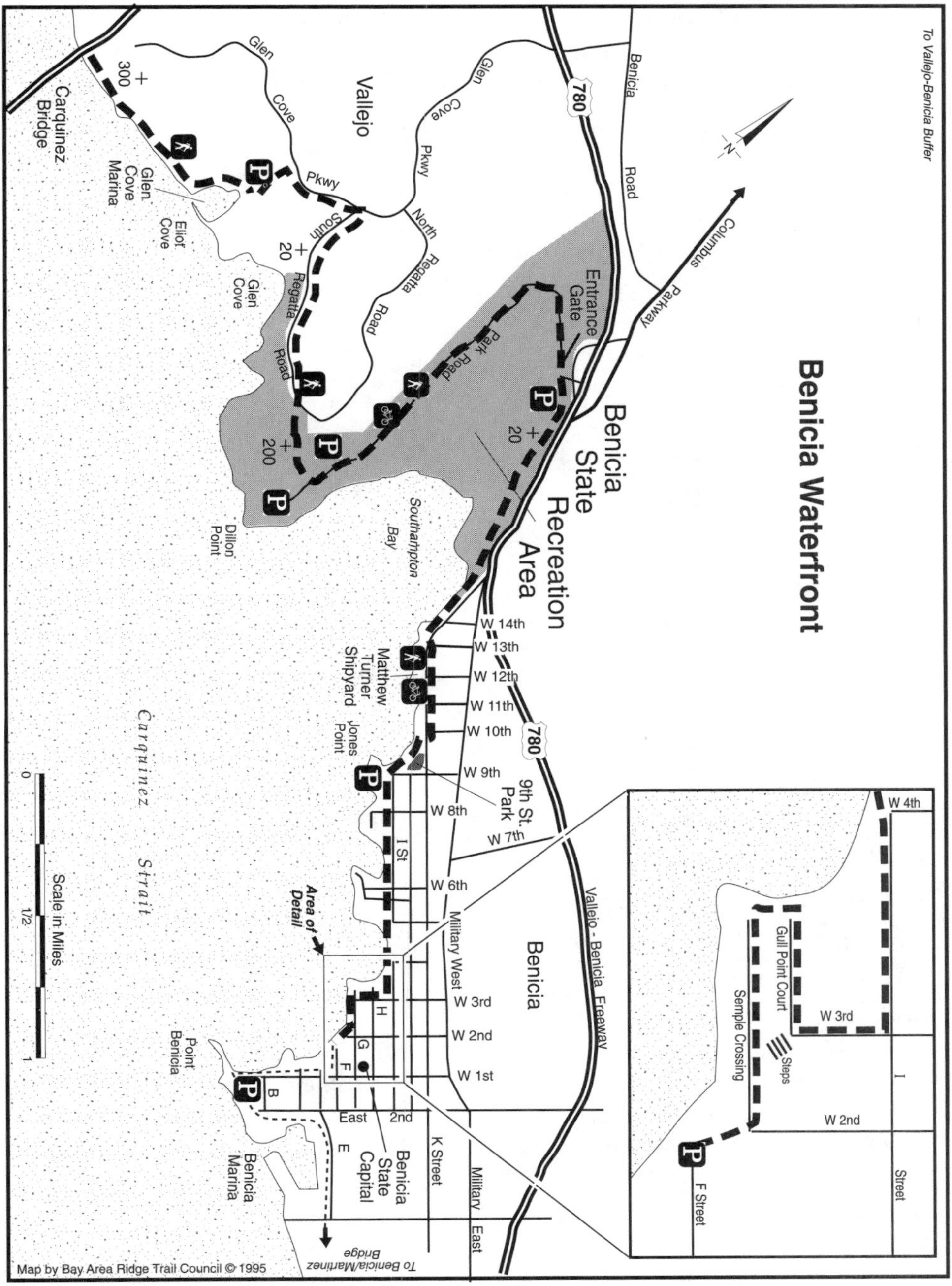
Benicia Waterfront
Benicia State Recreation Area
Vallejo
Benicia
To Vallejo-Benicia Buffer
Benicia Road
Columbus Parkway
780
Glen Cove Pkwy
Glen Cove Pkwy
North Regatta Road
South Regatta Road
Park Road
Entrance Gate
Carquinez Bridge
Glen Cove Marina
Eliot Cove
Glen Cove
Dillon Point
Southampton Bay
Matthew Turner Shipyard
Jones Point
9th St. Park
Carquinez Strait
Area of Detail
Point Benicia
Benicia Marina
Benicia State Capital
Military West
Military East
K Street
Vallejo - Benicia Freeway
W 14th
W 13th
W 12th
W 11th
W 10th
W 9th
W 8th
W 7th
W 6th
W 3rd
W 2nd
W 1st
I St
H
G
F
B
E
East
2nd
300
200
20
20
To Benicia/Martinez Bridge
Scale in Miles
0
1/2
1
W 4th
Gull Point Court
W 3rd
Semple Crossing
Steps
W 2nd
I
Street
F Street
Map by Bay Area Ridge Trail Council © 1995

Benicia Waterfront

From Benicia State Recreation Area to Benicia Point at F Street

Take two trips through Mexican and early California history beside the strait that funnels San Joaquin and Sacramento river waters into San Francisco Bay.

Length   East on Benicia Waterfront Trail—3.5 miles; west on Vallejo Waterfront Trail to Carquinez Bridge—3.5 miles.

Location   In Solano County in the cities of Benicia and Vallejo along Carquinez Strait.

Trail Characteristics   Benicia Waterfront Trail is paved and relatively level from Benicia State Recreation Area to F Street. Routes mostly level, except for 300-foot elevation gain to vista point above Carquinez Bridge. Trail westward from paved road in Benicia State Recreation Area to gate at South Regatta Dr. is unpaved. Sidewalks and city streets from there to Glen Cove Marina at Eliot Cove; crushed granite path to vista point above Carquinez Bridge. Brisk breezes off the water and occasional fog.

Ridge Trail Accessibility
- Hikers, bicyclists, and wheelchair users—Benicia State Recreation Area main entrance to F Street and paved road to Dillon Point within Recreation Area.
- Hikers only—Unpaved trails within Recreation Area and on path from Glen Cove Marina to vista point above Carquinez Bridge.
- Not suitable for equestrians.

Trail Management
- Benicia State Recreation Area—State of California, Department of Parks and Recreation: 707-745-3385.
- Waterfront Trail—City of Benicia: 707-746-4285.
- City of Vallejo sidewalks—707-648-4315.
- Unpaved trail from Glen Cove Marina to vista point at Carquinez Bridge—Greater Vallejo Recreation District: 707-648-4600.

Rules
- Benicia State Recreation Area—Open 6 A.M. to $\frac{1}{2}$ hour after sunset, current State Park fee schedule applies. No dogs. State fishing license required for those 16 years and older.
- City of Benicia Waterfront Trail and city of Vallejo Trail—Open daylight hours. No bicycles on unpaved trails.

Amenities
- Benicia State Recreation Area—Picnic tables, barbecues, water, restrooms, fishing, and parking.
- City of Benicia 9th Street Park—Beach, windsurfing, restrooms, water, telephone, launching ramp, and parking.

Getting There

Benicia State Recreation Area—From I-80 take I-780 (Vallejo-Benicia Fwy.) to exit marked Benicia State Recreation Area. Curve around right, make a quick jog left (south) and turn right to recreation area gate. Day-use fee required.

On The Trail East

Starting from the Benicia State Recreation Area head southeast on the paved trail that skirts the marshlands rimming Southampton Bay. Among the shorebirds and waterfowl feeding in the marshes you may see the 30-inch-tall, stately white egret. You will certainly see many runners, strollers and bicyclists enjoying this trail.

To the south across Southampton Bay lies Dillon Point, named for Patrick Dillon, the rancher who, in 1855, bought the 400 acres that now lie within the state recreation area. Dillon set out orchards and a vineyard and built a hilltop home. He also had a quarry and a brickyard. Today, his homesite is marked by towering eucalyptus, and a few of his fruit trees remain, but the grapevines, quarry, and brickyard are gone.

When the Waterfront Trail reaches K Street, it continues on the sidewalk. Near West 14th Street you see the first of many signs marking historical sites. This one tells of the famous 1889 boxing match between James J. Corbett and "Battling Joe" Choynski. The first rounds were fought in Fairfax, and the fight was continued a week later on a barge in Southampton Bay.

At West 12th Street turn right (south) to the Matthew Turner Shipyards Park, where 169 ships were launched around the turn of the century. Today, you'll find benches, picnic tables and pretty gardens, another historical marker, and your first close-up view of the water rushing through Carquinez Strait toward San Francisco and the Golden Gate. Across the strait lies Port Costa, once an important depot for

Commodore Thomas Jones Park on Carquinez Strait commemmorates the founder of the US Naval Academy.

transporting grain by barge, ship, and rail. The Southern Pacific Railroad still runs transcontinental freight and passenger trains here on its waterfront tracks.

Now return to K Street and a bluff-top path that runs diagonally across the Ninth Street Park to Jones Point, commemorating Commodore Thomas Jones, founder of the U.S. Naval Academy. Southampton Bay is named for one of his supply ships. As Commander of the Pacific Fleet in the 1840s, Jones feared war with Mexico and advocated a port here in Benicia's deep offshore waters. Modern-day sailors launch their craft beside Jones Point to ply these same waters.

From the park take I Street on sidewalks or on the road's edge past houses with charming gardens. In the 1860s two tanneries near here processed hides brought from vast inland cattle ranches. Each hide was marked with the ranch's unique registered brand. On beyond, where barriers exclude motor vehicles from I Street, Ridge Trail signs assure bicyclists and pedestrians that they can pass. At 4th Street they find picnic tables and children's play equipment overlooking a small crescent-shaped bay.

Turn right (south) at West 3rd Street and proceed to Gull Point Court, which **bicyclists** must use to reach Semple Crossing, the street below. **Hikers** can descend on a stairway near a handsome, restored Victorian house. From Semple Crossing **hikers** and **bicyclists** continue on an unpaved path to F Street, where at this writing the Benicia Waterfront Trail ends.

But your tour of historic Benicia need not end. At West First and G streets is the centerpiece of the town's attractions—an imposing, red brick building with white, two-story columns, our state's third capitol. Although the legislature convened here only in 1853, the building is now faithfully restored and open as a state historic park. Next door, and now open for tours, is the Fischer-Hanlon house, a fine example of Victorian architecture, until recently occupied by the original owner's descendants.

You are in the heart of Benicia's old town, where saloons, hotels, and the 1847 Von Pfister adobe (to be restored) bring to life the years before and after the Gold Rush. If you continue down West First Street to Benicia Point, you'll see where 400-foot-long barges once ferried trains across to Port Costa. Cars too were ferried across the strait until the Benicia-Martinez bridge was built. And just a few minutes away are the military buildings of the 1850s, the Benicia Arsenal with its landmark clock tower, the Camel Barn Museum, and the Commandant's House.

Today Benicia bustles with activity matching its former days—huge ships unload Japanese cars at its port, and slick condominiums, shopping malls, and subdivisions cover the hillsides and crowd its shores. However, thanks to far-sighted citizens, the cities and former capitals of California that bear General Mariano Vallejo's family names are joined by a waterfront and a buffer trail. See *Vallejo-Benicia Buffer* for more about the Vallejo family.

On The Trail West

To take another waterfront trail, again begin at the entrance to Benicia State Recreation Area and follow the park road as it skirts the marshes and western shore of Southampton Bay. Hikers use the shoulder of this paved road, open to bicyclists, which leads out to Dillon Point, about 1.5 miles from the entrance gate.

Just past the first picnic area on this road, **hikers** take the path, marked by a Bay Area Ridge Trail sign, over the low hill running north-south through the park. Along this footpath you will see some of Patrick Dillon's surviving fruit trees. When you reach the crest of the hill, look due west to the Carquinez Bridge. Your route in the city of Vallejo lies along the bluffs that reach the heights above the bridge.

To get there, take the short footpath descending to a gate in the fence that you can see from the hilltop. (Don't veer off into the long swale on your left.) Once through this gate to South Regatta Drive in the city of Vallejo, turn left. From here to Eliot Cove, the Bay Area Ridge Trail route is on sidewalks through several new subdivisions. For the first $\frac{1}{2}$ mile you have an unobstructed view out to the strait and its maritime traffic. Then you can look west through the trees to Glen Cove, where the city of Vallejo is planning a shoreline park. In the future, the Ridge Trail will go through this park.

In the meantime, continue on South Regatta Drive to Glen Cove Drive—0.9 mile from the Benicia State Recreation Area gate—and turn left. On the north side of the street is Vallejo's Glen Cove Park, with attractive plantings and brightly painted children's play apparatus. In just 0.2 mile along Glen Cove Drive, turn left again on Glen Cove Marina Road, and go 0.1 mile downhill to a cul-de-sac and the entrance to the Glen Cove Marina.

At the marina is a handsome Victorian building that was the residence for personnel at the former Carquinez Lighthouse and Life Saving Station. It was situated just west of the Carquinez Bridge at the mouth of the Napa River. After the lighthouse was automated in 1955, the building was sold to a private party and barged to its present site at Eliot Cove in 1957. It now serves as the Glen Cove Marina's yacht club. This handsome three-story building, painted white with gray trim, now presides over the yacht basin filled with boats whose sails and decks are bright with nautical blue covers.

On the west shore of the yacht basin look for the Bay Area Ridge Trail **hiker's** route heading uphill through a broad easement on the bluffs above the strait. As you climb the path surfaced with crushed granite, you look down on a steady stream of ship traffic—tankers and freighters from ports around the world, barges, naval vessels, and pleasure craft. On a foggy day, the horns of ships and the bells of buoys reverberate eerily from the strait's watery canyon. High above the strait, the double strand of the Carquinez Bridge carries its noisy load of land-based traffic.

In the adjoining subdivision, connecting trails from tiny parks intersect with this segment of the Bay Area Ridge Trail. Just above the park on Waterview Place, the trail ends at a dramatic vista point above the bridge. From here you see the swiftly moving river joining San Pablo Bay. On beyond, Mt. Tamalpais and the coast ranges stand as a backdrop. Out of sight on the west side of the Carquinez Bridge are two once-important, now historic, maritime facilities, the Mare Island Naval Shipyard and the California Maritime Academy, situated on opposite sides of the Napa River.

When you turn around, your downhill trip brings views of the port communities of Vallejo, Benicia, and Martinez, with Mt. Diablo looming in the distance. This Waterfront Trail, also the route of the Bay Trail, will someday cross the river to Martinez and Contra Costa County's bayfront and ridgeline trails. See *Carquinez Strait Regional Shoreline to John Muir National Historic Site* for a Bay Area Ridge Trail segment in Contra Costa County. ∎

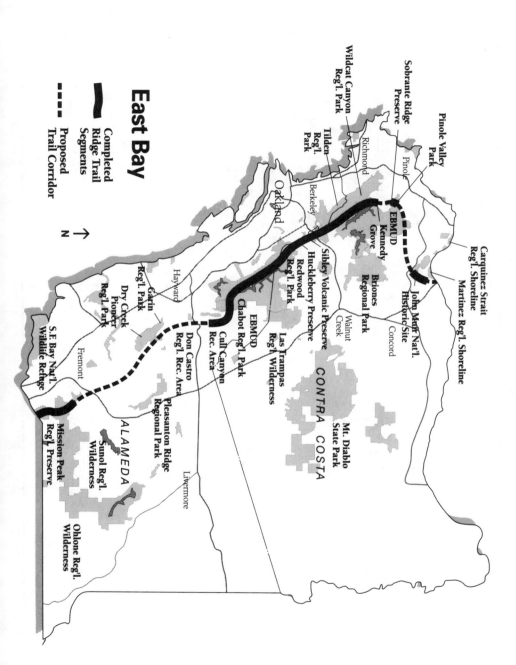

East Bay

Completed
Ridge Trail
Segments

Proposed
Trail Corridor

N →

Wildcat Canyon
Reg'l. Park

Sobrante Ridge
Preserve

Pinole Valley
Park

Tilden
Reg'l.
Park

Richmond

Pinole

EBMUD
Kennedy
Grove

Briones
Regional Park

Carquinez Strait
Reg'l. Shoreline

Martinez Reg'l. Shoreline

Oakland

Berkeley

Sibley Volcanic Preserve

Huckleberry Preserve

Redwood
Reg'l. Park

Walnut
Creek

Concord

John Muir Nat'l.
Historic Site

EBMUD
Chabot Reg'l. Park

Las Trampas
Reg'l. Wilderness

CONTRA
COSTA

Mt. Diablo
State Park

Hayward

Cull Canyon
Rec. Area

Garin
Reg'l. Park

Dry Creek
Pioneer
Reg'l. Park

Don Castro
Reg'l. Rec. Area

Pleasanton Ridge
Regional Park

Fremont

S.F. Bay Nat'l.
Wildlife Refuge

ALAMEDA

Sunol Reg'l.
Wilderness

Livermore

Mission Peak
Reg'l. Preserve

Ohlone Reg'l.
Wilderness

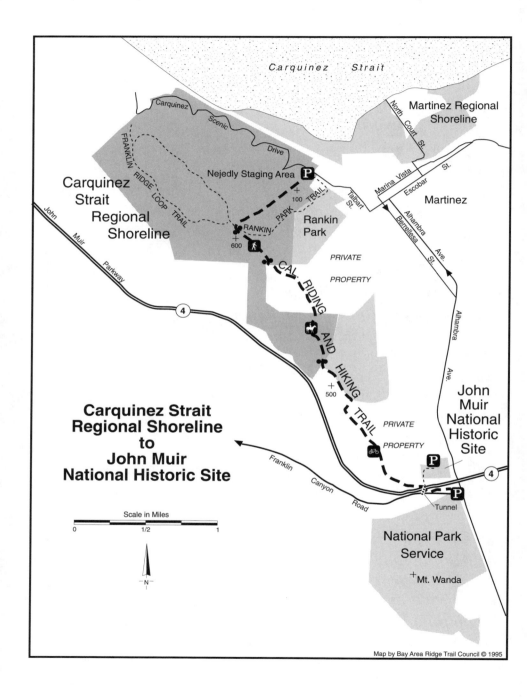

Carquinez Strait

Martinez Regional Shoreline

Carquinez Scenic Drive

Nejedly Staging Area

Carquinez Strait Regional Shoreline

FRANKLIN RIDGE LOOP TRAIL

Martinez

Marina Vista

Escobar St.

North Court St.

Talbart St.

Alhambra

Berrellesa St.

Rankin Park

RANKIN

600

100

PARK TRAIL

PRIVATE PROPERTY

CAL. RIDING AND HIKING TRAIL

500

John Muir Parkway

4

PRIVATE PROPERTY

Alhambra Ave.

John Muir National Historic Site

Carquinez Strait Regional Shoreline to John Muir National Historic Site

Franklin Canyon Road

4

Tunnel

Scale in Miles

0   1/2   1

-N-

National Park Service

+ Mt. Wanda

Map by Bay Area Ridge Trail Council © 1995

Carquinez Strait Regional Shoreline to John Muir National Historic Site

From Nejedly Staging Area to Visitor Center

On broad ranch roads, roam rolling ridgelands across northern Contra Costa hills with views of Carquinez Strait and Mt. Diablo and, at trail's end, make a visit to John Muir's home.

Length 3 miles.

Location In Contra Costa County on the hills above Martinez.

Trail Characteristics First and last legs of trail short and steep. Most of trail is on wide, unpaved service roads on gently rolling terrain. Except for first 0.3 mile, no tree cover on trail. Elevation gain 615 feet.

Ridge Trail Accessibility
- Hikers, equestrians, and bicyclists.

Trail Management
- Carquinez Strait Regional Shoreline—East Bay Regional Park District (EBRPD): 510-635-0135.
- John Muir National Historic Site—National Park Service (NPS): 510-228-8860.

Rules
- Trail open from 8 A.M. to ½ hour after sunset. Dogs on leash allowed in staging area, under voice control in open space.
- John Muir National Historic Site—Open Wed. through Sun., 10 A.M. to 4:30 P.M. Park fee.

Amenities
- Carquinez Strait Regional Shoreline, Nejedly Staging Area—Parking, picnic tables, restrooms.
- John Muir National Historic Site—Visitor center, audio-visual program, water, restrooms, self-guiding tour of Muir House, Oval Garden, orchards, and Martinez Adobe.

Getting There

By Car
North entrance, Carquinez Shoreline, Nejedly Staging Area—From I-80 or I-680 in Contra Costa County take Hwy 4 (John Muir Pkwy.) to Martinez. Take Alhambra Ave. exit and go 1¾ miles north through Martinez, turn left on Escobar, right on Talbart, veer left on Carquinez Scenic Dr. Just after cemeteries, turn left into Nejedly Staging Area.

South entrance, John Muir Site—Follow directions above to Alhambra Ave. exit, but immediately after turning north on Alhambra Ave., look for John Muir National Historic Site on your left at 4202 Alhambra Ave. Limited parking on site. Additional parking at southwest corner of Alhambra Ave. and Franklin Canyon Rd. with access to the trail from Franklin Canyon Rd. through a tunnel under Hwy 4.

By Bus
Contra Costa County Connection bus 116 to Alhambra Ave. and Marina Vista and to Alhambra Ave. and Franklin Canyon Rd. from BART stations daily except Sundays.

On The Trail

This trip follows the alignment of the old California Riding and Hiking Trail, a round-the-state trail system planned in the late 1940s and early '50s. One of the few scattered segments remaining, this leg runs along the ridge south of Carquinez Strait and ends in the Alhambra Valley of Martinez.

The original name for this valley, derived from an 1842 land grant, was *Cañada del Hambre y las Bolsas del Hambre*, the Valley of Hunger. It was renamed Alhambra Valley when Mr. and Mrs. Strentzel, parents of John Muir's wife, settled there in the 1880s.

Begin your trip from the Nejedly Staging Area by heading uphill toward the East Bay Regional Park District's green gate emblazoned with a prominent Bay Area Ridge Trail sign. (An alternate route through adjoining Rankin Park takes off to the left behind the uppermost picnic table.) After closing the gate to the EBRPD Trail, take the path that cuts across a wide flat and soon enters a glade of bay and buckeye trees with an understory of toyon and poison oak.

Then, in an oak woodland beside a seasonal creek, you begin a steady ascent, gaining over 500 feet in elevation in less than a half mile. A couple of switchbacks take you out into grassland, but soon you return to shaded woodland. In winter, you may find burnished, brown buckeye balls (seedpods) and deer or bobcat prints on the trail. In spring, you may see the long, wavy leaves of soap plant promising evening blooms of delicate, bluish-white flowers on tall stalks. In a series of three steep pitches, followed by short, level stretches, you make a last upward rise to a gate at the Franklin Ridge Loop Trail. If you turn right and circle the knoll, there are picnic sites overlooking the strait and a view west of Mt. Tamalpais.

To proceed southeast on the Ridge Trail, bear left at the gate, and at the next fork, take the gravelled road on the right, descending into a saddle between grassy, rounded hilltops. In the valley to your left is a small pastoral scene of orchard, windmill, and water tank reminiscent of the farming that flourished in this area when John Muir and his family lived here.

Now the Bay Area Ridge Trail route is a series of rises to hilltops followed by dips into little hollows. The hollows below the trail are often filled with clusters of evergreen oaks, while the hilltops are devoid of any vegetation higher than the oatgrass—all the better for seeing the views and enjoying the birds and flowers.

On your left are Carquinez Strait, the Benicia-Martinez Bridge, and the Navy's mothball fleet in Suisun Bay. Across the strait are the Benicia foothills, along which the route of another leg of the Ridge Trail lies. (See *Vallejo-Benicia Buffer*.)

Anywhere above these open grasslands you may see kestrels fluttering in place, and red-tailed and northern harrier hawks riding the updrafts, each searching for its prey. At your feet orange poppies and blue-eyed grass brighten the trail.

When you go through the next gate, you are on private property over which the EBRPD has a trail easement. Signs remind you to stay on the trail. Ahead is a brown horse barn on your right and a yellow house on your left. Watch for the Ridge Trail sign that sends you right toward the barn, then continue on the trail past it.

At the trip's highest point, Mt. Diablo's twin summits loom ahead, in sight for the rest of the trip. The view is especially fine at sunset, when a soft, pink glow cloaks the mountain.

Although John Muir's real love was the Sierra Nevada, he often wandered these hills with his daughters, and he set aside a special hilltop for evening strolls with them. Surely Muir, the father of our National Park System, would have appreciated the Bay Area Ridge Trail Council's effort to join 75 Bay Area parks with a 400-mile regional ridgeline trail. As he wrote, "Everybody needs beauty as well as bread, places to play in and pray in where Nature may heal and cheer and give strength to body and soul alike."

Wheat stalks dry near John Muir's fruit trees.

From the next hilltop let your gaze travel south to Franklin Ridge and a succession of gently rounded hills rising above tree-filled canyons. Directly beneath this hilltop is the canyon named for Edward Franklin, who bought a portion of the Ignacio Martinez estate in 1853 and lived in this canyon until 1875. Strands of many powerlines strung on tall transmission towers march across the hilltops here, and your way crosses under them on a long descent.

A Bay Area Ridge Trail sign directs you onto a narrow, paved road leading into a tight little canyon. You continue until the paving veers right; there you go straight ahead onto a dirt trail from which you can see the town of Martinez below. Martinez, now the Contra Costa County seat, was named for Ignacio Martinez, who was born in Mexico City in 1774, and became *comandante* of the San Francisco Presidio from 1822 to 1827. In recognition of his military service, Martinez received the vast *Rancho El Pinole* in 1823. It was on these lands that Col. William M. Smith laid out the town of Martinez in 1849.

From the top of a steep hill, you make a quick descent on a Caltrans easement above Highway 4, the John Muir Parkway. (Bicyclists should dismount.) At the trail's terminus is a fenced cross trail. By going left, you reach a gate into the John Muir Historic Site. By going right, you continue on the California Riding and Hiking Trail through a tunnel under the John Muir Parkway to Franklin Canyon Road. Then turn east to the parking area at Alhambra Avenue. You could have a shuttle waiting at one of these parking areas. If not, your route back to the Nejedly staging area will afford fine views west, north, and east.

If you stop at the John Muir visitor center, the National Park Service will treat you to a delightful movie of Muir's life, from his childhood in Wisconsin to his trip in Yosemite with President Theodore Roosevelt. Just a stone's throw beyond are the orchards, barns, and lovely Victorian house where John Muir and his family lived. You can wander through the grounds, visit the old Vicente Martinez adobe, and browse through Muir's home.

At the desk in his study Muir wrote many of the books and articles that inspired political action to save wildlands and wildlife. He helped establish conservation as a national policy, reflected today in environmental legislation and in our excellent National Park System.

The next Bay Area Ridge Trail segment, due to be opened soon, will travel south across the Contra Costa County hills to connect with Kennedy Grove Regional Recreation Area.   ∎

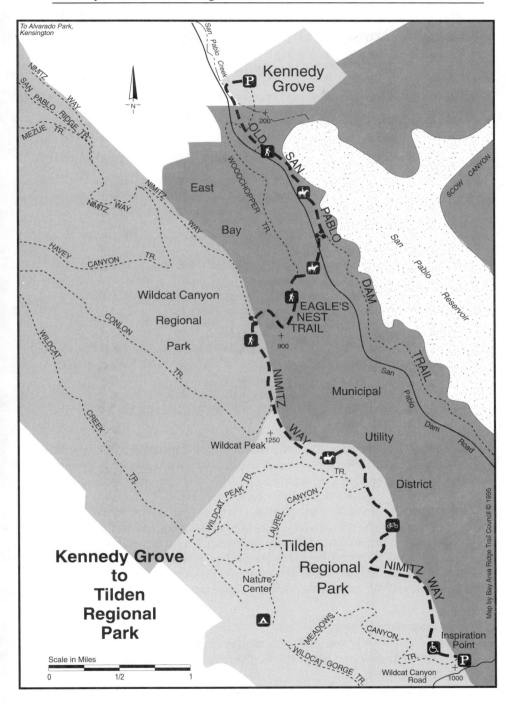

To Alvarado Park,
Kensington

P Kennedy
Grove

NIMITZ WAY

SAN PABLO RIDGE TR.

MEZUE TR.

NIMITZ WAY

NIMITZ WAY

OLD SAN PABLO DAM TRAIL

WOODCHOPPER TR.

East

Bay

200

SCOW CANYON

San Pablo Reservoir

HAVEY CANYON TR.

Wildcat Canyon

Regional

Park

CONLON TR.

WILDCAT CREEK TR.

EAGLE'S
NEST
TRAIL

900

NIMITZ WAY

San Pablo Dam Road

Municipal

Utility

District

Wildcat Peak
1250

WILDCAT PEAK TR.

LAUREL CANYON TR.

TR.

Tilden

Regional

Park

NIMITZ WAY

Nature
Center

MEADOWS

WILDCAT GORGE TR.

CANYON TR.

Inspiration
Point

P

Wildcat Canyon
Road   1000

**Kennedy Grove
to
Tilden
Regional
Park**

Map by Bay Area Ridge Trail Council © 1995

Scale in Miles

0   1/2   1

Kennedy Grove to Tilden Regional Park

From the Grove to Inspiration Point

From a shady grove in a remote canyon, climb to a ridgecrest trail that leads to Inspiration Point and far-flung views over the San Francisco Bay Area.

> **Length** 4.4 miles.
>
> **Location** In Contra Costa County on San Pablo Ridge above Berkeley and Richmond.
>
> **Trail Characteristics** Except for narrow first 0.3 mile, trail is on wide service roads to ridgecrest. Last 2.4 miles of the trip, on Nimitz Way, are paved. Elevation gain 810 feet.

Ridge Trail Accessibility

- Hikers and equestrians—Kennedy Grove and East Bay Municipal Utility District lands.
- Hikers, equestrians, bicyclists, and wheelchair users—Nimitz Way from Wildcat Canyon Park to Inspiration Point in Tilden Park.

Trail Management

- Kennedy Grove Regional Recreation Area, Wildcat Canyon Regional Park and Tilden Regional Park—East Bay Regional Park District (EBRPD): 510-635-0135.
- San Pablo Reservoir Recreation Area and watershed lands on San Pablo Ridge—East Bay Municipal Utility District (EBMUD): 510-254-3778.

Rules

- Kennedy Grove Regional Recreation Area, Wildcat Canyon Regional Park and Tilden Regional Park—Open from 5 A.M. to 10 P.M., or as posted. Dogs must be on leash in parking lots, at picnic sites, and on lawns; under voice control on Nimitz Way. Fee for dogs and for parking at Kennedy Grove.
- San Pablo Reservoir Recreation Area—Fishing, boating, picnicking, water, restrooms and telephone. Old San Pablo Dam Road along the reservoir's west shore open from sunrise to 1 hour before sunset. No swimming in reservoir.
- Eagle's Nest Trail from San Pablo Dam Rd. to Wildcat Canyon Park—Trail use permit required for hikers and equestrians. No dogs. No bicycles. Same hours as reservoir area. Cattle grazing—close gates behind you.

Amenities

- No water along entire trail.
- Kennedy Grove—Water, restrooms, telephone, picnic areas, children's playground, volleyball and horseshoe facilities, large playing field, and senior citizen's center.
- Wildcat Canyon and Tilden Parks—Many trails lead from Nimitz Way to

Wildcat Peak, Jewel Lake, International Peace Grove, Redwood Grove, Tilden Nature Area, and Wildcat Creek.

Getting There

By Car

North entrance, Kennedy Grove—From I-80 in Richmond area take San Pablo Dam Rd. exit, go east 4 miles to park entrance on left, 0.5 mi south of Castro Ranch Rd.

From Berkeley, Oakland, Orinda and Walnut Creek area take Hwy 24 to Orinda exit and turn north on Camino Pablo, which becomes San Pablo Dam Rd. After passing San Pablo Reservoir Recreation Area, continue 1 mile to Kennedy Grove entrance on right.

South entrance, Inspiration Point—From Hwy 24, take Fish Ranch Rd. exit, go 1 mile, and turn right on Grizzly Peak Blvd. In 1.3 miles, beyond Lomas Cantadas Rd., turn right on South Park Dr. and go $1\frac{1}{2}$ miles. Turn right on Wildcat Canyon Rd., and in about $1\frac{1}{2}$ miles turn left into large parking area at Inspiration Point. When South Park Dr. is closed to motor vehicles during the salamander migration season, November to March, continue on Grizzly Peak Blvd. to Golf Course Dr., turn right and then, past the clubhouse, turn right again on Shasta Rd. Quickly turn right on Wildcat Canyon Rd. and continue about 1 $\frac{1}{2}$ miles to Inspiration Point.

From I-80 in Berkeley—Take University Ave. exit, and go 2 miles east to U.C. campus. Turn left (north) on Oxford, right (east) on Rose, go one block, turn left (north) on Spruce and go to top of hill. Veer right (east) on Wildcat Canyon Rd. and continue about 2 miles to Inspiration Point.

By Bus

AC Transit 69 and 71 to San Pablo Dam Rd. at Castro Ranch Rd. daily. 67 to Tilden Park weekends and holidays.

On The Trail

From Kennedy Grove, this trip takes you through lands once part of the 17,754-acre Rancho El Sobrante. Granted to Juan José and Victor Castro in 1841, the rancho consisted of lands remaining between other established ranchos, hence its name "the left-over place." Here the Castros maintained a flourishing ranch, grazed cattle on the surrounding hillsides, and shipped hides and tallow via bayside ports.

But by the 1870s, the Castros were beset by struggles with squatters and newly arrived settlers over legal rights to the land. Finally, a settlement ensued granting the Castros only a small portion of the former rancho. However, they and their heirs continued operations on the remaining land into the 1980s. Modern-day place names—nearby Castro Ranch Road, El Sobrante, and Sobrante Ridge—remind us of these early landowners.

Hikers, bicyclists, and equestrians, start your trip in Kennedy Grove by proceeding from the main parking area toward the spacious lawns and eucalyptus groves. On the lawn just off the paved area, look for a boulder bearing a bronze plaque telling of an 1890s railroad that ran through this valley enroute to Orinda from Emeryville and Berkeley. This wood-burning, narrow-gauge train, the California and Nevada Railroad, never reached Nevada, but did carry freight and farm products between Orinda and Oakland.

Although the railroad was plagued by washouts in winter, dust in summer, and continual financial problems, it introduced picnickers and vacationers to many recreation sites along San Pablo Creek. Today's picnickers can see the train's former roadbed cutting a wide swath between the rows of eucalyptus trees in Kennedy Grove. The 0.33-mile Kennedy Loop Trail encircling the upper lawn passes picnic sites named for stops on this historic railroad.

After absorbing this bit of history, proceed west between the Senior Center and the lawns to the south edge of the next parking area. On your left, just beyond the center, a small Bay Area Ridge Trail sign marks the trail entrance. Go downhill beside an intermittent stream and cross San Pablo Creek, easily forded except after heavy rains. Then bear left, cross the Grove's entrance road, and go through a gate into EBMUD land. Climbing up the west side of San Pablo Dam, you reach Old San Pablo Dam Road, now a trail.

Following this trail to the top of the dam, you arrive at lake level beside the vast body of water behind the dam. Impounding the waters of San Pablo Creek, this dam was built to supply water for the growing population in Berkeley and surrounding areas. It was constructed by Anthony Chabot, who used hydraulic mining techniques to whittle away hillside rock and soil and sluice it to the dam site.

Although the lake now fills the canyon for 3 miles southeast, it was not always so full. Begun in 1916 and completed in 1921, it stood empty during many drought years. Not until 1936, when an aqueduct brought water from the Mokelumne River, did it reach capacity.

Glimpses of the lake and Sobrante Ridge above it will reward you along Old San Pablo Dam Road, as well as from the ultimate heights of this trip. While traversing the lake's edge, you may also reflect on glimpses of man's prehistory here. When in the 1970s the reservoir was drained to rebuild the dam according to modern earthquake standards, archaeologists looked for clues to Native American settlements in the San Pablo Creek valley. In shell mounds and graves, they found native artifacts. But since most of these indigenous people had been removed to Mission San José by 1810, little is known of their life here. A few Native Americans remained to work on the Castro ranch, but pneumonia wiped them out in 1850.

Found too, were former farm sites of early American settlers. During the period before the dam was built, ranchers ran both dairy and beef cattle, grew hay, and raised goats in this valley. Several dairies flourished, notably the Scow Dairy, for which Scow Canyon (due east of Kennedy Grove) is named, and the Varsity Creamery.

As you continue on Old San Pablo Dam Road, pass the road to the Oaks Picnic

Bicyclists enjoy long rides on Nimitz Way.

Area on your left and veer right, uphill. At a log gate beside San Pablo Dam Road bear left, continuing on the road shoulder for $\frac{1}{8}$ mile to a crosswalk. On the other side of the road is a gate leading into EBMUD watershed lands on the east side of San Pablo Ridge. Before continuing on this trail for **hikers** and **equestrians** only, turn around to see the dam's recreation complex, where visitors can enjoy picnicking, fishing, and boating.

Now your route, the 0.9-mile Eagle's Nest Trail, crosses the Woodchopper Trail, veers left and almost immediately goes right. From here the trip to the top of San Pablo Ridge lies over a wide fire trail through eucalyptus groves and open grasslands. These eucalyptus trees were planted here and all over the Berkeley and Oakland hills around 1910. During the late 1930s, Civilian Conservation Corps and WPA workers planted Monterey pines, Douglas firs, and redwoods in many East Bay parks to rehabilitate and stabilize eroded hillsides.

Where the trail makes a wide swing to the right, you can look across the lake to identify landmarks. Sobrante Ridge rises from the east shore, creased by canyons where little streams named for early settlers, including Sather and Dutra, flow into the south end of the lake. Up Scow Canyon you can see the Nunes Ranch, operating here since 1914, which still retains one of its original ranch buildings.

When you reach the ridgetop, go through a gate into Wildcat Canyon Regional Park. Now, turn left (south) on Nimitz Way, named for World War II Admiral Chester Nimitz, who in his retirement walked here daily, scattering wildflower seeds. This paved trail, part of the 31-mile East Bay Skyline National Recreation Trail and also the Bay Area Ridge Trail, runs for 4 miles along the crest of San Pablo Ridge from a former Nike site northwest of here all the way to Inspiration Point.

From this trail there are remarkable views: directly west across the Bay lies San Francisco, with Mt. Tamalpais on the north side of the Golden Gate; Marin County is joined to the East Bay by the Richmond-San Rafael Bridge; northwest are Pinole and Hercules peaks; and due east, Mt. Diablo's 3,849-foot summit rises above the surrounding plain.

Equestrian rides on Nimitz Way after leaving East Bay Municipal Utility District Lands on east side of San Pablo Ridge.

Continuing south along Nimitz Way, you pass the Conlon Trail and then you meet the Wildcat Peak Trail on the right, a side trip for hikers only, which leads to the International Peace Grove and to a vista point on Wildcat Peak enclosed by a double semi-circle of low rock walls. Established by Rotary International and EBRPD, the grove and the vista point offer the opportunity to contemplate the significance of friendship across the waters beyond the Golden Gate. Returning to Nimitz Way, continue to the Laurel Canyon Trail, where another side trip would lead you to the Sequoia Grove, planted by the Berkeley Hiking Club.

On the last half mile of your trip on Nimitz Way, as you near Inspiration Point, you'll be in the company of casual walkers, hikers, bicyclists, roller-bladers, neighbors walking their dogs, and parents pushing strollers. Signs warn those on wheels to reduce their speed and call out before passing. Benches spaced conveniently along the way invite you to rest and enjoy the passing parade. Occasionally you can see Vollmer Peak, a high point on the Bay Area Ridge Trail route southeast through Tilden Regional Park.

Soon you skirt the stone pillars at the end of Nimitz Way and move to the viewing area at Inspiration Point. Below you lies the many-fingered lake behind San Pablo Dam, nestled between the rounded hills of San Pablo and Sobrante ridges. At the far north end of the lake lies Kennedy Grove, a 4.4-mile, mostly downhill return, back to your starting point. If you have an EBMUD permit, you could take the Inspiration and Lakeview trails downhill (east) to connect with the Old San Pablo Dam Road going north to Kennedy Grove.

If you have a car shuttle waiting here, drive east down Wildcat Canyon Road to its junction with San Pablo Dam Road. On the northeast corner of this junction, an American rancher, General Theodore Wagner, built a hotel. Scant foundations of this building, which served passengers on the California and Nevada Railroad, remain today. Wagner also built a fine home southeast of this intersection, which is now the rural campus of John F. Kennedy University. It was General Wagner who surveyed and built Wildcat Canyon Road in 1889, though it was not paved until 1930.

If you are continuing on the Bay Area Ridge Trail, see the description of the next segment on the following pages for *Tilden Regional Park to Redwood Regional Park.* ■

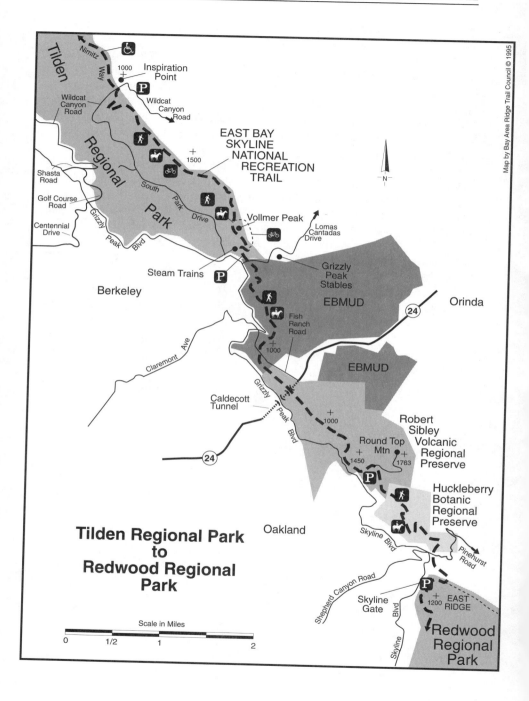

**Tilden Regional Park
to
Redwood Regional
Park**

Scale in Miles

0   1/2   1   2

Tilden Regional Park to Redwood Regional Park

From Inspiration Point to Skyline Gate

Steep climbs to dramatic views followed by descents to wooded streamsides and traverses through open grasslands make this a challenging, varied day's trip along the spine of the East Bay Hills.

Length 9.3 miles.

Location In Contra Costa County Hills between Berkeley and Oakland.

Trail Characteristics Trail surface varies from rocky to soft, duff-covered. Trail changes from wide, multi-use service road to narrow, occasionally overgrown path. Some sections are open, with little shade, others are sheltered and tree-covered. Ridgetops are often breezy, sometimes shrouded in fog. Considerable elevation gains and losses occur in short stretches of trail; e.g., a gain of 860 feet in Tilden Park, a loss of 600 feet in Sibley Preserve.

Ridge Trail Accessibility
- Hikers and equestrians—Tilden Regional Park, Sibley Regional Volcanic Preserve, Huckleberry Botanic Regional Preserve and East Bay Municipal Utility District (EBMUD).
- Bicyclists—Tilden Regional Park to Lomas Cantadas Rd.

Trail Management
- East Bay Skyline National Recreation Trail, including sections through EB-MUD lands—East Bay Regional Park District (EBRPD): 510-635-0135.

Rules
- East Bay Skyline National Recreation Trail through EBRPD preserves, Tilden, Sibley and Huckleberry, open from 5 A.M. to 10 P.M. Dogs must be on leash.
- EBMUD segments of East Bay Skyline National Recreation Trail—No dogs or bicycles. EBMUD backcountry permits not required.

Amenities
- Tilden Regional Park—Water (no water at Inspiration Point), restrooms, phone, visitor center, food concessions, swimming, picnic areas; group picnics by reservation: 510-636-1684. Youth group camping only, by reservation: 510-562-2267 (CAMP).
- Sibley Regional Volcanic Preserve—Water, picnic tables, self-guiding volcanics tour pamphlet and restrooms at visitor center.
- Redwood Regional Park—Water, telephone and restrooms at Skyline Gate.

Getting There

By Car

North entrance, Inspiration Point—From Hwy 24 take Fish Ranch Rd. exit, go 1 mile, and turn right on Grizzly Peak Blvd. In 1.3 miles, beyond Lomas

Cantadas Rd., turn right on South Park Dr. and go 1½ miles. Turn right on Wildcat Canyon Rd., and in about 1½ miles turn left into the large parking area at Inspiration Point. When South Park Dr. is closed to motor vehicles during the salamander migration season, November to March, continue on Grizzly Peak Blvd. to Golf Course Dr., turn right and then past the clubhouse, turn right again on Shasta Rd. Quickly turn right on Wildcat Canyon Rd. and continue about 1½ miles to Inspiration Point.

From I-80 in Berkeley—Take University Ave. exit and go 2 miles east to the U.C. campus. Turn left (north) on Oxford, right (east) on Rose, go one block, turn left (north) on Spruce and go to top of hill. Veer right (east) on Wildcat Canyon Rd. and continue about 2 miles to Inspiration Point.

South entrance, Skyline Gate—From Hwy 24 take Fish Ranch Rd. exit, go 1 mile, and turn left onto Grizzly Peak Blvd., which leads onto Skyline Blvd. After passing Shepherd Canyon Rd., go 0.1 mile to Skyline Gate and parking on east side of Skyline Blvd.

By Bus
AC Transit 67 serves Tilden Regional Park on weekends and holidays.

On The Trail
This 9.3-mile section of the Ridge Trail is part of the 31-mile East Bay Skyline National Recreation Trail (EBSNR Trail), also known as the Skyline Trail, which forms the backbone of a vast trail network in the East Bay. The Skyline Trail traverses lands of the East Bay Regional Park District and those of the East Bay Municipal Utility District, linking Wildcat Canyon Regional Park in Richmond with Cull Canyon Recreation Area in Castro Valley. Signposts carry the Bay Area Ridge Trail logo as well as the EBSNR Trail symbol.

Three entry points provide the opportunity to take this 9.3-mile trip in shorter sections—at Tilden Park's Inspiration Point, at Lomas Cantadas Road near the Steam Trains overflow parking lot, and at the Sibley Regional Volcanic Preserve parking area.

Starting from the north end, the first segment of 3.0 miles begins at Inspiration Point in Tilden Park. Before beginning your trip, walk over to the north side of the point's parking area for impressive views of the reservoirs and coastal hills. Then leave from the west side of the parking area, go around the stone gates to Nimitz Way and immediately drop down left onto the Curran Trail. After you pass the Meadows Canyon Trail on the right, take the next trail on the left, heading uphill to Wildcat Canyon Road.

Cross the road here to a broad, multi-use trail, Tilden Park's Sea View Trail, which climbs steadily to reach the vistas that its name promises. Unfolding at every step are panoramic views (if the day is clear) through the Golden Gate to the sea; of San Francisco Bay and its surrounding cities; and of our tallest mountains—Tamalpais, St. Helena and Diablo.

For 1.3 miles on the Sea View Trail, the Ridge Trail route for **hikers, equestri-**

ans, and **bicyclists** traverses the heights of San Pablo Ridge, uplifted some ten million years ago by stresses on the nearby Hayward and Moraga faults. At the junction of the Sea View/Lupine trails, **bicyclists** go straight ahead on the wide Sea View Trail. From this trail are splendid views of the North Bay hills traversed by other segments of the Bay Area Ridge Trail. As you rise to the highest point of the trail, look east across the ridges and valleys of Contra Costa County to Mt. Diablo, which dominates the landscape. Continuing around the northeast side of Vollmer Peak (1,913′), you then descend to the Lomas Contadas/Grizzly Peak Boulevard intersection and the end of the signed Ridge Trail route for bicyclists.

At the Sea View/Lupine trails junction, **hikers** and **equestrians** turn right downhill (south) on the Lupine Trail. (Do not take the Arroyo Trail, which goes north from this junction.) Follow the Lupine Trail, marked Bay Area Ridge Trail and East Bay Skyline National Recreation Trail, past an unmarked trail on your right. Continue along a coyote bush-wild blackberry-tangled hillside below Vollmer Peak to the Vollmer Peak Trail junction. Here, on a shoulder of Vollmer Peak, you make a very sharp turn left uphill (east) on the Vollmer Peak Trail. Then, after 200 feet on this rocky path, you veer right, still on the Vollmer Peak Trail, and contour around the steep hillside on this narrow trail, passing through grasslands dotted with purple lupine and yellow mule ears in spring. Then the Vollmer Peak Trail emerges from a bay-tree woods and ends at the Steam Trains overflow parking area. Hikers and equestrians pass through the parking area, rejoin bicyclists on the wide, paved service road, and go downhill to reach the picnic area by the Steam Trains at Lomas Cantadas Road.

The second segment of this trip extends from Lomas Cantadas Road to the Sibley Preserve, a 3.4-mile trip. On the south side of the road, the **hiker's** and **equestrian's** Bay Area Ridge Trail route takes a downhill trail to a gate into EBMUD's lands. On this trail you travel through eucalyptus groves and along hillsides carpeted with a variety of annual grasses and native, perennial bunchgrasses. In an oak woodland you pass the De Laveaga Trail descending east to Orinda, but you veer right, out into the grasslands again. Looking out over a peaceful scene of ranches nestled in valleys and cows grazing on hillsides, you can easily forget the proximity of nearby urban centers.

Soon you make a couple of zigzags, curve around below Grizzly Peak Boulevard, and descend to Fish Ranch Road. Cross the road and open the gate to the well-marked Skyline Trail, the Ridge Trail route for hikers and equestrians. (Please close the gate).

Now 1.45 miles from Lomas Cantadas Road, you take a narrow trail, in some places bordered by masses of poison oak and thistles, but fragrant with sticky monkey flower and cow parsnip blossoms in spring and summer. Heading uphill to cross over the Caldecott Tunnel, you can hear the traffic on Highway 24 below, but near the top you will find a quiet, peaceful rest stop at a rustic bench in a mature oak woodland.

In an opening in these woods, proceed a few hundred yards along an old wagon road to a wooden gate on your right. Here you enter Sibley Volcanic Regional

Step up to the open-air visitor center at Sibley Volcanic Regional Preserve to learn about the preserve's volcanic origins.

Preserve, and then continue 1.95 miles on the EBSNR Trail. Under a canopy of large evergreen oaks, multi-trunked bays and tall bigleaf maples you keep to the north side of a creek. After crossing a bridge over this creek, the trail turns due south, following the west side of the creek. Then you ascend a wide fire road, gaining 300 feet in elevation before reaching the Sibley Preserve parking area.

The third segment, 2.9 miles, starts at the entrance to the Sibley Preserve. Just to the left (north) of the visitor center take the narrow trail 0.2 mile through pine forests and pass a gated road on your left, where a side trip on the Round Top Loop Trail begins. If you take this trip with the explanatory brochure available at the visitor center, you can learn about the exposed volcanic rocks extruded from nearby Round Top, an extinct volcano that last erupted over nine million years ago. Deposits from this volcano underlie some of the ridges over which you have just traveled.

To continue along the Skyline Trail, your Bay Area Ridge Trail route, cross the gated Round Top Loop Trail and the paved road to the water tank, and follow a narrow trail 0.16 mile through a fragrant pine forest. Then you cross the paved road, which leads to Round Top's 1,763-foot summit, and arrive at the top of a steep, rocky hillside. Here, the other end of the Loop Trail comes in from the east, but you make a rugged, precipitous descent on a south-facing hillside into San Leandro Creek Canyon, where you enter the East Bay Regional Park District's Huckleberry Botanic Regional Preserve. On your descent, you may see the brittleleaf and the pallid manzanitas, found in only two places in the world.

Then under a dense cover of oak and bay trees grown spindly in their search for light, you cross San Leandro Creek by a defunct dam, turn sharp right (west) and start uphill on the north-facing slope. (A preserve gate bars an old trail, not recommended, along the creek.) On a well-designed trail with a lush understory of ferns, ocean spray, and huckleberry, continue through this delightful, verdant section. This preserve receives heavy winter rainfall and dense summer fogs. In the wet season, you may be crossing full-flowing rivulets coursing down the ravines.

After about two hundred yards on your uphill way, there is a junction from where a gated trail goes straight ahead, uphill, to the Huckleberry Preserve's parking area on Skyline Boulevard. However, you make a sharp left turn (southeast) in front of this gate, contour along the hillside through a damp oak-and-bay forest, and then make a steep climb up and around the head of a ravine. When you reach the Huckleberry Preserve Nature Trail junction, go left on the EBSNR Trail. Here, on warmer slopes, you are in an oak-and-madrone forest.

Shortly you reach Pinehurst Road and cross it at its junction with Skyline Boulevard. Proceed south along the east side of Skyline Boulevard, looking to your left for a trail entrance. From it climb steeply through a eucalyptus grove, then continue over the hilltop to the junction with the East Ridge Trail in Redwood Regional Park. Here you turn right (southwest) on the East

The Ridge Trail in Sibley Preserve winds through a fragrant pine forest.

Ridge Trail, also the Skyline National Recreation Trail, a broad service road. Continue about ¼ mile to the Skyline Gate and the end of your trip. If you have a shuttle car waiting here, you can make this a one-way trip. Equestrians able to travel greater distances in a day than hikers can probably make this a round trip.

The next leg of the Bay Area Ridge Trail, an 8.3-mile trip, continues through Redwood Regional Park to Bort Meadow in Anthony Chabot Regional Park. See *Redwood Regional Park and Anthony Chabot Regional Park.* ■

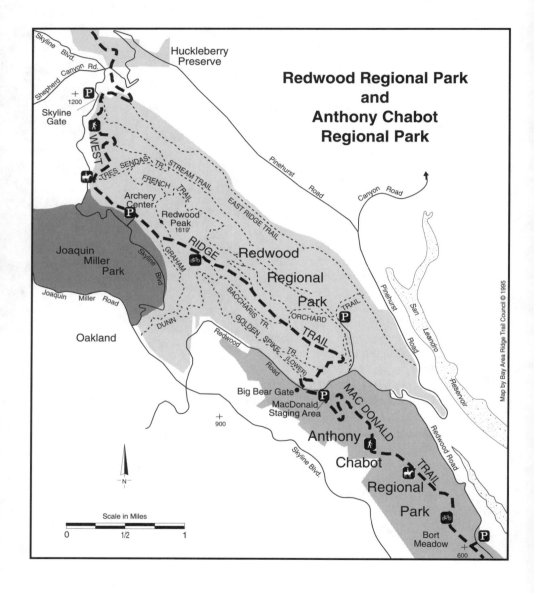

Redwood Regional Park
and
Anthony Chabot
Regional Park

Redwood Regional Park and Anthony Chabot Regional Park

From Skyline Gate to Bort Meadow

Through second-growth forests and along open grasslands, this segment stays on the ridgeline except for a quick descent and subsequent rise halfway to Bort Meadow.

Length 8.3 miles.

Location In Alameda County east of Oakland and Piedmont between Skyline Blvd. and Pinehurst/Redwood roads.

Trail Characteristics West Ridge and MacDonald trails are wide, unpaved service roads, in shade part way. Occasional fog, often strong sunshine in summer on open ridgetop sections. West Ridge Trail climbs 200 feet, drops 900 feet. MacDonald Trail climbs 500 feet, drops 300 feet to Bort Meadow.

Ridge Trail Accessibility
- Hikers, equestrians, and bicyclists.

Trail Management
- East Bay Regional Park District (EBRPD): 510-635-0135.

Rules
- Open from 5 A.M. to 10 P.M. or as posted. Fee for group picnics, camping, parking, and dogs (allowed on leash only).

Amenities
- Redwood Regional Park—Water, restrooms, telephone, and parking at Skyline and Redwood gates. Group picnic reservations: 510-636-1684. Youth group camping only, by reservation: 510-562-2267 (CAMP).
- Anthony Chabot Regional Park
  MacDonald Staging Area—Restrooms and parking.
  Bort Meadow—Water, restrooms, picnicking, and large group camping (up to 500) by reservation: 510-562-2267.
  Bort Meadow Staging Area—Parking.

Getting There

By Car
North entrance, Skyline Gate—From Hwy 24 take Fish Ranch Rd. exit, turn left onto Grizzly Peak Blvd., which leads onto Skyline Blvd. After passing Shepherd Canyon Rd., go 0.1 mile to Skyline Gate and parking on east side of Skyline Blvd.

South entrance, Bort Meadow Staging Area, also marked Big Trees—From Hwy 13 in Oakland, take Redwood Rd. northeast through Redwood Regional

Park. At the Pinehurst Road junction, veer east, and continue on Redwood Road for 2 miles to Bort Meadow Staging Area on south side of road.

By Bus
AC Transit bus 46 to Skyline Blvd. at Roberts Recreation Area, weekends only.

On The Trail

This segment of the Bay Area Ridge Trail route continues southeast on the EBRPD's 31-mile East Bay Skyline National Recreation Trail (EBSNR Trail). Redwood Regional Park, midway on the Skyline Trail, was once the site of a magnificent redwood forest. Trees in this primeval forest measured more than 20 feet in diameter, larger than the greatest redwood of the North Coast. It is said that ships entering the Golden Gate, sixteen miles away, used two of the tallest trees to steer their course across San Francisco Bay.

Sadly, this majestic redwood forest, part of early 19th century Spanish land grants, was felled to the last tree between 1840 and 1860 in the rapid building of Bay Area cities—San Francisco, Oakland, and the more distant cities of Benicia and Martinez. Even the tree stumps were rooted out for firewood. The new redwoods that sprouted from the remaining stumps were later cut to rebuild structures devastated by the 1906 earthquake. Finally the logging ceased. Today, some redwood trees tower above the ridges, reaching 100-foot heights, and former mill sites for the logging operations serve as picnic areas in the park.

Hikers, equestrians, and **bicyclists,** begin your trip through Redwood Regional Park by setting off from the park's Skyline Gate on the West Ridge Trail. You tread a wide, level path frequented by a variety of trail users—strollers, bicyclists, runners, and local residents escorting their toddlers or walking their dogs. The first half mile is quite open, although oaks, madrones, pines, and many eucalyptus trees fill the canyon below. On your right, after rains, there is a rivulet trickling down an assemblage of smooth, sandstone boulders.

When you reach the first clump of redwoods, the trail surface is sprinkled with soft duff, composed of redwood branchlets and small cones. These tall, second-growth redwoods, intermixed with luxuriant bay trees, support an understory of ferns and shade-loving, spring wildflowers in white and blue.

Rounding a bend, you pass the French Trail taking off to the left. If the day is very hot, the French Trail, for hikers and equestrians, offers a cool, though longer, alternate route which contours midway between the high West Ridge Trail and the Stream Trail on the canyon floor. (The Stream Trail too, is open only to hikers and equestrians.)

Continuing for 0.5 mile on the West Ridge Trail, **hikers, equestrians,** and **bicyclists** pass the Tres Sendas Trail on the left, a footpath which descends east to join the French Trail. Then, just beyond a short spur on your right that leads to the Moon Gate at Skyline Boulevard, you begin a steady climb around the flank of a hill dominated by communications equipment and a water tank. At the outer edge of the flank is a bench overlooking some of Redwood Regional Park's 2,000 acres north and east of here.

Second-growth redwoods tower over Redwood Regional Park

For the next half mile you follow the trail through an extensive forest of eucalyptus trees, turned brown from the severe frosts of 1990, yet now recovered. You may wonder about the origin of these trees. It seems that an Oakland real-estate developer planted vast eucalyptus forests in an ill-fated timber-harvesting scheme. At the same time, he built Skyline Boulevard to take investors to his project. However, eucalyptus wood was financially unprofitable for the developer and ecologically disastrous for this former redwood environment. Eucalyptus, a fast-growing and invasive import from Australia, inhibits the growth of native plant species, such as redwood and oak trees.

Yet, some native plants are springing up in the tangle of litterfall in dense, shaggy eucalyptus forests. Today, you can find robust toyon bushes on the hillside and wild huckleberry bushes flourishing in ravines where moisture is sufficient. You can recognize the huckleberries by their small, shiny green, oblong leaves on long, graceful branches. In late summer you may see their blue-black berries, much-favored by deer and blue jays. To the right of the trail, and much more noticeable than the huckleberries, are seven maple trees planted on Arbor Day, 1986, to commemorate the seven astronauts lost on the *Challenger*. A wooden plaque marks the site.

When you reach the Archery Center, where the Redwood Bowmen practice, cross the parking area and then veer slightly left to continue on the West Ridge Trail. In deep shade you walk on a wide path bounded by a fence with massive redwood posts draped with thick, green moss. This may be a trail built during the Depression years by Works Progress Administration (WPA) crews. These crews also built four stone huts along Redwood Creek in the canyon east of this trail, as well as trails and a few huts in the Sierra Nevada. From this path, kept damp and cool by fog moisture dripping from the redwoods' upper branches, look left for inviting picnic facilities in the Redwood Bowl.

At the Graham Trail junction, bear left (east) on the West Ridge Trail. (The Graham Trail leads off right to the swimming-pool complex, children's play equipment, and picnic tables in the Roberts Recreation Area.) In 500 feet you could take the Peak Trail left for a quick side trip, a 0.2-mile climb to 1,619-foot Redwood Peak, the highest point in Redwood Regional Park. Continuing on the Bay Area Ridge Trail beyond the Peak Trail turnoff, you are out of the woods. The West Ridge Trail lives up to its name as it traverses the long ridge that lies on the west side of the park. Following the ridgeline on a bare sandstone surface, this wide trail marks the limits of chaparral on the west and forest on the east. Best taken during the cool hours of a hot day, this trail's southwest-facing orientation is most welcome on cool but sunny winter days.

Passing the north and then the south end of the Baccharis Trail you come to the Orchard Trail, which drops into the canyon just east of the Orchard and Old Church picnic areas beside Redwood Creek. In the 1920s, settlers moved into the cut-over forest land, built small homes and a church, and set out orchards. Remnants of their fruit trees still send out fragrant blossoms in spring.

Before long the chaparral gives way to a fine, dense, mixed woodland of oak, madrone, bay, and occasional redwood, home to many deer. You may see them bounding across the trail or hear them crashing in the woods. Now the West Ridge Trail descends steeply to a park entrance road. **Bicyclists** stay on it, crossing a stone bridge at the Fishway Interpretive Site. Here, explanatory plaques tell the story of a unique native species of rainbow trout, *Salmo Iridia*, found in this creek and others of the San Leandro Creek drainage. Because the Lake Chabot Dam locked this species here, fish in these creeks are descendants of the pure native strain of the original rainbow trout. These fish are unique to this area and are the subject of scientific studies; therefore, fishing is not permitted in Redwood Creek. From the Fishway Interpretive Site **bicyclists** ride south on the park entrance road, turn right (west) on Redwood Road, and continue about $\frac{1}{3}$ mile to the MacDonald Gate Staging Area.

Hikers and **equestrians** may follow the West Ridge Trail too, but their more

Fishway in Redwood Creek protects unique endangered rainbow trout.

direct, half-mile Bay Area Ridge Trail route takes a short spur trail on the right (south) just before the West Ridge Trail makes a wide arc to the left (north). This spur trail then joins the narrow Golden Spike Trail for a pretty trip through the woods, across a rivulet, and down the hillside to the Lower Golden Spike Trail. Here you swing left and emerge in a clearing (probably the site of a former settler's home), marked by exotic plantings, several sizable redwood trees, and a plank bridge across Redwood Creek

Now cross Redwood Road to Anthony Chabot Regional Park and veer left cn the lovely, shady Big Bear Trail through Redwood Canyon. In spring, the white plum blossoms of fruit trees glow among the dark conifers at the creekside. In summer, their deep purple leaves add contrast to the various greens of maples, sycamores and bay laurels.

In a few minutes **hikers** and **equestrians** join **bicyclists** at the MacDonald Gate Staging Area to begin the second half of this trip. Now they travel through 4,927-acre Anthony Chabot Regional Park, named for a pioneer Californian who built an earth-fill dam across San Leandro Creek, forming Lake Chabot. Long before the time of Chabot, the Ohlone people lived in these hills, fished the streams, hunted small game, gathered acorns, and dug bulbs for food.

Begin your 3.2-mile trip through Anthony Chabot Park on the MacDonald Trail, which climbs steeply through oak woodlands to the park's central ridge. As you ascend the wide, multi-use trail and park service road, pause to look back northwest into wooded Redwood Canyon and over the vast public lands you have been traversing. Then, when you are almost at the crest of the ridge, search for a little side trail on the left that leads to a vista point. From a bench in this pleasant, shady spot you can see across a deep canyon to the opposite ridge where Pinehurst Road swings northwest. On beyond is Moraga, and towering above the ridges and valleys of the East Bay is Mt. Diablo, the central survey point for Northern California.

Returning to the MacDonald Trail, a segment of the EBSNR Trail, **hikers, equestrians,** and **bicyclists** now contour along close to the ridgetop through grassland and chaparral. In 1 mile the trail arcs right to a junction where the Parkridge Trail comes in from the park's south boundary. This trail crosses a narrow, transverse ridge that divides two drainages, the one to the east feeding the little creek that flows through Chabot's Grass Valley.

You bear left on the MacDonald Trail around a small knoll graced by a few oak trees and many wildflowers in spring. This trail continues for another 1.7 miles along the southwest-facing ridge, with no tree cover, so plan to do it in the cool hours. Above, on the ridgecrest, is a fringe of oak trees, and on the slope below is baccharis (coyote bush), now gaining a toehold. Although many informal trails take off from and re-enter the MacDonald Trail, you continue on the main park service road.

Before long you begin to see the grassy valley and tall trees of Bort Meadow. Please stay on the trail to the green gate. The end of this Bay Area Ridge Trail segment, the Bort Meadow Staging Area, is about 500 yards beyond the green gate. You can have a shuttle car waiting here to return to the Skyline Gate or to drive east on Redwood Road to family campsites in Anthony Chabot Park. (Use the Marciel Gate.)

Just beyond the green gate, a trail turns downhill to the valley. There you turn right (west) to find picnic tables, barbecues, water and restrooms in Bort Meadow. The eucalyptus trees around the periphery are remnants of vast plantings done by the People's Water Company in the 1910s, which greatly altered the landscape, but the EBRPD is now replanting with native trees. Group camping can be arranged for Bort Meadow through the EBRPD.

If you are continuing another 3.5 miles to Anthony Chabot campsites, head east on the Grass Valley Trail or the Brandon Trail after descending to the valley. See *Anthony Chabot Regional Park, Bort Meadow to Chabot Staging Area.* ■

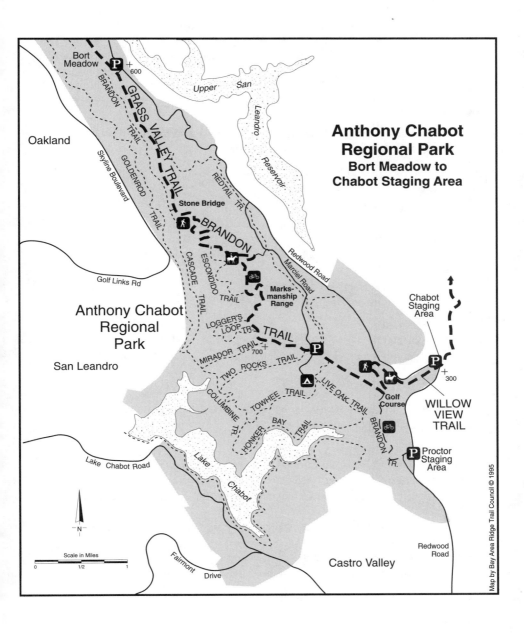

Bort Meadow

Oakland

Upper   San

Leandro

Reservoir

BRANDON TRAIL

GRASS VALLEY TRAIL

SKYLINE Boulevard

GOLDENROD TRAIL

REDTAIL TR.

Stone Bridge

BRANDON

Golf Links Rd

CASCADE TRAIL

ESCONDIDO TRAIL

Marksmanship Range

Redwood Road

Marciel Road

**Anthony Chabot
Regional Park**
**Bort Meadow to
Chabot Staging Area**

Chabot
Staging
Area

Anthony Chabot
Regional
Park

San Leandro

LOGGER'S LOOP TR.

MIRADOR TRAIL

TRAIL

TWO ROCKS TRAIL

COLUMBINE TR.

TOWHEE TRAIL

BAY TRAIL

HONKER TRAIL

LIVE OAK TRAIL

Golf
Course

BRANDON TR.

WILLOW
VIEW
TRAIL

Proctor
Staging
Area

Lake Chabot Road

Lake

Chabot

N

Scale in Miles

0   1/2   1

Fairmont   Drive

Castro Valley

Redwood
Road

Map by Bay Area Ridge Trail Council © 1995

Anthony Chabot Regional Park

From Bort Meadow to Chabot Staging Area

After traversing a long, grassy valley and climbing through eucalyptus forests, this trip follows a ridgetop trail and then zigzags down to the Chabot Staging Area on Redwood Road.

Length 6.1 miles.

Location In Alameda County between Redwood Rd. and Skyline Blvd. east of Oakland and San Leandro and north of Castro Valley.

Trail Characteristics Trails are wide park-service roads with compacted surface, except for the narrow Willow View Trail. Trip gradually gains 340 feet in elevation, then loses 660 feet in last 1.2 miles. About half the trails are in full sun, the rest in shade.

Ridge Trail Accessibility
- Hikers, equestrians, and bicyclists—From Bort Meadow to Willow View Trail junction.
- Hikers and equestrians—Willow View Trail.
- Bicyclists—Brandon Trail south to Proctor Staging Area.

Trail Management
- East Bay Regional Park District (EBRPD): 510-635-0135—Entire trail.
- Chabot Staging Area—East Bay Municipal Utility District (EBMUD): 510-254-3778.

Rules
- Open daily 5 A.M. to 10 P.M. or as posted. Fee for group picnics, camping, parking, and dogs (allowed on leash only).

Amenities
- Anthony Chabot Regional Park—Group picnic reservations: 510-636-1684. Camping reservations: 510-562-2267. Brochure available through EBRPD. Fees required at Equestrian Center, Marksmanship Range, and Lake Chabot Marina.
- Bort Meadow—Water, restrooms, picnicking, and large group camping (up to 500) by reservation.
- Anthony Chabot Family Camp—Year-round camping with hot showers.
- Chabot Staging Area—Parking and portable toilet. No water.

Getting There
North entrance, Bort Meadow Staging Area (also marked Big Trees)—From Hwy 13 in Oakland, take Redwood Rd. northeast through Redwood Regional Park. At the Pinehurst Rd. junction, veer east, and continue on Redwood Rd. for 2 miles to Bort Meadow Staging Area on south side of road.

South entrance, Chabot Staging Area—From Hwy 580 eastbound take Redwood Rd. exit and turn left (north), passing under freeway. Continue on Redwood Road about 3 miles. After the road narrows, pass the Willow Park Golf Course on your left. Where Redwood Rd. makes a hairpin turn to the left, the entrance to the Chabot Staging Area is on your right.

From Hwy 580 westbound take Castro Valley Blvd. exit, continue west on it to Redwood Rd. Turn right (north), following directions above.

Bicyclists, South entrance, Proctor Staging Area—Follow directions for Chabot Staging Area above, but after going 2 miles on Redwood Rd., watch for Proctor Staging Area on left.

On The Trail
From the Bort Meadow Staging Area take the gated service road beside the parking area (hikers can take the foot trail west of the parking area to the trail junction) to reach the broad service road in Grass Valley. To your right (north) lies Bort Meadow, a picnic and group camping area enclosed by high ridges and rimmed by tall eucalyptus and newly planted redwood trees.

To your left (south) is the Bay Area Ridge Trail route, the Grass Valley Trail, through mile-long Grass Valley. This area, the former 525-acre Grass Valley Ranch, was the major part of a 1951 East Bay Regional Park District purchase, first called Grass Valley Park, and now a part of 49,027-acre Anthony Chabot Regional Park. Later additions to today's park were parts of Mexican land grants made to Don Luis Maria Peralta (1840) and Don Guillermo Castro (1843), on which they grazed cattle and then sold the hides for leather. In the 1860s Don Castro's accumulated gambling debts led to the sale of his lands, which were later subdivided and sold to American owners who raised beef cattle. These lands east of Oakland became valuable watershed and were eventually consolidated into the East Bay Municipal Utility District. EBRPD now leases the Lake Chabot area, making it available for public recreation.

Grass Valley Creek flows under a willow-tree canopy between parallel trails, the Grass Valley Trail and the Brandon Trail. The Brandon Trail, on the west side of the valley, offers more shade and would be a good choice on hot summer afternoons. Either trail takes you to the Stone Bridge, where these trails converge.

This trip takes the Grass Valley Trail, which is the marked Bay Area Ridge Trail route and a segment of the East Bay Skyline National Recreation Trail. It traverses the east side of the valley at the foot of chaparral slopes, some recently revegetated to restore eroded, gullied areas. There may be cattle grazing on or near the trail, but even if you don't see them, heed the signs asking you to close gates. Up on the eastern ridge, powerline towers make perches for more indigenous creatures—the red-tailed hawks, who search the grasslands for rodents on broad, flat wings, and turkey vultures, whose wide, V-shaped wings and wobbly flight distinguish them from the hawks.

Just 1 mile from the trailhead, you pass the Redtail Trail on the left. Then the valley narrows, the trail edges closer to the creek, and it enters a eucalyptus grove, interspersed with coyote bush and some emerging redwoods. The huge forests of eucalyptus trees you see in this park, planted in the 1910s by the People's Water Company of Oakland, spread rapidly and greatly altered the ecology of the foothills. Severe freezes in the last 25 years turned the eucalyptus brown, but these hardy trees still survive. If you pass through eucalyptus groves on a foggy or rainy day, you will probably notice the trees' characteristic menthol fragrance.

Soon the Grass Valley and Brandon trails meet near the Stone Bridge, where the Grass Valley Trail terminates and the Brandon Trail crosses to the east side of the valley. Take a moment to walk out on the bridge to admire its huge sandstone block construction. Downstream from the bridge, Grass Valley Creek courses southeast through a tight canyon to reach Lake Chabot.

Now Ridge Trail users follow the Brandon Trail uphill, gently climbing into the heads of ravines and around bends. This wide trail and park-service road is part of the well-traveled Lake Chabot Bicycle Loop. In about 0.25 mile you pass an old trail that takes off left, but you continue on the broad Brandon Trail through the eucalyptus forest. In spite of the eucalyptus' dominance, the trail is edged with blackberries, ferns and seasonal blossoms—inconspicuous creamy-white miner's lettuce and white, four-petaled milkmaids bloom early in spring. In sunny areas, you may see the white clusters of Fremont lilies atop their long stalks and the vibrant orange hues of California poppies. Ubiquitous poison-oak plants explode each spring with shiny, green, three-lobed leaves. In fall, you can easily recognize poison oak by its brilliant red and orange leaves. At any time of the year, this plant should be avoided.

Almost a mile from the Stone Bridge the Escondido Trail arcs right, but the Bay Area Ridge Trail route continues straight ahead (east) on the Brandon Trail around the hillside, curving back into canyons and rounding shoulders of the hill. On the sandy surface of the trail are prints of many trail users—the corrugated tread of athletic shoes, the continuous pattern of bicycle tires, U-shaped prints of equestrians' steeds, spindly, three-toed bird prints, and the paw prints of many animals. If you look closely, you may see the sinuous track of a snake's passage. After you pass the other end of the Escondido Trail and make a deep sweep into the back of a ravine, you begin to hear rifles cracking in the forest. Unnerving as the noise may be, these weapons are contained in a marksmanship range.

You emerge from the shade of the eucalyptus groves to a south-facing, sloping grassland. On your right are the Logger's Loop and Mirador trails and then the Two Rocks Trail. However, to continue your trip on the Ridge Trail, stay on the Brandon Trail through the grasslands to the Marciel Road crossing. On the other side of Marciel Road are a parking area, restrooms, and the continuation of the Bay Area Ridge Trail south. If you plan to camp in the park, take the Towhee Trail right (south) to reach the campground kiosk.

Continuing on the Bay Area Ridge Trail for less than ¼ mile, you will find some trailside boulders, good perches for lunch or a pause to look northeast across two canyons to Dinosaur Ridge, the highest point of the next Ridge Trail segment. On clear days, the ridge's distinctive white rock is visible from here, almost 2 miles away. Beyond is an impressive vista of the East Bay's seemingly endless succession of rugged ridges.

When it's time to move on, start down the ridgetop trail flanked by evergreen oaks, toyon, and coyote bushes. At a sharp turn right, bicyclists veer off, following the Brandon Trail, the continuation of the Lake Chabot Bicycle Loop, for another 1.6 miles downhill to the Proctor Staging Area at the end of the bicyclist's segment.

But on the left, just before the bicyclists' sharp turn to the right, is the Willow View Trail entrance beside a bench in the shade of a beautiful evergreen oak tree. Hikers and equestrians take the Willow View Trail down into the woods on the east side of the ridge. Winding along the canyonside under oaks and madrones, you pass huge sandstone outcrops decorated with feathery moss and high trail banks festooned with ferns. Having dropped over 200 feet in 0.3 mile, you then travel upstream along a little tributary of San Leandro Creek, cross it, and follow it downstream for another 0.3 mile. This trail, delightfully cool on a hot day, could be muddy after heavy winter rains.

Although Redwood Road runs along the bank above this section of the Willow View Trail, a canopy of bushes and trees shields the trail from the road. On the right side of the trail is an old fence post entwined with wild cucumber vines, a remnant of former ranching days. A little farther down the trail lies a jumble of smooth-edged, lichen-encrusted boulders under overarching oak and bay trees from which you can watch the golfers on adjacent Willow Park Golf Course.

Then you follow the Willow View Trail north through a damp, woodsy flat where, in early spring, a fabulous garden of three-petaled trillium flowers blossom in shades of pink, mauve, and burgundy. These plants are worth a special trip to see. In the midst of this garden is a fork in the trail. The Bay Area Ridge Trail arcs right, crosses the creek, goes under Redwood Road, and then on to the Chabot Staging Area. However, after heavy rains, take the left trail out to Redwood Road, cross it, and continue on to the staging area.

The Chabot Staging Area is the end of this Bay Area Ridge Trail segment for hikers and equestrians. At the Proctor Staging Area, bicyclists end their trip. See *East Bay Municipal Utility District Lands to Cull Canyon Recreation Area* for the continuation of the Bay Area Ridge Trail.   ■

Look for this gate to reach campsites in 4,900-acre Anthony Chabot Regional Park.

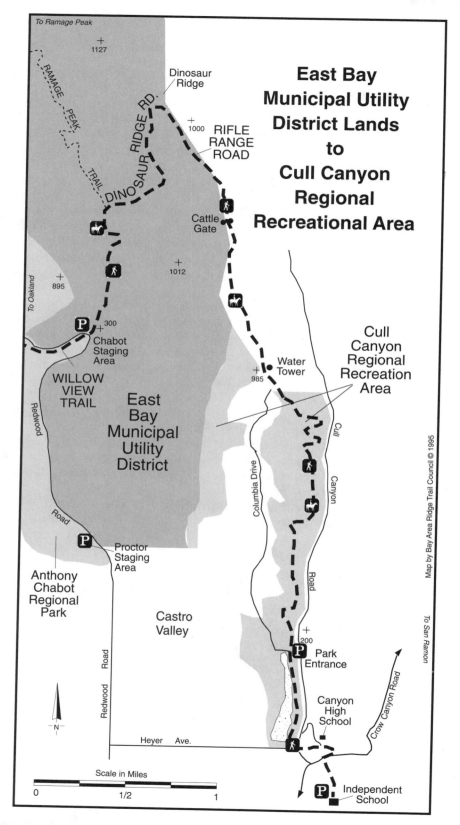

To Ramage Peak

RAMAGE PEAK TRAIL

+ 1127

Dinosaur Ridge

DINOSAUR RIDGE RD.

+ 1000

RIFLE RANGE ROAD

East Bay Municipal Utility District Lands to Cull Canyon Regional Recreational Area

Cattle Gate

+ 1012

To Oakland

+ 895

P + 300

Chabot Staging Area

WILLOW VIEW TRAIL

East Bay Municipal Utility District

Redwood Road

Water Tower

+ 985

Cull Canyon Regional Recreation Area

Cull Canyon Road

P

Proctor Staging Area

Anthony Chabot Regional Park

Castro Valley

Columbia Drive

P + 200

Park Entrance

Canyon High School

Crow Canyon Road

To San Ramon

Redwood Road

Heyer Ave.

P Independent School

—N—

Scale in Miles

0   1/2   1

Map by Bay Area Ridge Trail Council © 1995

East Bay Municipal Utility District Lands to Cull Canyon Regional Recreation Area

From Chabot Staging Area to Cull Canyon Picnic Area

Beginning with a steady, 2-mile ascent to Dinosaur Ridge and its 360-degree views, this segment follows a rolling ridgetop trail through open grasslands, then descends through oak woodlands to a shady trail bordering Cull Creek. From the recreation area hikers meander past new subdivisions to reach Independent School in Castro Valley.

Length   Chabot Staging Area to Cull Canyon Recreation Area—7.2 miles; Chabot Staging Area to Independent School—8.4 miles.

Location   In Alameda County near Castro Valley.

Trail Characteristics   About half the trails are on service roads through hilly cattle-grazing lands with little tree cover; others mostly in oak woodlands, 3 feet wide on a moderate grade. The last, short segment skirts suburban development. Elevation gain of 920 feet in first 2 miles. Very little shade until Cull Canyon.

Ridge Trail Accessibility
- Hikers and equestrians—Chabot Staging Area to Cull Canyon Regional Recreation Area.
- Hikers—Cull Canyon Recreation Area to Independent School.

Trail Management
- Chabot Staging Area to Cull Canyon Recreation Area—East Bay Municipal Utility District (EBMUD): 510-254-3778.
- Cull Canyon Recreation Area—East Bay Regional Park District (EBRPD): 510-635-0135.

Rules
- EBMUD trails from Chabot Staging Area to the water-tank clearing require a trail use permit, available for a small fee from the EBMUD office, 500 San Pablo Dam Rd., Orinda, CA 94563; 510-254-3778. No dogs or bicycles on EBMUD lands.
- EBRPD trail through Cull Canyon Regional Recreation Area to Independent School—Open dawn to dusk. No bicycles, no permit required. Dogs on leash on EBRPD trails.

Amenities
- Chabot Staging Area—Parking and portable toilet. No water.
- EBRPD—Year-round camping with hot showers available at Anthony Chabot Family Campground in Anthony Chabot Regional Park, 2 miles west on Redwood Rd. Use Marciel Gate entrance. EBRPD group picnic reservations:

510-636-1684. Family camping reservations: 510-562-2267. Fee per car/trailer for camping and for dogs.
- Cull Canyon Regional Recreation Area—Restrooms, water, picnic areas, fishing lake, swimming lagoon and snack bar in season. Fee for swimming.

Getting There

North entrance, Chabot Staging Area—From Hwy 580 eastbound take Redwood Rd. exit and turn left (north), passing under the freeway. Continue on Redwood Rd. about 3 miles. After the road narrows, pass the Willow Park Golf Course on your left. Where Redwood Rd. makes a hairpin turn to the left, the entrance to the Chabot Staging Area is on your right.

From Hwy 580 westbound take Castro Valley Boulevard exit, continue west on it to Redwood Rd. Turn right (north), following directions above.

South entrance, Cull Canyon Recreation Area—From Hwy 580 eastbound, take Center St. exit and go north on Center St. Turn right (east) on Heyer Ave., turn left (north) on Cull Canyon Rd., and then turn left into recreation area parking lots.

From Hwy 580 westbound, take Castro Valley exit, turn left (west) on East Castro Valley Blvd., and then go right (north) on Crow Canyon Rd. After 0.6 mile, turn left (northwest) onto Cull Canyon Rd. and proceed to recreation area.

South entrance, Independent School—From Hwy 580 eastbound take Crow Canyon Rd. exit, cross over freeway, turn right on East Castro Valley Blvd., cross Crow Canyon Rd., and turn left on Independent School Rd. Park outside school gates on cul-de-sac.

Westbound, take East Castro Valley Blvd. exit, turn right on it, and then left on Independent School Rd.

On The Trail

With your EBMUD permit in hand, **hikers** and **equestrians** leave the east side of the Chabot Staging Area and go a few paces along a gravelled road to EBMUD's Ramage Peak Trail entrance on your right. Also well-marked as the Bay Area Ridge Trail, this path leads into a shady glade, then winds uphill through oak woodlands on the east side of San Leandro Creek canyon.

About ¾ mile from the trail entrance, you drop into the Tamler Memorial Redwood Grove, dedicated to the father of Lou Tamler. Lou supervised the Conservation Corps crew that built this trail.

Shortly—¼ mile—you reach the Dinosaur Ridge Road/Ramage Peak Trail junction. Here the Bay Area Ridge Trail route veers right (east) following Dinosaur Ridge, a wide ranch road. After a couple of zigzags under the powerlines, this trail heads straight up the nose of a bare hillside. An elevation gain of 480 feet in less than ½ mile promotes frequent stops to enjoy views back across San Leandro Creek canyon and the forested ridges of Chabot Regional Park to San Francisco Bay.

Part way up, the trail curves around a knoll and levels off a bit, then dips into a saddle before beginning another ascent. Looking ahead to the heights of Dinosaur Ridge, you see large, white protrusions on the rounded mountaintop. Regularly spaced and jagged, they stretch across the summit. From here it's unclear what they might be.

Uplifted rocks with embedded fossilized shells surmount Dinosaur Ridge.

Then, at a trail junction just below the summit, about 2 miles from your start, a Bay Area Ridge Trail sign points east, away from the top. Wisely avoiding an old ranch road leading directly uphill, you contour around to the east flank.

Here, although the Bay Area Ridge Trail joins Rifle Range Road and turns right (south), take the short, gentle climb to the summit on your left. Well worth the detour, this 0.2-mile side trip reveals the derivation of the ridge's name. The jagged protrusions indeed look like the protective plates or fins of a giant dinosaur. And a closer look discloses white seashell fossils embedded in the rocks. Probably uplifted from the ocean floor during some ancient folding/faulting process, these rocks remained when softer materials eroded away.

From the top of Dinosaur Ridge you have Bay Area views around the compass— west to the Golden Gate guarded by Mt. Tamalpais, north to Mt. St. Helena, east to ridge after ridge of open space lands with Mt. Diablo capping the range, and south to Mt. Umunhum and Loma Prieta. Southeast lies your trail, undulating along the ridgetops toward Cull Canyon.

Retrace your steps from the summit and follow Rifle Range Road for about a mile, passing cattle grazing beside and on the trail. Although oak and bay trees fill the canyons below the trail, only a few offer shelter on this west-facing slope. However, wildflowers, including lupine, wild cucumber, and Indian paintbrush, bloom in an extravagant display of color in springtime. Watch for a trail junction on your left (east), where the Bay Area Ridge Trail leaves Rifle Range Road and follows a short connector trail uphill to a green cattle gate. (Be sure to close the gate.) Beyond this gate turn right (south) beside an electric cattle fence. For a little more than a mile you are on an easement through private land. (Please stay on the trail and respect private property rights.)

Now the views open up eastward—steep-sided ridges clothed in spring green or summer gold, canyons filled with dark green oak and bay trees, and Mt. Diablo's pyramid rising in the distance.

Through two more green gates, with shy cattle clustered nearby at watering troughs and salt licks, you enter a broad clearing behind a subdivision surmounted by a water tank. This is the EBMUD/EBRPD boundary and the north end of the Cull Canyon Regional Recreation Area.

Now 4 miles from Chabot Staging Area, you cross this clearing and descend into a beautiful forest on the Chabot to Garin Regional Trail. Wide-branched, symmetrically shaped specimen oaks stand at several switchbacks, immense bay trees grow around sandstone boulders, and shady stream canyons indent the steep hillside. On warm days, you will be pleased to plunge into these east-facing woods. Trailside gardens of blue hounds' tongue, blood-red trillium, and white milkmaids are early spring treats. Later in the year wild roses show their pink blossoms, and in the fall, white snowberries hang on bare-branched shrubs.

About halfway along this segment of the Bay Area Ridge Trail, you step out onto a knoll with views over Cull Canyon. Here the trail becomes a wide, bare path through a pygmy forest of coyote bush. Soon out on a grassy shoulder between two forested canyons, you can find sunny picnic places or sheltered rest stops under wide-spreading oaks. Also found here are yellow suncups, blue-eyed grass, and

Mt. Diablo's summit looms beyond Dinosaur and other East Bay ridges.

blue brodiaea blooming beside and along the trail when in season. Plunging back into the forest, you zigzag down the mountain. To the sound of frogs croaking and birds singing, you reach steep-sided Cull Creek. Easily forded on rocks at low water, it may be more difficult to cross in the wet season.

Up on the other side of the creek a surprise awaits—fluffy-furred, thin-legged, steely-eyed llamas grazing in a pasture. A charming Victorian house across the pasture brings reality to a momentary illusion of the high Andes. These sure-footed Andean creatures make fine pack animals for local mountains, too.

For almost a mile more the trail gently undulates along the stream, up and down its high, fern-draped banks, back into ravines to cross intermittent streambeds, through a flowery meadow, and again into the woods. The Bay Area Ridge Trail follows Cull Creek through a huge culvert under Columbia Drive and enters the park. Hikers and equestrians can take a path beside the creek through this culvert.

Now in Cull Canyon Regional Recreation Area, a little more than 7 miles from Chabot Staging Area, Ridge Trail adventurers will find opportunities to swim and fish in the lake, and to picnic at tables beside it. This popular recreation area is an attractive place to spend a few hours with friends who could meet you here after your trip.

The short trip south on the Bay Area Ridge Trail route to Independent School is suitable for hikers. **Equestrians** can ride back to the Chabot Staging Area from Cull Canyon Regional Recreation Area, for an approximately 14-mile round trip. Or they can have a horsetrailer waiting in the unpaved parking area at Cull Canyon Recreation Area.

To continue to Independent School, **hikers** follow the lake's east shore for about ½ mile on a path bordered by tall willow trees. To the tune of ducks quacking and red-wing blackbirds singing in the dense rushes, you continue until the trail rises to the side of Cull Canyon Road. At Heyer Avenue you cross Cull Canyon Road with the signal, and then proceed uphill, along the south side of Canyon School Road. The Bay Area Ridge Trail route stays on the road's unpaved shoulder to the crest of the hill, then descends on an asphalt service road to Crow Canyon Road. Here, you turn right and head downhill to a signalized crossing. On the other side of Crow Canyon Road, bear right, cross a side street on your left, and in a few paces enter a woodland trail on your left. Under arching oaks, this trail ascends the sheer side of the fern-draped canyon of Cull Creek.

As the trail climbs, the woodland thins out. You see straight down to new houses along the creek and above to fences, some quite elaborate, enclosing manicured gardens of an adjoining subdivision. After a last little rise, the trail edges Independent School's fenced playground and emerges at a cul-de-sac, the trail's end.

Since the trip back to Chabot Staging Area is more than 8 miles, hikers might prefer to avoid the long round trip by having a shuttle car waiting at the cul-de-sac near Independent School.

The next dedicated segment of the Bay Area Ridge Trail begins approximately 13 miles southeast in Mission Peak Preserve. See *Mission Peak Regional Preserve and Ed R.Levin County Park.*   ■

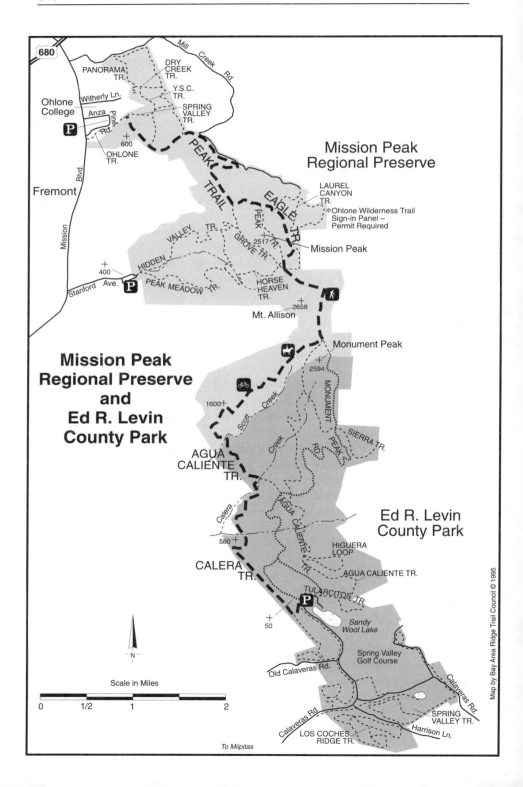

Mission Peak Regional Preserve and Ed R. Levin County Park

From Ohlone College to Sandy Wool Lake

Climb past three lofty peaks to high grasslands overlooking San Francisco Bay before descending to a pretty lake in a quiet valley.

Length 9.7 miles.

Location In Alameda and Santa Clara counties on the ridges above Fremont, Newark, and Milpitas.

Trail Characteristics Most of trail is on wide, unpaved park patrol roads. Trail to Mission Peak's summit is narrow, steep and rocky; final 4-mile downhill segment very steep. Elevation gain to Mission Peak, 2,100 feet; descends and regains 120 feet in elevation before final loss of 1,920 feet. Very little shade, can be windy on ridgetops.

Ridge Trail Accessibility
- Hikers and bicyclists—entire route.
- Equestrians—from Warm Springs Staging Area.

Trail Management
- Mission Peak Regional Preserve—East Bay Regional Park District (EBRPD): 510-635-0135.
- Ed R. Levin County Park—Santa Clara County Parks and Recreation Department: 408-358-3741.

Rules
- Mission Peak Regional Preserve—Open 5 A.M. to 10 P.M. or as posted. May be closed during extreme fire-danger periods. No fires or camping. Dogs under voice control permitted in open-space areas. 15 mph speed limit for bicycles.
- Ed R. Levin County Park—Open 8 A.M. to dusk. Dogs prohibited on this trail and all hiking trails in park. Dogs are allowed in certain designated areas, if kept on 6-foot leash. Bicyclists must wear helmets and observe 15 mph speed limit. Entrance fee on weekends.
- Cattle grazing along entire trail; close gates behind you.

Amenities
- No drinking water anywhere on trail.
- Ohlone College and Stanford Ave. Staging Area—Water, phone, parking, and restrooms. Equestrian staging facilities at Stanford Ave.
- Mission Peak Regional Preserve—Hang-glider facilities. Chemical toilet at Hidden Valley/Peak Trail junction.
- Ed Levin Park—Visitor center, hang-glider facilities, phone near hang-glider landing zone, picnic areas, water, children's play equipment, parking, eques-

trian staging facilities, fishing, and group camping. For reservations call 408-358-3751.

Getting There

By Car

North entrance, Ohlone College—From I-680 in Fremont take Mission Blvd. to Ohlone College, just south of Mission San José. Weekends and holidays, parking free in college lots. When college is in session, obtain parking permit for 50 cents at vending machines in Lot D or H, and park in any lot.

North entrance, equestrian staging area—At east end of Stanford Ave. off Mission Blvd., 2 miles south of Ohlone College.

South entrance, Ed Levin Park—From I-680 in Milpitas take Calaveras Rd. east to park entrance, turn left on Downing Rd., and continue to parking at Sandy Wool Lake. Find trailhead by the hang-glider landing zone across from parking area. Equestrian staging area near Sandy Wool Lake.

By Bus

AC Transit lines 24 and 28 daily and 37 Monday through Saturday to Ohlone College. Lines 22 and 28 daily to Mission Blvd./ Stanford Ave. intersection.

On The Trail

This entire trip takes place on lands once part of Mission San José de Guadalupe. Spanish colonizers established the mission in 1797 at the base of Mission Peak near the site of a Native American village, Oroysom. Eventually, the mission lands stretched from Oakland south to Coyote Hills and from the Bay east to Mt. Diablo.

The original mission church and outbuildings, built of wood with thatched roofs, were later reconstructed with adobe walls and tile-covered, hewn redwood roof beams. Surrounding the mission were orchards, vegetable gardens, and promenades. Behind the orchards on the rolling hills at the 400–500-foot level were extensive, flourishing vineyards. On the upper hills large herds of cattle ranged, said to number some 12,000 head. After the Mexican government took over Alta California and following the arrival of the Anglos in 1849, the mission complex fell into disrepair. All the buildings were severely damaged by the 1868 earthquake.

Today, the refurbished mission church and a museum lie just north of Ohlone College and the campus occupies some of the former mission gardens, promenades, and orchards. Mission Boulevard, which you followed to reach the college, approximates the trail that the Spanish explorers and mission padres traveled between the Santa Clara and San José missions. Some of the gnarled, gray-leaved olive trees lining the route remain from the mission plantings.

When the advance guard of mission founders chose this site, they noted it was "beside a perennial stream, found good tillable soil, . . . lime deposits and a rock formation called hewing stone, suitable for construction." Today on the Bay Area Ridge Trail, these features are still apparent.

Hikers and **bicyclists** begin your trip from the parking area at Ohlone College, cross the southern leg of Anza Pine Road, and pick up the adjoining, paved Ohlone Trail. Follow it uphill, turn right (east), and go past the swimming pool, where a dirt service road leads to the green gate into Mission Peak Regional Preserve. (There are many gates on this hike, each of which should be shut after you.)

Take the wide service road on your right (south), the Peak Trail, where a signpost bears a Bay Area Ridge Trail logo. The trail heads uphill under a string of powerlines. Views of the South Bay and its urban fringe unfold as you climb steadily around the west side of an unnamed 1,000-foot hill. With an early start you can do the bulk of the 2,100-foot-plus elevation gain before the day warms. Beginning early in the day allows you to enjoy a brief, ethereal glow illuminating the terrain as the sun rises above the often fog-shrouded peaks ahead.

On the Peak Trail the Bay is visible through a notch in the hills.

Continuing uphill past a small cave carved into the limestone bank, you bend north around the shoulder of the hill above a tree-canopied creek canyon. For the next half mile your uphill way lies in a narrow pass between high, rounded hills that are covered in early spring with masses of shiny, yellow-faced buttercups and luminous, purple lupines. At the top of the rise in a basin among three hills sits a seasonal pond, reserved for watering cattle and favored also, by swallows and red-wing blackbirds.

Follow the Peak Trail, bearing right under evergreen oak and bay trees. As you pass through this shady glen, small rabbits may dart across the trail and tiny quail skitter into the bushes while a sentinel parent cries its warning call from a nearby fence post. When emerging from the woods, your vista northeast takes in the grassy hills and tree-filled canyons that form the drainage of Mission Creek, which once powered the grist mill at Mission San José.

Now on a gravelled service road, you begin a gradual climb up the north shoulder of Mission Peak. Little clefts in the north-facing hillside are crowded with young trees that promise future shade on some rather open slopes. In springtime, watch for a jumble of lichen-splashed rocks where white phacelia push their hairy, curled necks from narrow crevices. Masses of yellow fiddlenecks crowd the surrounding fields.

Then Mission Peak appears, its sheared off, scarred west face dropping abruptly to the valley below. In a sometimes windy saddle, the Hidden Valley Trail comes in on your right, having risen 2.7 miles from the preserve's Stanford Avenue entrance, known as the Warm Springs Staging Area, the **equestrians'** entry to this Bay Area Ridge Trail trip. The Hidden Valley Trail, part of the Ohlone Wilderness Trail, is also a good hiker and bicyclist route to Mission Peak and the trail to Ed Levin Park.

From the Hidden Valley/Peak Trail junction veer left (east) and go $\frac{1}{4}$ mile to the Eagle Trail. Here you see the Peak Trail, for hikers only, forging right (south) up the eroded, rocky north flank of Mission Peak. You can climb to the summit from here or take the Eagle Trail, the Bay Area Ridge Trail route, around the peak's east side, then follow the Peak Trail up the summit's south flank. If you choose the south flank ascent, veer left at the Peak Trail/Eagle Trail junction and traverse a high, grassy plateau filled with wildflowers in spring. From here the Laurel Canyon Trail leads to the park boundary, whence trail users with permits can follow the Ohlone Wilderness Trail 25 miles east to Del Valle Regional Park. This trail traverses San Francisco Watershed lands and the beautiful, rugged Sunol and Ohlone Regional Wilderness preserves.

Whichever flank you choose, do not fail to make the less than half-mile ascent to 2,517-foot Mission Peak. If the day is clear, prominent peaks around the Bay Area are visible—from Loma Prieta and Black Mountain to Mt. Tamalpais in the west and from Mt. Diablo in the north to Mt. Hamilton in the south. On a tall post a few feet north of the summit are directional sighting holes pointing to other important landmarks of the Bay Area. And just below you on Mission Peak's craggy face, you occasionally see a herd of feral goats leaping from rock to rock.

To continue on the Bay Area Ridge Trail toward Ed Levin Park, descend the south flank of Mission Peak and follow the fence line across high grasslands. Drainage from Mission Peak and the surrounding high plateau flows into Agua Caliente Creek, which runs down the west side of Hidden Valley. In the Spanish era, warm water from this creek was carried by an aqueduct to Mission San José for laundering and bathing.

After following the fence line to a green gate, go through it and take the wide trail that heads southeast toward an array of antennae on the distant peaks. Gradually climbing, this trail passes remnants of ancient rock walls of uncertain origin, possibly predating the Ohlone period. The Spanish recorded that the hills "abounded in rocks which could be easily transported" to building sites. Here too are some of the springs the Spanish reported.

Passing a private road on the right, you soon curve around the east side of

**The 130-year-old McClure family farmhouse nestles in
Hidden Valley below Mission Peak. Monument Peak rises
in the distance.**

2,658-foot Mt. Allison, the highest on this three-peak trip. To the east you may see
the Ohlone Wilderness Trail ascending the west face of 3,817-foot Rose Peak on
Valpe Ridge.

Shortly you enter the land acquired in 1992 from the Wool family, whose ranch
lies off to the left. This 400-acre acquisition provided the link needed to join Mission
Peak Regional Preserve to Ed Levin Park in Santa Clara County. Mr. E. O. (Sandy)
Wool, a prominent 1900s rancher, once farmed the valley in Ed Levin Park, where
the lake now bears his name.

For more than a mile you travel through a high valley between Mt. Allison and
Monument Peak, both bristling with tall radio and TV towers—a veritable communications village or giant pincushion. Ignore all roads leading to these towers and
head due south. Then, trending west you surmount a small rise, and the Bay view
unfolds below you. In the South Bay are the salt ponds, tinged shades of blue-green
to rosy lavender, and the marshes, sloughs, mud flats, and open waters that make
up the San Francisco Bay National Wildlife Refuge. Due west along the Bay's shore
lies Jarvis Landing, an important grain and hide shipping port until the turn of the
century. Now, the expanding communities of Fremont, Milpitas, and Newark
stretch from foothills to shore. Yet, more than 4,000 mountainside acres through
which the Bay Area Ridge Trail travels remain in public open space.

For the next 4 miles your Bay Area Ridge Trail route, a wide ranch road, drops
2,000 feet in elevation down the very steep prow of these East Bay Hills to your
destination in Ed Levin Park. Caught between the Hayward and Calaveras faults,
the hills were uplifted through the eons by fault movement. Rocky knobs dotting
the hillsides are remains of sedimentary deposits formed as the Pacific Plate slid
northward along the edge of North America some 15 million years ago.

At a switchback where the trail makes a wide swing right, a multi-trunked bay tree grows in a heap of boulders, casting welcome shade on a southwest-facing slope. Although the steepness of the trail requires your close attention, pause occasionally to glance skyward for turkey vultures and red-tailed hawks wheeling on the updrafts, or for the golden eagles known to soar over these still-wild lands.

Notable too, are the spring wildflowers in rainbow hues, from magenta redmaids and frilly pink checkerblooms to yellow buttercups, tiny baby blue eyes, and tall purple brodiaea. Great swaths of orange California poppies glow on south-facing hillsides. By early summer, the drying grasses turn golden, contrasting with the dark green oaks that fill the lower canyons, nourished by Agua Fria, Toroges, Scott, Calera and other small, unnamed creeks.

Still descending and rounding shoulders of the mountains, you reach the wooded banks of Scott Creek, the Alameda/Santa Clara County boundary and the entrance to Ed R. Levin Park. In Levin Park, the Bay Area Ridge Trail follows the Agua Caliente Trail past a catch basin for watering cattle and, in about a half mile, reaches Calera Creek. Lining the creekside are lofty sycamore trees, their gray-and-white-patterned bark repeating the shades of the limestone deposits for which this creek is named. The Spaniards, and later the Mexican settlers, burned this stone in kilns to make mortar and whitewash for their adobes.

A park sign proclaims that Sandy Wool Lake lies 2.1 miles straight ahead. Following the wide road on a less precipitous route, now the Calera Creek Trail, you cross Calera Creek, staying close enough to its banks to hear the rushing water and to appreciate the trees shading the trail in the afternoon.

Then, leaving the creekside for a meadow filled with brilliant yellow mustard in spring, you ford a tributary of Calera Creek. An early settler remarked that the mustard stalks were so strong that "ground squirrels climbed them to get a better view."

The trail hugs a fence surrounding former Minnis Ranch fields, purchased in 1967 by Santa Clara County for Ed Levin Park. These lands were once part of the Tularcitos Ranch ("little tules"), granted to José Higuera in 1821 by Pablo Vicente de Solá, the last Spanish governor of Alta California. Of the numerous Higuera family adobes, only one remains, now the centerpiece of little Higuera Adobe Park in Milpitas.

After passing a fenced, private development of homes surrounding a golf course and a pond, continue to a paved road heading left. Take the Calera Creek Trail, the Bay Area Ridge Trail route, across this road and go through a gate to an unpaved path following the fence line for ¼ mile. At the next gate, you turn left and descend to another gate at the park road.

You have gone around a landing field where, especially on weekends, hang-gliders, strapped to their brightly colored wings, alight after their flight from Monument Peak. Just beyond are the picnic tables and greensward beside the blue waters of Sandy Wool Lake, a cool, refreshing place at trail's end. It was at this pretty picnic area on April 24, 1993, that Bay Area Ridge Trail volunteers celebrated the completion of this long-planned regional trail.

As you plan your trip, you might arrange with friends to meet you here for a picnic and a car shuttle after your exhilarating ridgetop trek. Although hikers would probably eschew a round trip, stalwart bicyclists and equestrians with an early start could make this a 20-mile trip with a considerable elevation gain on the return.

The next Bay Area Ridge Trail segment begins about 15 miles south at Coyote Hellyer Park in south San Jose. See *Coyote Hellyer County Park to Metcalf City Park.* ■

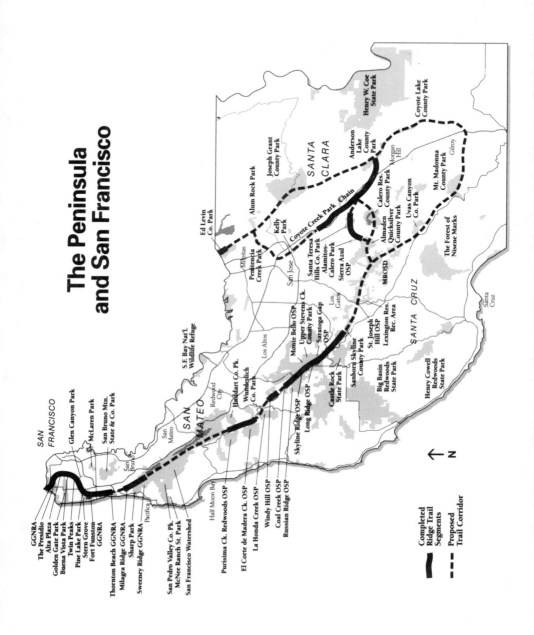

The Peninsula and San Francisco

Completed Ridge Trail Segments

- - - Proposed Trail Corridor

← N

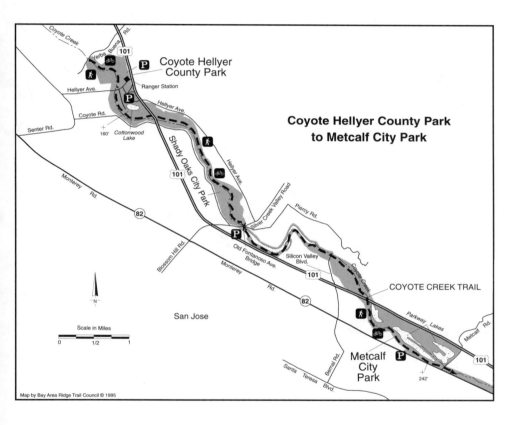

Coyote Hellyer
County Park

Ranger Station

Coyote Creek

Yerba Buena Rd.

101

Hellyer Ave.

Coyote Rd.

Hellyer Ave.

Senter Rd.

160' Cottonwood
Lake

Monterey Rd.

Shady Oaks City Park

101

Hellyer Ave.

82

Coyote Hellyer County Park
to Metcalf City Park

Piercy Rd.

Silver Creek Valley Road

Old Fontanoso Ave.
Bridge

Blossom Hill Rd.

Monterey

Rd.

Silicon Valley
Blvd.

101

82

Coyote Creek

COYOTE CREEK TRAIL

Parkway Lakes

Metcalf Rd.

101

N

Scale in Miles

0   1/2   1

San Jose

Santa Teresa Blvd.

Bernal Rd.

Metcalf
City
Park

P

242'

Map by Bay Area Ridge Trail Council © 1995

Coyote Hellyer County Park to Metcalf City Park

From Cottonwood Lake to Metcalf Road

Follow the route of Native Americans and explorers beside Santa Clara Valley's longest creek.

Length 6 miles.

Location In Santa Clara County on the east side of valley in south San Jose.

Trail Characteristics Wide, paved trail, mostly in shade with almost imperceptible elevation gain.

Ridge Trail Accessibility
- Hikers and bicyclists.

Trail Management
- Coyote Creek Trail, Coyote Hellyer Park and Parkway Lakes—Santa Clara County, in cooperation with Santa Clara Valley Water District (SCVWD): 408-358-3741.
- Shady Oaks and Metcalf parks—City of San Jose: 408-277-4000.

Rules
- Coyote Hellyer and Parkway Lakes—8 A.M. to dusk. Entrance fee. Dogs on maximum 6-foot leash at all times. No horses or motorcycles.
- Coyote Creek Trail—No horses or motorcycles. Dogs on maximum 6-foot leash at all times.
- Shady Oaks and Metcalf parks—Open during daylight hours.

Amenities
- Coyote Hellyer Park—Water, picnic areas, children's play equipment, fishing lake, velodrome, parking, and restrooms.
- Shady Oaks Park—Water, benches, playing field, children's play equipment, and basketball court.
- Metcalf Park—Water, restrooms, turf, play areas, and public parking.

Getting There

North entrance, Coyote Hellyer Park—From Hwy 101 in San Jose south of Fwy 280 take Hellyer Ave. exit to west side of Hwy 101 and then bear right (north). At park stop sign, continue straight ahead to parking beyond ranger station; or go left at park stop sign and then turn left to parking at Cottonwood Lake.

South entrance, Metcalf Park—From Hwy 101 in southeast San Jose take Bernal Rd. exit, go 1/4 mile on Bernal Rd., take Monterey Rd. exit, and turn left (southeast) on Monterey Rd. At Metcalf Rd. make a U-turn and go ½ mile northwest to Metcalf Park staging area on right.

On The Trail

This segment of the Bay Area Ridge Trail follows Coyote Creek for 6 miles along its meandering, 31-mile route from the Diablo Range to the shores of San Francisco Bay. Coyote Creek, the longest creek in Santa Clara County, rises in the steep, rugged ridges of Henry W. Coe State Park and then flows north through the eastern foothills.

Temporarily slowed by the Santa Clara Valley Water District reservoirs—Coyote and Anderson lakes—Coyote Creek drops out of the foothills to flow along the east side of the Santa Clara Valley. Joined and enlarged by waters of many tributaries, including Silver, Penitencia and Berryessa creeks, it threads its way in a corridor of riparian vegetation down to the Bay. There, in the San Francisco Bay National Wildlife Refuge, its fresh water mingles with salt water in a complex pattern of sloughs and marshes.

Seen from the air, Coyote Creek looks like a verdant, dark green serpent slithering through the Santa Clara Valley. On the ground, its broad, tree-lined course provides food, shelter and a travel route for wildlife, as well as a recreation corridor for the residents of urbanized Santa Clara Valley. Our Bay Area Ridge Trail route uses this Coyote Creek corridor from Coyote Hellyer Park to Metcalf Park as it passes through publicly owned lands and remnants of the agricultural history of Santa Clara County.

The eastern foothills rise beyond Coyote Creek's lush streamside vegetation.

Before the coming of European settlers, the Ohlone people used trails along Coyote and other creeks to reach settlements of other tribes with whom they traded shells, salt, cinnabar, arrowheads, and stone knife blades. When the Spanish explorers came this way, they followed the Coyote on Ohlone routes, keeping to high ground above the water's edge.

From the days of American settlement, early inhabitants built their homes along

Coyote Creek, using its water for home, farm, and orchard. In those days, periodic floods were a serious problem, destroying homes and inundating crop lands.

As more people came to the Santa Clara Valley, wells were dug to satisfy thirsty fields and a burgeoning population. By the 1930s the need to control floods, to provide drinking and irrigation water, and to reduce ground subsidence gave impetus to a Santa Clara Valley Water District plan to dam the valley's major streams—Guadalupe, Los Gatos, Stevens, Calero, Los Alamitos and Coyote. To recharge the groundwater supply, the plan called for percolation ponds along some of the watercourses.

In the 1970s park planners, public officials, and interested citizens began planning for recreation trails along these creeks, as well as creeks in the foothills and mountains, and beside the Bay. They planned a network of trails linking city, county, and regional parks throughout Santa Clara County. The resulting Trails and Pathways Master Plan, adopted into the County General Plan by the Santa Clara County Board of Supervisors in November 1980, guided the development of county trails. Cities, too, integrated their trails plans with the county network. Today, the trail we follow along Coyote Creek is the result of these city and county plans formed in cooperation with the Santa Clara Valley Water District. A comprehensive Countywide Trails Master Plan, nearing completion, includes the Coyote Creek Trail.

The Bay Area Ridge Trail trip on the Coyote Creek Trail begins in Coyote Hellyer County Park and heads 6 miles upstream (south) to percolation ponds known as the Parkway Lakes at Metcalf Road. From any of several parking areas in Coyote Hellyer County Park, take the paved hiking and bicycle trail under a leafy canopy of cottonwood, sycamore, and oak trees. A veil of poison-oak vines and elderberry bushes often hides the creek here, but there are many places where you can see the creekbed. In summer there is very little running water, but during winter storms this creek can be a raging torrent.

In Coyote Hellyer Park you pass picnic tables, lawns, and pretty Cottonwood Lake. When this section of the Ridge Trail was dedicated in October 1990, children lined up along the lakeshore to vie for its stocked trout and bluegill.

The trail follows the creek upstream as it curves east to dip under the Highway 101 bridge. Here under tall cottonwoods the creek flows in a wide, gravelly flat tangled with berry vines and reeds. Soon the trail rises to the bluffs high above the creek, where venerable oaks shade the way. These ancient oaks send their roots deep to tap the creek's underground moisture. Closer to the water are the white-barked, big-leaved sycamore trees and the cottonwoods, whose roots prefer a streamside location.

The trees, along with an understory of shrubs, grasses, and flowers, make a hospitable environment for trail users, as well as for birds, mammals and reptiles. You will probably see swallows and blue jays flitting in and out of the trees and hear mourning doves and quail calling. At dusk you may see deer or smaller animals searching for food or going to the creek for a drink. You may also see a fenced area enclosing native plants, such as live oaks and wildflowers, put in by the California

At full flood Coyote Creek can be a raging torrent.

Department of Transportation as mitigation for creek encroachment at the new Silver Creek Valley Road bridge, a few miles farther south on the trail.

On your right, about 2 miles south from Coyote Hellyer Park, is a wide, wooden-plank bridge arching over the creek. Cross it to the City of San Jose's Shady Oaks Park, a pleasant place under the oak and pepper trees for your backpack lunch. In this neighborhood park you'll find restrooms, drinking water, acres of invitingly green turf, basketball courts, and young children's play equipment.

Returning to the trail, you meander for another mile under wide-spreading oaks, passing a few truck gardens and unkempt walnut orchards. When you go under the large, newly built Silver Creek Valley Road bridge leading to an industrial park and new housing developments, you turn sharply right onto the former Fontanoso Avenue auto bridge. Now closed to motor vehicles, this bridge is the trail route to the creek's west side.

Here, on the south side of Silver Creek Valley Road, is a staging area, another entrance to the Coyote Creek Trail. From it, the paved path descends to creek level, flanked by rangy sycamore trees whose mottled, white trunks grow at odd angles. In the creekbed, tall reeds, cattails, and grassy thickets make good nesting sites for migratory and resident ducks and grebes.

Veering away from the creek, you pass through an old prune orchard and then travel beside widely spaced oaks and tall black walnut trees. On the low eastern foothills across the creek there are still a few truck gardens and greenhouses. As the creek swings left, the trail follows it past acres of percolation ponds. During drought years, these ponds, which depend upon water from upstream reservoirs, may be dry.

Between the trail and the freeway to the west is a large floodplain planted to orchards and bordered by a few houses. This still semipastoral setting is particularly delightful on a summer evening when sunset casts its slanting, golden light.

Before you reach Silicon Valley Boulevard, new commercial and industrial development fills the land between the Coyote Creek Trail and the freeway. As yet, the bridge over the creek at the end of the boulevard has not been rebuilt, so cross the road stub and continue south along the wide, shallow creekbed. Here too is another Caltrans riparian-habitat planting project installed to mitigate for wetlands lost during completion of the Highway 85 extension. Just beyond here, the trail, protected by cyclone fencing, comes close to the freeway before passing under it.

Soon you see the first Parkway Lakes percolation pond on your left. These ponds are the largest freshwater lagoons in the county, harboring many year-round and migratory bird species. Look for white egrets and terns, black cormorants, and blue-gray kingfishers as you travel the last part of this trail.

A trailer park and a large new subdivision on your right fill once-open land, but you can still look west to Santa Clara County's high peaks, Mt. Umunhum and Loma Prieta. You will find some magnificent ancient oak trees that still border the lakes and shade the Coyote Creek Trail as it meanders through Metcalf City Park.

Although the Bay Area Ridge Trail route ends here, the Coyote Creek Trail continues another 7 miles south to the Anderson/Burnett Ranger Station. In addition to this paved trail, a separate equestrian trail traverses this still rural landscape.

The Bay Area Ridge Trail will someday lead south from Ed Levin Park along the ridges higher up on the eastern hills. But for now, this Coyote Creek Trail is one to treasure and travel often. The next segment of the Ridge Trail begins $3\frac{1}{2}$ miles west of Metcalf Road in Santa Teresa County Park at the end of Bernal Road. See *Santa Teresa County Park and Los Alamitos/Calero Creek Park Chain.*   ■

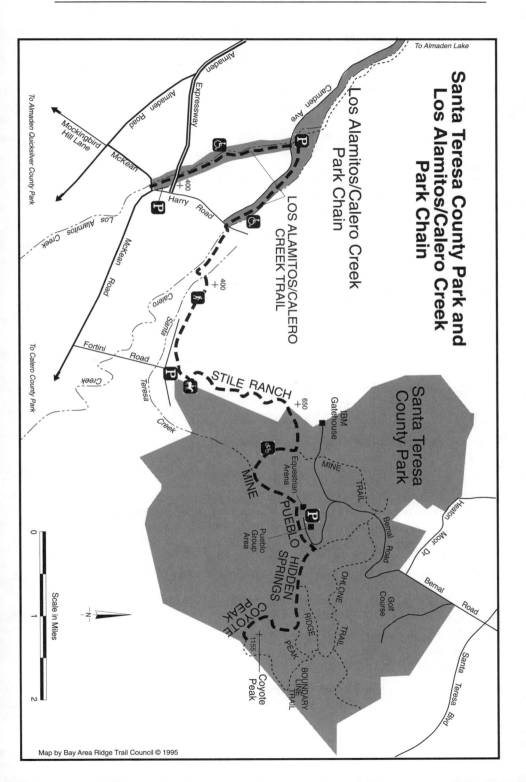

Santa Teresa County Park and
Los Alamitos/Calero Creek
Park Chain

Map by Bay Area Ridge Trail Council © 1995

Santa Teresa County Park and Los Alamitos/Calero Creek Park Chain

From Pueblo Group Picnic Area to McKean Court/Harry Road Junction

Take this trip through high, oak-studded grasslands and beside tree-lined, year-round creeks for spring wildflower displays, coast range views, and the sound of running water.

Length 6.3 miles.

Location In Santa Clara County in the Santa Teresa Hills and Almaden Valley.

Trail Characteristics Pueblo, Mine, Stile Ranch, and Calero Creek trails east of Harry Rd.—Well-graded, unpaved, with little shade. Los Alamitos/Calero Creek Trail—Wide, paved, partially shaded in late afternoon.

Ridge Trail Accessibility
- Hikers, equestrians, and bicyclists.
- Wheelchair users—Los Alamitos Creek Trail.

Trail Management
- Pueblo, Mine, Stile Ranch trails—Santa Clara County Parks and Recreation Department: 408-358-3741.
- Los Alamitos/Calero Creek Trail—City of San Jose, with cooperation of Santa Clara Valley Water District: 408-277-4000.

Rules
- Open during daylight hours.
- Dogs on leash only.

Amenities
- Santa Teresa County Park—Water, restrooms, picnic areas, and parking at Pueblo Group Picnic Area. Parking at southwest corner of park just off Fortini Rd.
- Los Alamitos/Calero Creek Park Chain, Camden Ave. at Villagewood Dr.—Parking area.
- McKean Ct./Harry Rd. junction—Limited street parking.

Getting There

By Car
East entrance, Santa Teresa County Park—Take Hwy 101 to Bernal Rd. exit, turn south and go 1.6 miles to park entrance. Continue 1 mile uphill on Bernal Rd. and turn left to Pueblo Group Picnic Area and parking.

West entrance, Los Alamitos/Calero Creek Trail—In south San Jose take

Almaden Expwy. to Harry Rd., and turn right (south). In next 300 yards look for street parking on Harry Rd. or on adjacent McKean Ct.

Limited parking at west end of Stile Ranch Trail, reached by going south from Harry Rd. on McKean Rd. for 1.1 mile. Turn left (east) on Fortini Rd. and continue to its end.

By Bus
Santa Clara County Transit buses 67 and 68 to Santa Teresa Blvd./Bernal Rd. intersection daily; 13 to Harry Rd. daily.

On The Trail

This Bay Area Ridge Trail trip begins in 1,677-acre Santa Teresa County Park, at the southern end of the Santa Teresa Hills. Portions of these hills and some of the adjacent valleys were part of Joaquin Bernal's vast Rancho Santa Teresa. Bernal received the 9,646-acre land grant as compensation for investigating mineral deposits in California. There were no productive mines in present-day park land, but Bernal and his family lived near here and ran cattle on these hills for many years.

Santa Teresa Park is one of a cluster of three Santa Clara County parks in south San Jose—Santa Teresa, Almaden Quicksilver, and Calero Reservoir parks—which encompass 7,400 acres in the narrowest part of the Santa Clara Valley. The Ridge Trail route in Santa Teresa Park includes a round trip southeast to Santa Teresa Park's Coyote Peak and a trip southwest on county park trails to join the city of San Jose's Los Alamitos/Calero Creek Trail ending at the McKean Court/Harry Road junction.

Starting from the Pueblo Group Picnic Area, go a few yards uphill to find the Pueblo Trail, where you turn left (east) for the 2-mile round trip to the highest point in the park, 1,155-foot Coyote Peak. The Pueblo Trail soon intersects the Hidden Springs Trail, on which you turn right and cross a bridge over an unnamed creek. For a short while your way is shaded by lovely, broad-branched oaks, and in spring by flowering buckeye trees. As you climb, however, the shade trees disappear. Pass the park's own Ridge Trail coming in on the left and very shortly turn right on the Coyote Peak Trail.

For the next $\frac{1}{2}$ mile you contour up and around the peak with westward views to the wooded heights of the Santa Cruz Mountains. When the trail swings around to the south slope of the peak, take the left (northwest) turn to reach the summit, which offers sweeping panoramas of the Santa Clara Valley. This fertile land, once known as the Valley of Heart's Delight, the fruit bowl of America, has developed industrial plants, shopping malls and subdivisions. Yet, thanks to far-sighted citizens who many years ago voted funds for park acquisition, the county's foothill and mountain parks and its creekside and baylands parks preserve some of the valley's former characteristic environment.

Now retrace your steps to the Pueblo Group Picnic Area and on the Pueblo Trail begin your 5.3-mile Ridge Trail trip west. Traversing the base of the rocky slope above the picnic area, you soon come to the equestrian arena, which is open at both ends. Follow the trail through the arena, unless some equestrian activity is in progress. On the far side of the arena, bear left (south) on the Mine Trail, which descends gently to a little stream, Santa Teresa Creek, that drains the park's lush central meadow, now closed off for wildlife habitat protection.

Following the west side of the stream, bordered by a few oaks and many bay trees, you descend through a little valley. The south-facing hillsides, punctuated by lichen-encrusted, igneous rocks interspersed with gray sage bushes, come alive with blue brodiaea, orange poppies and magenta Clarkia after winter rains. Among the rocks you may see gray-green serpentine, the California State Rock and a known indicator of earthquake faults. According to the geologic maps, a small fault runs through this valley.

From the heights of Coyote Peak, Santa Teresa Park and the northern hills extend northwest between populated valleys in Santa Clara County.

Curving north, you climb away from the creek to a ridgetop where a clump of gnarled oak trees with small, leathery, dull-green leaves stands beyond the fence on your left. This native California tree, mostly found on serpentine soil, is known as the leather oak. You will see other specimens of leather oak as you traverse sections of this trail cut through serpentine rock.

Now you descend into a quiet, grassy swale sprinkled with fine old valley oak trees and pierced by an intermittent stream. After you cross the stream, the Mine Trail continues right (north) through the swale, but you take the Stile Ranch Trail, which cuts off to the left (west). This trail weaves through the sloping grasslands at a very manageable grade. Switchbacks carry you uphill through tall grasses, ungrazed for several years. In early morning or late afternoon, you may see deer going to drink from the stream in a little notch in the hills.

As you zigzag up an east-facing ridge on a trail cut through solid rock and lined with chunks of serpentine, you can appreciate the persistent, indefatigable volunteer trail builders' work. With the combined efforts of the County Parks Department, which funded the trail construction and now maintains it; the Trail Center, which directed the trail crews; and International Business Machines (IBM), which granted an easement over its land, this 1.6-mile Stile Ranch Trail was completed in 1991. IBM, whose facility stands out on a distant ridge, also donated funds to help develop and print the Bay Area Ridge Trail guides. A dedication ceremony on September 14, 1991, celebrated the trail opening and lauded these cooperative efforts.

Reaching the top of the ridge, the trail levels out and passes a couple of 6-foot-high sentinel rocks splashed with orange and red lichen. One rock set farther back from the trail could serve as a traveler's bench and rest stop to enjoy this remote oak-dotted grassland. As you dip into another valley among clumps of bunchgrass, light-pink-flowered buckwheat, and tall stalks of white yarrow, a couple of switchbacks take you to a plank bridge across a wash (dry in summer). Then you begin ascending an east-facing ridge, a veritable Persian carpet of multi-colored wildflowers in spring. Even in July this hillside glows with the magenta haze of Clarkia blossoms. A few oaks and an occasional bay tree offer shade in the late afternoon. As you reach a switchback, look east to see the white domes of the Lick Observatory atop Mt. Hamilton in the Diablo Range.

At the ridgecrest there is a panoramic vista west of Loma Prieta and Mt. Umunhum standing guard along the ramparts of the Santa Cruz Mountains. Loma Prieta, the tallest mountain in this range, lies south of Mt. Umunhum, which you can identify by the tall structure on its summit. In the valley below, subdivisions and ranchettes are replacing the vineyards and orchards of yesteryear. Feeder roads in the valley bear former ranchers' names—Fortini and Rakstad, among others.

As you descend rapidly down numerous switchbacks, note a fine old rock wall that undulates uphill and down, defining an early boundary, which is now also delineated by a barbed-wire fence. On the far side of the wall are bluebird boxes attached to tall posts. This open, rolling grassland, graced by great oaks, is typical habitat for the rusty-breasted Western bluebird, but rapid urbanization has decreased its natural nesting sites and reduced this beautiful bird's numbers. Yet it is known that bluebirds can be lured to nest in bird boxes.

When you reach the bottom of the hill, follow the trail between a double row of newly planted oaks and go right (west), continuing along the trail between the road and the fence. Now on the city of San Jose's Calero Creek Trail, you head west for less than ¼ mile and cross a log barrier. Proceed along the base of the slope past wide fields, planted or plowed according to the season. Signs request that you stay out of these fields. (There is no outlet on the other side.)

Carry on for ½ mile, then angle left (south) between two barbed wire fences. The trail dips down into the channel of intermittent Santa Teresa Creek, which drains the terrain through which you just traveled. This streamcourse is a cool, damp place under a tall canopy of trees—delightful on a hot day, but potentially difficult to cross after heavy rains.

On the other side of the stream, you pass a well-kept, fenced walnut orchard on the right and a small model-plane landing strip on the left. When you reach the next line of trees, veer right (west) and follow a wide track for ½ mile beside Calero Creek. Greeted by the sounds of running water, leaves rustling in the breeze, and birds singing in the trees, you wander along the creek bank sheltered by tall, white-barked sycamores and broad-branched oaks. Through openings in the understory of elderberry, poison oak, and wild roses, you can see the creek flowing toward its confluence with Los Alamitos Creek.

Riders look up to Loma Prieta from the Los Alamitos/Calero Creek Trail.

You ramble along beside the creek until you come to Harry Road. Cross the road, jog left on the bridge over the creek, and then turn right on the paved trail that meanders through a wide easement between the creek and Camden Avenue. Although the creek is completely hidden from view, its wooded corridor adds charm to the neighboring community.

About 1 mile from Harry Road, Camden Avenue crosses Los Alamitos Creek, which joins Calero Creek just beyond. Here, at the confluence of the two creeks, in a wide half-moon-shaped easement, is a parking area on the site of a proposed park. Beyond here the City of San Jose's Los Alamitos/Calero Creek Trail extends 2.7 miles to Almaden Lake, a water sports/picnic park, from which a trail will someday follow the Guadalupe River to San Francisco Bay.

However, to continue on the Bay Area Ridge Trail from Camden Avenue south to the McKean Court/Harry Road junction, take one of the paths on either side of Los Alamitos Creek. These paths are built on raised levees between the generous creekbed and the adjoining subdivision roads. Shaded by indigenous and newly planted oaks, sycamores, and cottonwoods, these wide trails meander for 1 mile upstream. Choose the paved trail on the east side of the creek for shade in the afternoon on a hot day. Equestrians use the unpaved trail on the west side.

Los Alamitos Creek originates in Almaden Quicksilver County Park, west of the trail. Long before Europeans settled in this valley, Native Americans traveled upstream along Los Alamitos Creek to gather cinnabar (which contains mercury) in the hills of today's Almaden Quicksilver Park. They crushed the rock to make the red pigment with which they decorated their bodies. Cinnabar rock was mined here during the Gold Rush days.

Today, residual mercury in the soil and streams is known to be highly toxic. Prominent signs along the trails warn that fish in the creek are contaminated by mercury and should not be eaten. Some areas of the abandoned Almaden Quicksilver mines are closed to the public. Plans to expand the use of Almaden Quicksilver Park have been delayed by the state until the toxicity is remedied, but many miles of park trails are still open to hikers, runners, and equestrians. In the near future, it is hoped that the Bay Area Ridge Trail route will extend to the park and continue west to join ridgeline trails in the Santa Cruz Mountains.

In the meantime, continue on the creek trail as it dips under the broad span of the Almaden Expressway bridge. Bay Area Ridge Trail users will be joined on this last leg of the trip by children on bicycles, neighbors strolling or walking their dogs (which must be on leash), runners, and parents teaching youngsters to ride bikes. For the time being, the Ridge Trail segment terminates at the intersection of McKean Court and Harry Road. You can retrace your route to Santa Teresa Park or have a shuttle car waiting at one of two parking areas along the route, either at Camden Avenue or at a new parking place at the foot of the Stile Ranch Trail on park lands off Fortini Road.

The next segment of the Bay Area Ridge Trail traverses the crest of the Santa Cruz Mountains in western Santa Clara County. See *Sanborn County Park and Castle Rock State Park.*   ■

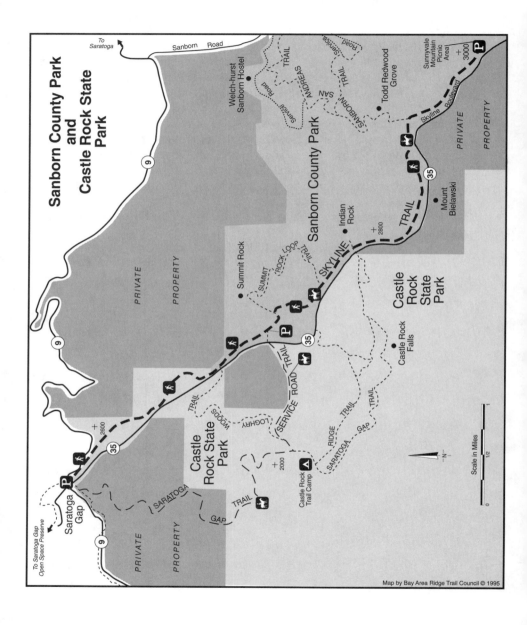

Sanborn County Park
and
Castle Rock State
Park

To
Saratoga

Sanborn   Road

Welch-hurst
Sanborn Hostel

Service   Road

ANDREAS

SAN

SANBORN   TRAIL

Service   Road

Todd Redwood
Grove

Sunnyvale
Mountain
Picnic
Area
+
3000

P

Skyline   Boulevard

PRIVATE   PROPERTY

9

35

Mount
Bielawski

Sanborn County Park

Indian
Rock
+
2800

TRAIL

Summit Rock

ROCK LOOP   TRAIL

SUMMIT

SKYLINE

Castle
Rock State
Park

PRIVATE   PROPERTY

P

35

SERVICE ROAD   TRAIL

TRAIL

LOGHRY   WOODS

Castle
Rock
Falls

RIDGE   TRAIL

GAP   TRAIL

N

Scale in Miles

1/2

0

+
2600

35

+
2000

Castle Rock
Trail Camp

TRAIL

9

P

Saratoga
Gap

SARATOGA

GAP

PRIVATE   PROPERTY

To Saratoga Gap
Open Space Preserve

Map by Bay Area Ridge Trail Council © 1995

Sanborn County Park and
Castle Rock State Park

From Sunnyvale Mountain Picnic Area to Saratoga Gap

In forests of Douglas fir, oak, and madrone, traverse the ridgeline of two vast parks, passing impressive sandstone outcrops and vestiges of early homesteaders' orchards and dwellings.

Length 6 miles—hikers; 10 miles—equestrians.

Location In Santa Clara County west of Saratoga on the crest of the Santa Cruz Mountains.

Trail Characteristics Easy trip on relatively level trail of varying width; northern segment through Castle Rock State Park narrow with steep side slope, unsuitable for equestrians. Entire trail in mixed evergreen forests, thus ideal for warm days; occasionally foggy when Santa Clara Valley is hot.

Ridge Trail Accessibility
- Hikers and equestrians—Sanborn County Park.
- Hikers only—East side of Castle Rock State Park.
- Equestrians—Use alternate route on service road and Saratoga Gap Trail through west side of Castle Rock State Park.

Trail Management
- Sanborn County Park—Santa Clara County Parks and Recreation Department: 408-358-3741.
- Castle Rock State Park—State of California, Department of Parks and Recreation: 408-879-2952.

Rules
- Parks open 8 A.M. to dusk. No dogs or bicycles on trails.

Amenities
- Sanborn County Park—No water, restrooms or telephone beside the trail. Camping 1.6 miles downhill on Sanborn Trail; reservations: 408-358-3751.
- Sanborn Hostel, Welch-hurst, 2.2 miles downhill on Sanborn and San Andreas trails, open year-round, reservations advisable: 408-741-0166.
- Castle Rock State Park—Backpack camping at park headquarters 2.7 miles west of Castle Rock Skyline Blvd. parking area.

Getting There
Take Skyline Blvd. (Hwy 35) to its intersection with Hwy 9 at Saratoga Gap.

South entrance, Sunnyvale Mountain Picnic Area—On Skyline Blvd. (Hwy 35) drive 4.7 miles south of Saratoga Gap to Sunnyvale Mountain Picnic Area on east side of road.

North entrance, Saratoga Gap—Parking area is just 500 feet south of Saratoga Gap on east side of Skyline Blvd. (Hwy 35); some spaces available at trailhead on northeast side of Hwy 9.

On The Trail

The Skyline Trail roughly follows the route of the old Summit Road through Sanborn County Park and Castle Rock State Park. Sections of this wagon road that served early settlers' homesteads, linked by new paths, wind along the protected east side of the crest of the Santa Cruz Mountains.

To begin your Bay Area Ridge Trail trip on this trail, leave the north side of the Sunnyvale Mountain Picnic Area, skirt the edge of an overgrown orchard and head northward on the wide, old farm road. At a fork in the trail, keep to the left for a gentle climb under a canopy of mature Douglas fir trees. Before long you reach a clearing where fragments of a sea captain's garden mark the former Seagraves residence. Just beyond the homestead in a forest opening on a clear day, you may see south across Monterey Bay to the Monterey Peninsula and its mountains.

Back in forest the trail descends to a shady redwood grove. Here are two picnic tables beside the stone wall which flanked the now-closed entrance to the Seagraves' place. Beyond here the trail narrows, continuing in a dense forest, as it contours into and around steep-sided canyons, the headwaters of streams named for early settlers—Todd, McElroy, and Bonjetti.

You soon pass the first of several wind- and water-eroded sandstone outcrops, uplifted over the millennia by folding and faulting along the San Andreas Rift Zone.

Keeping left at the next junction, you'll pass a few pear trees, temptingly adorned with fruit in fall. Many deer tracks in the dust of the trail, the sharp call of blue jays, and the chatter of squirrels in the trees attest to the presence of others who may enjoy this feast.

Then on a wide swing east around the shoulder of a ridge, you meet the Sanborn Trail, 1.2 miles from your starting point. Just 0.3 miles down the Sanborn Trail is the Todd Redwood Grove, where a few venerable giants remain after the logging of the late 1800s. Take this trail for backpack campsites, 1.6 miles downhill in Sanborn Park, or find the Sanborn Hostel set in a grove of majestic redwoods off the San Andreas Trail. The hostel, known as Welch-hurst, was built as a mountain retreat by former Santa Clara County Judge James Welch in the early 1900s. It is now on the National Register of Historic Places.

The Skyline Trail continues northwest, cut into the steep sides of Todd Creek canyon. Now the Douglas fir forest is interspersed with madrones and tanoaks, and it offers occasional glimpses of the Santa Clara Valley. But for the best views, continue to Indian Rock, 1.6 miles uphill from the Sanborn Trail intersection and just 0.1 mile uphill from the main trail. Here you find exposed sandstone rocks set among gnarled oaks and madrones. Rock-climbers and casual hikers clamber up on them for east and south views over the Santa Clara Valley to the high points of the South Bay—Mt. Hamilton and Mission Peak. The dramatic dropoff on the east side of the rocks is a breathtaking 150 feet.

Shortly after returning to the main Skyline Trail, you see a sign for Castle Rock

Loma Prieta Mountain looms south of Sanborn County Park.

State Park. Most of the park's 3,000 acres lie in the semiwilderness lands across Skyline Boulevard on the steep west face of the Santa Cruz Mountains. There you will find hiking trails to waterfalls, shady forests, and even more extensive sandstone outcrops. The trail camp for backpackers is 2.7 miles west from the Skyline Boulevard parking area.

But the Bay Area Ridge Trail heads north on the Skyline Trail, passing the south end of the Summit Rock Loop Trail, which descends into Bonjetti Creek Canyon. Continuing on the Skyline Trail you meet the north end of the loop trail after curving around yet another settler's homesite, where exotic plantings remain in the clearing.

In the late 1800s immigrants from mountainous regions of Europe settled these hillsides, set out orchards and vineyards, and built wineries. But the 1906 earthquake struck hard here, causing landslides and severe property damage. Eventually most of the hillside farms were abandoned. After Santa Clara County bought the parklands in the 1970s, the dwellings were removed. As you walk the route of the old road joining their farms, imagine the hard work and tenacity required to carve out an existence on these steep hillsides far from the fertile Santa Clara Valley.

At the junction where the Summit Rock Loop Trail rejoins the Skyline Trail, you bear left, unless you take a 0.2-mile side trip east to Summit Rock. Here you will find another huge sandstone outcrop. Perches some 20 feet off the ground offer a hawk's-eye view of Sanborn County Park and Monte Bello Ridge to the north. If you take this detour, retrace your steps to the turnoff and follow the wide, old roadbed northwest past some big mahogany-barked, broad-branched madrones.

When you pass between two boulders marking the trail entrance from a parking area near Skyline Boulevard, **hikers** veer right, staying on a narrow ridge until you join the old Summit Road going north. **Equestrians** cross Skyline Boulevard to Castle Rock State Park and take the 1.5-mile Service Road Trail, then head north for 4.5 miles on the Saratoga Gap Trail.

As you leave Sanborn County Park, you enter the 120 acres of Castle Rock State Park that lie on the east side of the Skyline ridge, formerly known as Loghry Woods. The Skyline Trail, now a narrow footpath for hikers only, continues through mixed woodland, swinging around the east side of a 2,920-foot rise.

Then, skirting a fenced, private inholding, you once again pick up old Summit Road, with tall, fragrant firs overhead, soft forest duff underfoot, and moss-covered rocks at trailside. Fern fronds and clumps of iris edge the trail, while fine-leaved ocean spray and hazelnut bushes often overhang it. In spring you may find blue hound's tongue blooming on tall stalks.

For the last 0.3 mile, you traverse a very steep hillside on a narrow footpath for hikers only. After crossing a couple of sturdy wooden bridges over gullies and passing some sizable sandstone boulders, you come to the Saratoga Gap parking area. Here, hikers join equestrians, and all can continue on the next leg of the Bay Area Ridge Trail.

On the north side of Highway 9, the Bay Area Ridge Trail continues through the forests of Saratoga Gap Open Space Preserve, into Upper Stevens Creek County Park, and then on to the west-side ridgelands. See *Saratoga Gap to Skyline Ridge Open Space Preserve.*

For those who left cars at the Sunnyvale Mountain Picnic Area, it's time to turn around and make the trip southeast to your starting point.   ■

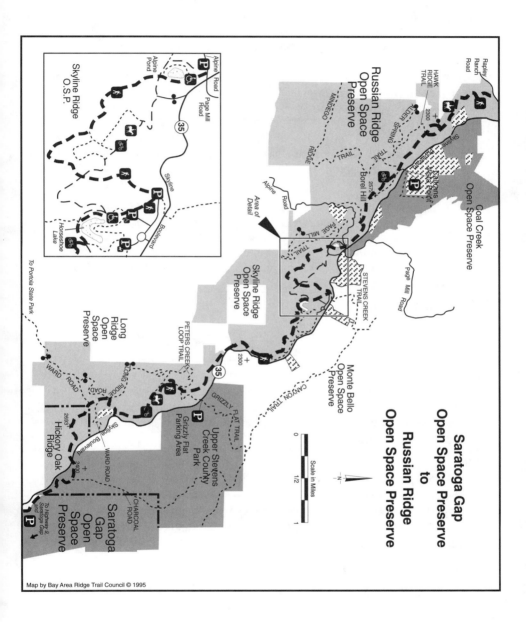

Saratoga Gap
Open Space Preserve
to
Russian Ridge
Open Space Preserve

Scale in Miles

0   1/2   1

Map by Bay Area Ridge Trail Council © 1995

Saratoga Gap Open Space Preserve to Skyline Ridge Open Space Preserve

From Saratoga Gap to Horseshoe Lake

Along the crest of the Santa Cruz Mountains, this segment passes through diverse terrain, from damp evergreen forests and oak-madrone woodlands to high grasslands with stunning coast and Bay views.

Length 7.8 miles.

Location In Santa Clara, Santa Cruz, and San Mateo counties on the ridge above cities of Saratoga, Cupertino, Mountain View, Los Altos, Los Altos Hills, and Palo Alto.

Trail Characteristics Width varies from narrow path to wide patrol road. Surface soft in forests and on creeksides, firm and bare on patrol road through grasslands. Elevation loss of 400 feet from Saratoga Gap to Horseshoe Lake with several elevation gains and losses of 100–300 feet enroute. Exposed ridgetops can be foggy and windy, protected west- and south-facing slopes often hot in summer.

Ridge Trail Accessibility
- Hikers, equestrians, and bicyclists.
- Wheelchair users—Skyline Ridge OSP: lakeside parking and trail at Horseshoe Lake.

Trail Management
- Saratoga Gap, Long Ridge, and Skyline Ridge open space preserves— Midpeninsula Regional Open Space District (MROSD): 415-691-1200.
- Upper Stevens Creek County Park—Santa Clara County Department of Parks and Recreation: 408-358-3741.

Rules
- MROSD preserves—Open from dawn to ½ hour after sunset. Bicyclists must observe 15-mile-per-hour speed limit and wear helmets.
- Dogs on leash allowed in designated area of Long Ridge Open Space Preserve just north of Grizzly Flat entrance; maps available from MROSD office.
- Upper Stevens Creek County Park—Open 8 A.M. to sunset. Helmets required for bicyclists. No dogs on trail.

Amenities
- No water on entire route.
- Skyline Ridge OSP—Picnic table on knoll above Horseshoe Lake, restrooms at Horseshoe Lake parking area. Special handicapped parking area near lake, wheelchair-accessible to Ridge Trail along lakeshore.

- Saratoga Summit Fire Station, 0.7 mile north of Saratoga Gap on west side of Skyline Blvd.—Phone and water.
- Overnight accommodations—Car-camping reservations: 408-358-3751 and hostel reservations: 408-741-0166 at Sanborn County Park, 6 miles southeast of Saratoga Gap on Sanborn Rd. Hidden Villa Hostel: 415-949-8648, open September to June, 6 miles north on Page Mill Rd., and then 1 mile east on Moody Rd. in Los Altos Hills. Backpack camp on Black Mountain in Monte Bello Open Space Preserve by reservation with MROSD: 415-691-1200.

Getting There

South entrance, Saratoga Gap—Take Skyline Blvd. (Hwy 35) to its intersection with Hwy 9 at Saratoga Gap. Parking area is just 500 feet south of Saratoga Gap on east side of Skyline Blvd.; some spaces available at trailhead on northeast side of Hwy 9.

North entrance, Skyline Ridge OSP, Horseshoe Lake—Take Page Mill Rd. to Skyline Blvd. (Hwy 35), turn left (south), and go 0.75 mile to preserve entrance on west side of road.

On The Trail

This 7.8-mile trip from Saratoga Gap to Horseshoe Lake traverses three MROSD preserves and one Santa Clara county park. It can be taken in two segments—a shady, moderately level, 2-mile trip from Saratoga Gap through Upper Stevens Creek County Park to the Skyline Boulevard trail crossing at the Hickory Oak Ridge gate in Long Ridge OSP, and a 5.8-mile trip from the Hickory Oak Ridge gate to the Horseshoe Lake parking area in Skyline Ridge OSP.

The Bay Area Ridge Trail roughly follows the old Summit Road, a wagon route used by early settlers. After the advent of motor vehicles, Skyline Boulevard replaced the old road with a straighter, more level route. Today, self-propelled Ridge Trail users can travel the old roadway past former homesites set in magnificent forests and on ridges with spectacular vistas.

Hikers, equestrians, and **bicyclists** enter Saratoga Gap OSP under a canopy of great oaks and meander around bends and into hollows above a steep-sided canyon. With Douglas firs towering overhead you skirt massive wind- and rain-pocked sandstone outcrops. These rocks were probably uplifted when the Pacific Plate dipped under the North American Plate in the geologic processes that built these Santa Cruz Mountains eons ago.

With a dropoff on your right too sheer for farming or cattle-grazing, this mountainside has remained relatively untouched. The rather unusual California nutmeg tree, which you can recognize by its flat, prickly needles, which distinguish it from Douglas fir tree needles, is taking hold here. A springhouse remains in a steep ravine below the trail. Fallen leaves from ancient madrones carpet the ground with shades of mauve, yellow and gold.

After reaching Upper Stevens Creek County Park, you swing east into a clearing at the top of historic Charcoal Road. This unpaved road was once used for hauling

The Ridge Trail appeals to all ages and a variety of users.

charcoal, a fuel made from trees on these steep mountainsides; this road descends through second-growth forests to Stevens Creek in Monte Bello OSP. Do not take Charcoal Road. Instead, cross the clearing and continue on a trail that contours northwest through an oak-madrone woodland to reach Skyline Boulevard.

Then cross Skyline Boulevard to the gate into the Hickory Oak Ridge Area of Long Ridge OSP. Rising to the ridgetop, you head north on sections of old Summit Road, now MROSD patrol roads, through a forest of the area's namesake—mature, widely spaced hickory oaks, also called canyon live oaks, some at least 5 feet in diameter. The canyon live oak bears dark green, prickly leaves that are powdery or gray underneath. Its acorns have a furry golden ruff around the cup, giving it yet another name, the golden cup oak. Regardless of your name preference, you will surely notice how well this species grows along the west side of the Skyline ridge.

Beyond the woods the main Bay Area Ridge Trail route continues on the patrol road, but you can veer left on a narrow trail to the preserve's 2,693-foot high point. Here more sandstone outcrops, lichen-splotched and weather-etched, stand near the lip of an abrupt decline into tree-filled Oil Creek canyon. From this vantage point the panorama of successive forested ridges creased by wooded stream canyons is an uncluttered, pastoral scene to nourish your spirit.

To return to the patrol road, continue on the narrow trail around the shoulder of this knoll and zigzag downhill through the hickory and live-oak woods. Now on the main Bay Area Ridge Trail route, you make several descents into broad swales and subsequent climbs to hilltop viewpoints. In spring and summer bright orange poppies nestle against boulders, and pink checkerblooms peek out from the grasses; in fall vinegary-smelling blue curls add trailside touches of color to this spectacular trip.

From the junction from which Ward Road descends west to reach Portola State

Park on Pescadero Creek, you ascend right, around a shoulder of the ridge. On the ridgetop watch for a junction where the multi-use Bay Area Ridge Trail route goes right (east) into the woods and then heads north on a 1.6-mile leg. An alternate route continues along the ridge and down the Peters Creek Loop Trail, a 2.1-mile trip. The two routes converge at the last Peters Creek crossing.

The main Ridge Trail route zigzags down through an oak forest to cross the earthen dam that holds back the waters of Peters Creek. On the dam's east side, turn left and follow the former wagon road, an avenue of welcome shade in summer, a moist trail under leafy arches in winter.

Past homesteaders' moss-covered fence posts and remnants of an apple orchard, you traverse a secluded valley where willow thickets mark the creek's course. Soon you and the creek arc right into a tight little canyon with delicate fern fronds draping the hillsides and exposed, gnarled tree roots growing around moss-covered boulders. After crossing the Peters Creek bridge, you can make a gentle, 0.5-mile ascent through the woods and into the grasslands to reach Long Ridge OSP's Grizzly Flat entrance on Skyline Boulevard.

The Grizzly Flat gate in Long Ridge Open Space Preserve is one of several entrances to this leg of the Ridge Trail.

However, in 1995 MROSD installed a connector trail between the Peters Creek crossing and the southern entrance to Skyline Ridge OSP. Parts of this 1-mile trail, open to hikers, bicyclists, and equestrians, adjoin private lands. Please respect fences, close gates, and observe trail directions.

The connector trail terminates in Skyline Ridge OSP on a knoll overlooking a hillside orchard of widely spaced chestnut and walnut trees. If you come here in fall, you can buy harvested nuts from the orchard's former owners. From the knoll the next leg of the Ridge Trail meanders downhill through the orchard, contouring above a tributary of Lambert Creek under a canopy of overhanging trees. In spring, fronds of creamy Solomon's seal drape over moist, fern-clad banks and heavenly blue and light yellow irises bloom on erect stalks.

Passing an ancient oak with fire-scarred heart, you again tread on old Summit Road until you leave the woods. Then turn sharply left and watch for Bay Area Ridge Trail signs that guide you up and down hills on a gravelled road bordering a Christmas tree farm. You pass straight, tight rows of conically pruned conifers on one side and graceful, untamed native forest on the other. Beginning in early November, this farm, leased from MROSD, draws eager urbanites searching for the perfect Christmas tree. After a final uphill pitch on the gravelled surface, pause to look across Stevens Creek canyon and the San Andreas Rift Zone to Monte Bello Ridge. Creased by tree-filled canyons, the rounded, grassy ridge is surmounted by 2,800-foot Black Mountain, its summit marked by tall antennae.

From this viewpoint on the hill, the 0.6-mile **hikers-only** route angles left up to a ridgetop crowned by venerable, 3-foot-diameter Douglas firs. After wending your way along the ridge under these magnificent trees for 0.2 mile, you then abruptly descend around switchbacks on an oak- and fir-forested, west-facing, steep-sided slope to Horseshoe Lake, the headwaters of East Lambert Creek.

In the meantime, **bicyclists** and **equestrians** continue on the gravelled road, a relatively level, wide route that curves around the northeast side of the ridge that the hiker's route traverses. All users meet on the east side of Horseshoe Lake. **Hikers** and **bicyclists** proceed southwest around the lake to the dam. Then, to reach the Horseshoe Lake trailhead and parking area from the dam, they take parallel routes on the west side of the lake, going north to the handicapped parking area. They then proceed uphill (northeast) on the same trail, crossing a sloping meadow to the preserve's Horseshoe Lake north parking area. **Equestrians** leave the hiker/bicyclist/equestrian junction on the east side of the lake and proceed north through woods of oak and buckeye to the equestrian parking area.

But, before you leave Horseshoe Lake, note that the lake does indeed resemble an equine shoe, with arms wrapped around the base of a high, tree-thatched knoll. Home to red-wing blackbirds and several species of ducks, Horseshoe Lake is known to attract a pair of black-shouldered kites. These large, white birds with black-tipped wings are often seen here searching the lakeshore for the frogs and water snakes that make up their diet.

You too can enjoy this scene by circling the lake on the foot trails that reach the picnic tables at the tip of the knoll above the lake. Here is a delightful spot to enjoy a knapsack lunch or snack and savor your experiences on this beautiful segment of the Bay Area Ridge Trail.

From the handicapped parking area, **wheelchair users** can take the gently graded Ridge Trail route along the lake's reed-lined west shore, cross the bridge over the dam on the south side, and then traverse the wooded east side of the lake.

The next leg of the Bay Area Ridge Trail continues northward from the Horse-shoe Lake parking areas. See *Skyline Ridge and Russian Ridge Open Space Preserves*. Adding this 4.8-mile trip, with a car shuttle at Russian Ridge, makes it possible for the trail user to spend a full day and 12.6 miles in the finest of coastal, mixed-evergreen forests and on untrammeled grasslands with unsurpassed views. If you choose to return to Saratoga Gap from Horseshoe Lake, it will be a round trip of almost 16 miles. ■

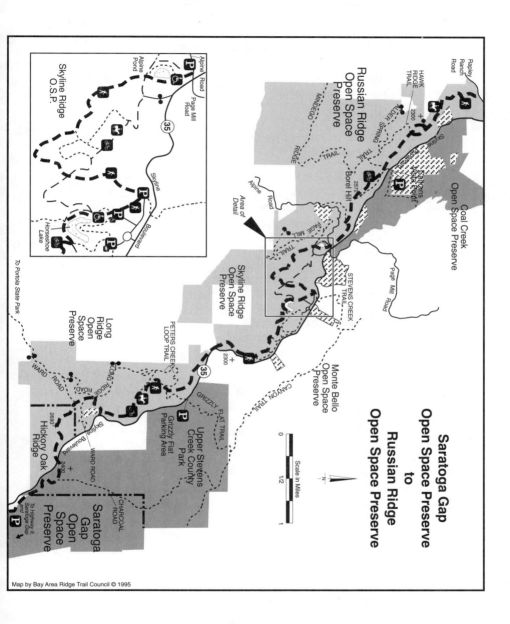

Saratoga Gap
Open Space Preserve
to
Russian Ridge
Open Space Preserve

Scale in Miles

0   1/2   1

Map by Bay Area Ridge Trail Council © 1995

Skyline Ridge and Russian Ridge Open Space Preserves

From Horseshoe Lake to Rapley Ranch Road

Enjoy the Midpeninsula's finest views of Bay and ocean from ridgeline trails that climb high knolls on open grasslands.

Length 4.8 miles.

Location In San Mateo County on the crest of the Santa Cruz Mountains above Palo Alto and Portola Valley.

Trail Characteristics Skyline Ridge OSP trail surfaces vary from duff-covered to gravelly and in width from narrow (hikers only) to wide, paved and unpaved ranch roads. Hikers' route from Horseshoe Lake to Alpine Pond gains 300 feet in 1.3 miles; bicycle/equestrian route gains 400 feet in 0.6 mile. Russian Ridge OSP trail surfaces are firm, unpaved, some rather rocky, with gradual elevation gains of 200 to 300 feet. Trails in both preserves offer only intermittent shade on south- and west-facing slopes. Ridgetops can be foggy and windy.

Ridge Trail Accessibility
- Hikers—Entire route.
- Equestrians—To Rapley Ranch Rd. gate.
- Bicyclists—To Hawk Ridge Trail junction.
- Wheelchair users—Trails around Horseshoe Lake and Alpine Pond.

Trail Management
- Midpeninsula Regional Open Space District (MROSD): 415-691-1200.

Rules
- Open dawn to ½ hour after sunset. Bicyclists must wear helmets and observe 15-mile-per-hour speed limit. No dogs on trail.

Amenities
- No water on entire route.
- Horseshoe Lake—Picnic tables on knoll above lake. Trails for physically limited.
- Horseshoe Lake and Russian Ridge OSP parking areas—Restrooms.
- Alpine Pond—David Daniels Nature Center has observation deck and periodic environmental displays. Trails for physically limited circle pond.

Getting There
South entrance, Skyline Ridge OSP, Horseshoe Lake—Take Page Mill Rd. to Skyline Blvd. (Hwy 35), turn left (south), and go 0.75 mile to preserve entrance on west side of road.

North entrance, Russian Ridge OSP, Rapley Ranch Rd./Skyline Blvd.—

Take Page Mill Rd. to Skyline Blvd. (Hwy 35), turn right (north), and go 2.7 miles to roadside parking on west side of road at Rapley Ranch Rd.

On The Trail

Throughout this northern part of Skyline Ridge OSP hikers follow a different route from equestrians and bicyclists. **Hikers** leave the northwest parking area at Horseshoe Lake and make a long, gradual ascent southwest on a steep, grassy hillside above East Lambert Creek. Particularly striking here in late spring are lemon-yellow mariposa lilies and blue brodiaea rising above drying oat grass.

After 0.9 mile, swing around to the west side of the preserve and walk through pungent chaparral punctuated by patches of small oaks. When you reach a dramatic parapet chipped out of a sheer sandstone butte, a 180-degree sweep of forests, stream canyons, ridges, and grasslands unfolds below you. On clear days, you can see the ocean. In almost any weather you can find Butano Ridge, which forms the western rampart above Portola State Park and Pescadero and Memorial county parks. Now you can reach these parks from the Bay Area Ridge Trail via Ward Road in Long Ridge OSP, and someday Old Page Mill Road in Portola State Park will connect to the Bay Area Ridge Trail through Skyline Ridge OSP.

After bending into folds of the mountain and traversing sloping grasslands for 0.4 mile, you then follow a short forest trail flanked by great canyon live oaks. On a knoll above the Old Page Mill Road junction is the site of former Governor James Rolph's 1930s "Summer Capital," which was topped by a gold-painted, papier-maché dome. "Sunny Jim" owned this land, as well as present-day Russian Ridge Open Space Preserve. Many years earlier, before the settlers arrived, the Ohlones came here to gather acorns, which they ground on nearby rocks.

Continuing on the Bay Area Ridge Trail, you go around reed-lined Alpine Pond, cross Alpine Road to the Russian Ridge OSP parking area, and rejoin the bicyclists and equestrians.

Bicyclists and **equestrians** leave the Horseshoe Lake parking areas (bicyclists use the northwest area, equestrians the northeast) and follow the marked routes down to the patrol road above the handicapped parking area at Horseshoe Lake. Here you go over a stile, veer right (south), and then bend northwest for a steep climb out of East Lambert Creek canyon. Then, after crossing the hikers' route, continue uphill (northwest) on an old, hard-surfaced, farm road through the preserve past lands now cleared of Christmas trees and replanted with native oaks by volunteers. At Alpine Pond, use the trail on the west side and cross Alpine Road to the Russian Ridge OSP parking area.

On a clear day the Pacific Ocean is visible from the Ridge Trail on Skyline

From the north side of the parking area **hikers**, **equestrians** and **bicyclists** take the multi-use Bay Area Ridge Trail route that zigzags up through the grasslands toward 2,572-foot Borel Hill. Although this hill was named for former owner Antoine Borel, a San Francisco banker and Peninsula resident, the preserve's name commemorates a Russian emigrant who lived east of the ridge from 1920 till 1950.

In years of ample rain this ridge in springtime is a wondrous wildflower sight. On both sides of the trail as far as you can see, extravagant palettes of color sweep over the hillsides and knolls. Often beginning in January you will find perky johnny jump-ups turning their yellow-orange faces to the sun. Then goldfields, cream cups, orange poppies, pink checkerblooms, red maids, and blue lupines follow. These beautiful flower fields may approximate what John Muir saw on his trips across California.

After 0.7 mile and just before you reach Borel Hill, a fork in the trail invites you to veer left (northwest) and follow the gently graded, multi-use Bay Area Ridge Trail route around the west side of the ridge. From this trail you can look past the preserve's boundary to Mindego Hill, an ancient, extinct volcano. Beyond lie a

Mindego Hill, an extinct volcano, lies west of the Ridge Trail in Russian Ridge OSP.

succession of rounded, grassy hills creased by almost a dozen streams that join San Gregorio Creek on its way to the San Mateo coast. This west fork of the Ridge Trail descends to a cleft in the ridgeline from where the Mindego Ridge Trail goes right (east) to reach the Caltrans Vista Point on Skyline Blvd., a convenient parking area where you could put a shuttle car. However, to continue toward the Russian Ridge north boundary, make a slight jog (less than 0.1 mile) to the left (west) on the Mindego Ridge Trail and then turn right (northwest) on the Bay Area Ridge Trail. A short steep climb to a 2,400-foot ridgetop will reward you with wonderful views of the Bay Area. North lie San Francisco and Mt. Tamalpais. Across the Bay is Mt. Diablo, and farther south of it are Mission and Monument peaks, where another

Bay Area Ridge Trail segment traverses East Bay ridgetops. Southeast beyond San Jose is Mt. Hamilton. If you look due south on very clear days, you can see the Santa Lucia Mountains rising beyond Monterey Bay.

After 0.5 mile on this top-of-the-world trail, look right for a Ridge Trail turnoff marked RAPLEY RANCH ROAD, where **hikers** and **equestrians** bear right. Here **bicyclists** can angle sharply left to return down the beautiful 0.6-mile Hawk Ridge Trail, joining the Alder Spring and Mindego Ridge trails to reach the Caltrans Vista Point on Skyline Boulevard.

Hikers and **equestrians** proceed to the Skyline Boulevard/Rapley Ranch Road junction on a 1.6-mile trip. Follow the old ranch fence line, curving around the south and east sides of another 2,400-foot hill crowned by telephone-relay and electric-transmission-line towers. Abruptly you enter a woods of tall oak trees that shade both you and the low-growing shrubs of elderberry, hazelnut, gooseberry, and thimbleberry. As the trail straightens out on the north side of the hill, you pass a wooden platform, a perfect picnic site for your backpack lunch or early evening supper.

Continuing north under a canopy of broad-branching oaks with lichen- and moss-covered trunks, you make a long, downhill switchback. Looking back, you note the transmission towers outlined against the sky contrasting with an earlier, but still operative, form of energy—a windmill. When strong ocean winds blow across this ridge, you can hear the powerline wires singing and the windmill paddles whirring.

A few switchbacks carry you downhill, across a service road and below a fascinating, glass-fronted, circular private home high above on the crest of the hill. In the wooded ravine far below the trail is another windmill set in a pretty garden. Contouring around a few curves midway between the woods and the ridgecrest, you pass great boulders splattered with lichen and bedecked with healthy patches of poison oak. In late summer the pearly everlasting's tufted, creamy flowers edge the trail cut into a steep hillside.

After passing through a little woods, nourished by an intermittent stream in a draw, you skirt a small meadow, and then round a shoulder of the ridge with a close-to-vertical dropoff. Then you enter another woods before reaching the locked gate at Rapley Ranch Road. **Hikers** crawl through the brown pipe gate and on the left note the large barn with electric fence, once used to pen a flock of sheep. Enjoy this picturesque, but off-limits, pastoral scene and carry on to the right for just 0.1 mile to roadside parking on Skyline Boulevard. Until MROSD can install a stile at this gate, **equestrians** must turn around here and return to the Russian Ridge parking area at Alpine Road.

Someday the Bay Area Ridge Trail will bridge the short gap from here to Windy Hill Open Space Preserve. (See the following trip description.) In the meantime, plan a car shuttle at Skyline Boulevard or retrace your steps to the Alpine Road parking area. If you are making a round trip, try the alternate return route described above for bicyclists, using the Hawk Ridge, Alder Spring, and Mindego Ridge trails to reach the Bay Area Ridge Trail going south. ■

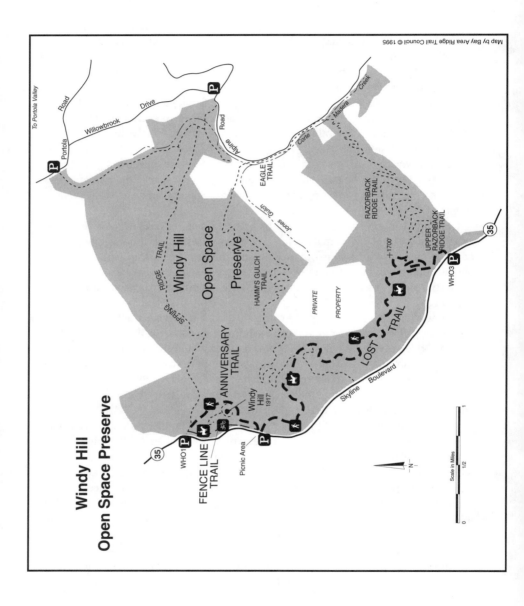

Windy Hill
Open Space Preserve

Windy Hill Open Space Preserve

From Upper Razorback Ridge to top of Spring Ridge

First following a beautiful, sheltered forest trail, then traversing rolling grasslands, this segment of the Ridge Trail finally climbs the heights of Windy Hill, a Peninsula landmark.

Length 3.5 miles.

Location In San Mateo County along the east side of Skyline Blvd. above Portola Valley.

Trail Characteristics After an initial 320-foot elevation loss, the route gradually gains 234 feet to the Windy Hill knobs on the Anniversary Trail segment. Trail varies from narrow footpath to broad, old wagon road. Possible strong winds and/or coastal fog.

Ridge Trail Accessibility
- Hikers and equestrians—Upper Razorback Ridge, Gate 3 (marked WHO3), to picnic area and then to Anniversary/Fence Line trails junction.
- Hikers only—Beyond junction of Anniversary/Fence Line trails, continue on Anniversary Trail to top of Spring Ridge, Gate 1 (marked WHO1).
- Equestrians—Upper Razorback Ridge to picnic area, then Anniversary and Fence Line trails to top of Spring Ridge.
- Bicyclists—From picnic area on Anniversary and Fence Line trails to top of Spring Ridge.

Trail Management
- Midpeninsula Regional Open Space District (MROSD): 415-691-1200.

Rules
- Open from dawn to ½ hour after sunset. No dogs on Lost Trail or Connector Trail, dogs on leash on Anniversary Trail and top of Spring Ridge.

Amenities
- Picnic area just off Skyline Blvd. at intersection of Anniversary Trail and Connector Trail. No water or restrooms.

Getting There
South entrance, Upper Razorback Ridge, Gate 3 (WHO3)—Take Skyline Blvd. (Hwy 35) south 4.3 miles from La Honda Rd. (Hwy 84) at Skylonda or north 3 miles from Page Mill Rd. Off-road parking for 6 cars at trail entrance.

North entrance, Top of Spring Ridge, Gate 1 (WHO1)—Take Skyline Blvd. (Hwy 35) south 1.8 miles from La Honda Rd. or 5.5 miles north from Page Mill Rd. Ample off-road parking.

Picnic Area, Skyline Blvd.—Take Skyline Blvd. 2.0 miles south from La Honda Rd. or 5.3 miles north from Page Mill Rd.

On The Trail

Just beyond the stile at the top of Razorback Ridge at Windy Hill Gate 3 (WHO3) is a MROSD sign and a left-arrow Bay Area Ridge Trail logo directing hikers and equestrians downhill. Bicyclists' access to this preserve begins at the picnic area. Leaving the whirr of Skyline Boulevard traffic behind, **hikers** and **equestrians** take the wide trail, an old farm road, through a mixed woodland where feathery moss and clusters of lichen decorate the trees. After 0.4 mile and a couple of zigzags on the steep hillside you reach the Windy Hill Loop Trail junction. From here the Ridge Trail traverses the upper reaches of the preserve on the 1.7-mile Lost Trail segment of the Loop Trail.

Bear left on the Lost Trail, heading northwest, to contour through a fir forest at approximately the 1,700-foot level. You wind in and out of little ravines and cross headwaters of streams named for settlers who once farmed this mountainside. Water seeping from the hillside and onto the trail feeds the creeks that empty into perennial Corte Madera Creek on the lower east side of the preserve.

This mountainside was once part of a huge land grant known as Rancho El Corte de Madera. Deeded to Maximo Martinez and Domingo Peralta in 1834 by Governor José Figueroa, its Spanish name means "the wood-cutting ranch." As you travel through the forest, try to picture its former grandeur. Before the mid-19th century, redwood trees 8 to 10 feet in diameter covered the mountains above present-day Portola Valley and Woodside. From these primeval redwood forests came the wood that built Mission Santa Clara and the Pueblo of San José. Then severe logging for building Gold Rush San Francisco in the 1850s and a disastrous fire in the '60s left hardly a tree standing here.

Today a second-growth forest of Douglas firs and redwoods flourishes, protected in the 1,130-acre Windy Hill Open Space Preserve. Some trees have grown to considerable girth, aided by natural springs, heavy rainfall, and coastal fogs that often shroud this ridgetop.

After 1.3 miles from the start, you emerge from the dense forest at the head of Jones Gulch. Down in the gulch lies a forested private inholding, the former Lauriston estate. In 1915 Herbert E. Law began the land purchases that eventually amounted to 627 acres of meadows, mountains and valleys. His holdings, known as Willow Brook Farm, included the magnificent villa, Lauriston, and acres of lath houses for his agricultural enterprises.

In 1937 John Francis Neylan, a San Francisco attorney, purchased the estate. Subsequent owners, Ryland Kelley and partners, gave part of the estate to the Peninsula Open Space Trust (POST). Sold to MROSD in the early 1980s, this land became the original Windy Hill Open Space Preserve.

A rusty wheelbarrow chained to a tree recalls days when hand work built roads for settlers' wagons. Below the trail are some rotting fence posts that marked boundaries of old ranches. When passing some high sandstone cliffs draped with

Stop for lunch at a picnic site near this sign.

ferns and berry bushes, one can speculate that this may have been the site of Herbert Law's quarry for his Lauriston villa.

Now you skirt a chaparral-clothed, south-facing flank of the mountain and cross a dirt access road from Skyline Boulevard. Then, bending west toward Skyline Boulevard, you tread a boardwalk over a marshy area fed by springs that empty into Hamms Gulch. At the right turnoff for the trail that bears this settler's name, you veer left along the edge of the gulch where several immense Douglas firs cling to the hillside. If you went right on the Hamms Gulch Trail, you'd zigzag downhill for 2.4 miles to a stone bridge over Corte Madera Creek and the ornate iron gates of the former Lauriston estate.

But continuing on the Bay Area Ridge Trail and the 0.6-mile Connector Trail to the picnic area, you thread through grasslands that are sprinkled with wildflowers in spring and summer and come upon Bob's Bench, named for the first executive director of POST, Bob Augsburger. Just beyond, a large wooden sign thanks contributors to the Windy Hill Loop Trail and the trail crews, under the direction of Jane Ames, who built this 8.4-mile loop trail up, down, and around this preserve.

Shortly you reach the picnic area set in a flat next to Skyline Boulevard near the site of the pioneering Brown Ranch. Settlers Brown and his neighbor to the north, Orton, must have traversed the Lost Trail route you just followed. Until Skyline Boulevard was built in the 1920s, this old wagon road between farms, known as the Ridge Road, stayed below the ridgecrest.

Hikers, equestrians, and **bicyclists** begin the northbound leg of this trip together on the Anniversary Trail. Then at the first swale, **equestrians** and **bicyclists** veer left on the Fence Line Trail while **hikers** continue on the Anniversary Trail. This 0.75-mile trail was constructed with funds from POST to mark the tenth anniversary of the establishment of the Windy Hill Preserve. Equestrians and bicyclists using the Fence Line Trail, which contours north above Skyline Boulevard, have splendid ocean views when the day is clear, and then they join the hikers at the top of Spring Ridge.

On the Anniversary Trail, **hikers** make a gradual ascent around the east side of the Windy Hill knobs past side trails reaching their summits. These treeless protrusions above the long sweep of grasslands descending to Portola Valley are prominent landmarks on the Peninsula. When you climb them on a clear day, commanding views of the entire Bay Area and the San Mateo coastside spread out before you. On a day true to its name, the 1,917-foot summit can be a challenge to steady footing, yet a delight for kite flyers and model-glider enthusiasts. From the summit it is a quick descent to the north parking area at the top of Spring Ridge, the end of this Bay Area Ridge Trail segment.

Since this is a short trip, hikers and equestrians may want to do the 7-mile round trip. If not, park a shuttle car at the picnic area or at the top of Spring Ridge and do the shorter trip. The next segment begins in Wunderlich Park, about 5 miles north of Windy Hill. See *Wunderlich County Park to Huddart County Park.*   ∎

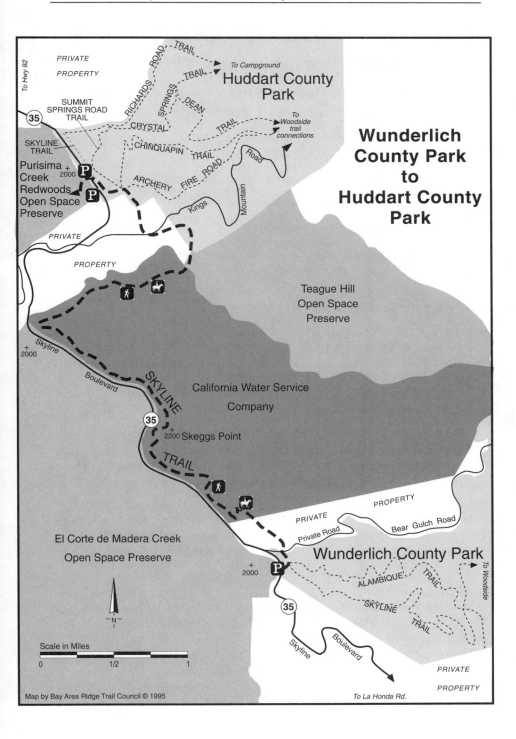

PRIVATE
PROPERTY

To Hwy 92

SUMMIT
SPRINGS ROAD
TRAIL

35

SKYLINE
TRAIL

Purisima
Creek
Redwoods
Open Space
Preserve

+2000

RICHARDS ROAD TRAIL

SPRINGS TRAIL

DEAN

CRYSTAL

CHINQUAPIN TRAIL

ARCHERY FIRE ROAD

TRAIL

Kings Mountain Road

To Campground

Huddart County
Park

To
Woodside
trail
connections

Wunderlich
County Park
to
Huddart County
Park

PRIVATE

PROPERTY

Skyline

+2000

Boulevard

SKYLINE

35

+2200 Skeggs Point

TRAIL

Teague Hill
Open Space
Preserve

California Water Service

Company

El Corte de Madera Creek

Open Space Preserve

–N–

Scale in Miles

0   1/2   1

PROPERTY

PRIVATE

Private Road

Bear Gulch Road

+2000

P

Wunderlich County Park

ALAMBIQUE TRAIL

To Woodside

35

SKYLINE

TRAIL

Skyline

Boulevard

To La Honda Rd.

PRIVATE

PROPERTY

Map by Bay Area Ridge Trail Council © 1995

Wunderlich County Park to Huddart County Park

From Wunderlich West Gate to Purisima Creek Trailhead

Follow this gently graded trail just below the crest of the Santa Cruz Mountains to discover unusual spring wildflowers in tall coniferous forests.

Length 6.2 miles.

Location In San Mateo County near Woodside.

Trail Characteristics An easy trail with only small changes in elevation. Shaded and cool, often foggy.

Ridge Trail Accessibility
- Hikers and equestrians.

Trail Management
- San Mateo County Parks and Recreation Department: 415-363-4020.

Rules
- Open 8 A.M. to sunset. No dogs, no bicycles.

Amenities
- No water or restrooms along the trail. Restrooms on Redwood Trail in Purisima Creek Redwoods Open Space Preserve, which is across Skyline Blvd. from Ridge Trail's north entrance at Huddart Park.
- Camping (organized groups—youth, equestrian, and backpack) in Huddart County Park by reservation only: 415-363-4021.

Getting There

South Entrance, Wunderlich Park—Take Skyline Blvd. (Hwy 35) 3 miles north from La Honda Rd. (Hwy 84) junction or 10 miles south from Half Moon Bay Rd. (Hwy 92) junction. Limited parking on west side of Skyline Blvd. Cross road to trail entrance.

North entrance, Huddart Park—Take Skyline Blvd. (Hwy 35) 6.5 miles south from Half Moon Bay Rd. (Hwy 92) or 6.5 miles north from La Honda Rd. (Hwy 84) to parking at Purisima Creek trailhead on west side of Skyline Blvd. Cross road to trail entrance.

On The Trail

Winding through fir and redwood forests, this section of the Bay Area Ridge Trail is on San Mateo County's Skyline Trail, paralleling Skyline Boulevard. For most of its length it follows the route of the old California Riding and Hiking Trail. This is one of the few remaining segments of a trail system established in 1954, a part of an ambitious plan for trails up and down the state.

In Wunderlich Park's northwest corner the trail descends on switchbacks through a redwood forest, losing 100 feet in elevation. You cross private Bear Gulch Road, then head north below a subdivision, continuing for 4 miles through the upper slopes of the California Water Service Company watershed (formerly the Bear Gulch Water Company). The trail is shaded by redwoods and firs grown tall since most logging ended here in the mid-1860s. Try this trail on a summer day when you need a retreat from the valley heat.

Winding in and out of small ravines, you are often close enough to Skyline Boulevard to hear the murmur of traffic. But not so close that you cannot hear the calls of Steller's jays, the crested blue-black cousins of the blue (scrub) jays of the foothill woodlands.

By the edge of the trail, blue hound's tongue of early spring is followed by masses of Douglas iris in shades of lavender. In May you will find the bright, rose-red flower clusters of the uncommon Clintonia. Also found in these woods is the elegant, lacy-leaved, pink bleeding-heart, nestled in damp ravines.

On clear, bright days occasional glimpses of the valley below open through the trees, though fog often shrouds the view. But it is the forest in all its variety that delights at every turn. Tall Douglas firs are part of the new forest taking hold here after the logging of the 1800s. A contrast to the dark conifers is the light foliage of bigleaf maples growing in ravines where water is plentiful.

The size of the redwood stumps gives us an idea of the scale of the ancient forest, known to the Spanish as the Pulgas Redwoods, which covered the eastern slopes of the Santa Cruz Mountains above present-day Woodside and Portola Valley. These immense trees, some of which were 2,000 years old, flourished in the heavy rainfall along the ridge—as much as 40 inches a year, with frequent fogs adding to the precipitation.

After traveling 1.5 miles along the trail you will see old moss-covered stumps of the largest redwood trees, some 10 feet or more in diameter. Note the horizontal slots cut about six feet from the ground, which held boards on which loggers stood to fell the trees. This whole forest was cut to supply redwood to build Gold Rush San Francisco. Logs dragged down the steep hills by oxen to sawmills were then

Nineteenth century logging in Huddart Park left hardly a tree standing.

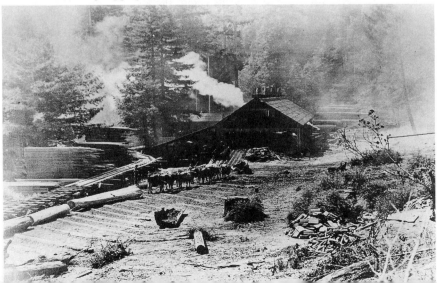

taken to the port of Redwood City to be barged up the Bay. So great was the demand for wood that by 1870 hardly a redwood remained standing on this mountainside. Logging finally ceased in this watershed because Bear Gulch Creek water formerly used in the sawmills was needed to supply a grist mill and then to provide water for the growing communities in the valley.

After rounding a wide curve in the trail below Skeggs Point, you come to a wooden bench and memorial plaque, dedicated by the local Sierra Club chapter to Clara May Lazarus, an ardent trail advocate. Here is a peaceful place for enjoying the forest's solitude.

You continue for nearly a mile through forest and beside occasional meadows, flower-filled in spring. Skirting a few homes of a mountaintop settlement, you climb back into the forest. Here the trail veers east, bringing spectacular views south as far as Black Mountain in Santa Clara County. Through oak woodland and chaparral the trail contours along a south-facing ridge to Teague Hill Open Space Preserve, where it begins a gentle descent northwest through a redwood forest to Kings Mountain Road. Follow the footpath beside the road to a marked pedestrian crossing leading to Huddart Park.

After passing a large, private parcel of open, rolling grassland, the trail reaches redwood forest again and a park crossroads. At this point the Skyline Trail, which is also the Bay Area Ridge Trail, turns west on a gravelled service road through open woodland. The Skyline Trail continues 0.3 mile to an exit to Skyline Boulevard, where this segment of the Bay Area Ridge Trail ends. Across the road on the west side of Skyline Boulevard is the trailhead and parking for the next segment of the Ridge Trail in Purisima Creek Redwoods Open Space Preserve. (See the trip description under that name.)

The Skyline Trail continues north, meandering 0.8 mile on a gentle grade through a redwood forest on the east side of Skyline Boulevard to the west boundary of Huddart Park. Someday the Skyline and Bay Area Ridge trails route may be extended north through the recently acquired Phleger Estate lands and then continue to a point opposite the north entrance of Purisima Creek Redwoods OSP. From the Huddart Park west boundary, the Crystal Springs Trail descends 2 miles to a woodsy setting in the park where group campsites, with picnic tables and restrooms, are available for equestrian and hiker groups by reservation only. Here is a pleasant place to camp before continuing on to the next leg of your Ridge Trail trek.   ∎

The Ridge Trail leads through conifer and oak forests from Wunderlich Park to Huddart Park.

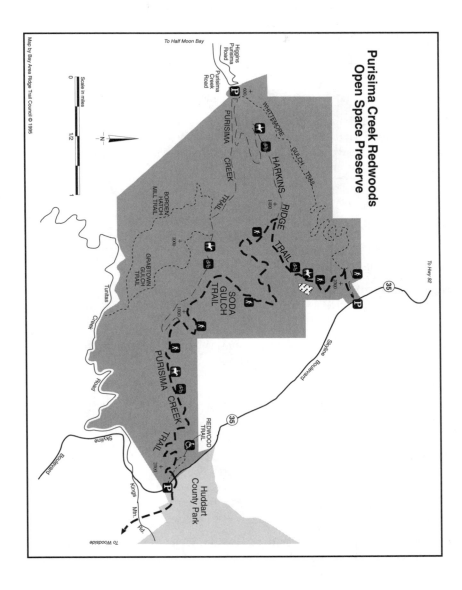

Purisima Creek Redwoods
Open Space Preserve

Map by Bay Area Ridge Trail Council © 1995

Purisima Creek Redwoods Open Space Preserve

From Purisima Creek Trailhead to Preserve's North Entrance

Parts of five trails through forested canyons and over high ridges make up the Ridge Trail route in Purisima Creek Redwoods Open Space Preserve.

> **Length**   5.7 miles— hikers; 7.7 miles—equestrians and bicyclists.
>
> **Location**   In San Mateo County near Woodside.
>
> **Trail Characteristics**   A loss of 1,000 feet elevation in the first 2 miles requires a steady climb out of the canyon to regain this elevation at the north end of the trail. Forested areas can be bathed in fog in summer, while the open, south-facing ridges may be hot.

Ridge Trail Accessibility
- Hikers—Entire route
- Hikers only—Soda Gulch and Whittemore Gulch footpaths.
- Equestrians and bicyclists—Purisima Creek, Harkins Ridge trails, and Whittemore Gulch service road.
- Wheelchair users—Redwood Trail.

Trail Management
- Midpeninsula Regional Open Space District (MROSD): 415-691-1200.

Rules
- Open from dawn to ½ hour after sunset. No dogs. Helmets required for bicyclists, mandatory 15-mph-speed limit.

Amenities
- Restrooms at south and north ends of trail. No water. Several trailside benches. Two picnic tables on Redwood Trail.

Getting There

South entrance, Purisima Creek Trailhead—Take Skyline Blvd. (Hwy 35) 6.5 miles south from Half Moon Bay Rd. (Hwy 92) or 6.5 miles north from La Honda Rd. (Hwy 84) to parking at Purisima Creek trailhead on west side of Skyline Blvd. Disabled parking 0.1 mile farther south at head of Redwood Trail on west side of Skyline Blvd.; several general parking spaces.

North entrance—Take Skyline Blvd. (Hwy 35) 4.5 miles south from Half Moon Bay Rd. (Hwy 92) or 8.5 miles north from La Honda Rd. (Hwy 84) to large parking area on west side of road; equestrian trailer parking available.

On The Trail

Wheelchair users start from the head of the Redwood Trail and follow the well-graded path northwest through a beautiful redwood grove, where shade-loving wildflowers in season and shiny-leaved huckleberry shrubs thrive at trailside. Your path crosses the Purisima Creek Trail and continues 0.2 mile to a flat where a picnic table affords a place to have a snack and enjoy the forest view.

Hikers, equestrians, and **bicyclists** start from the parking area at the Purisima Creek trailhead on the west side of Skyline Blvd. As you descend into the canyon under tall second-growth redwoods and tanoaks, perhaps you can imagine the forest scene here in the late 19th century—loggers felling primeval redwoods by hand, several streamside mills cutting the wood into shingles, and oxen teams pulling wagons loaded with logs up the steep mountainside.

Into the 20th century logging continued sporadically until MROSD completed its purchases of 2,511 acres in 1984. Now historic logging roads make fine trails linked by newly built footpaths through the woods.

At wide openings in the forest, once used as landings for the logs, springtime gardens of blue ceanothus, scarlet columbine, and invasive yellow Scotch broom blossom. In fall, the brilliant yellow of bigleaf maples accents the forest greens.

After 1.8 miles of steady downhill on the Purisima Creek Trail, look for a Bay Area Ridge Trail sign on the right side of a hairpin turn. Here, 1,000 feet lower than your starting point, is the secluded entrance to the Soda Gulch Trail, reserved for hikers only.

Equestrians and **bicyclists** continue downhill to the western terminus of the Purisima Creek Trail and then turn uphill on the Harkins Ridge Trail. At the Whittemore Gulch service road, you turn northeast to reach the parking area on Skyline Boulevard, having regained the 1,630 feet in elevation lost on the downhill leg of your 7.7-mile trip.

The Soda Gulch Trail for **hikers only** contours along the forested east side of No Name Gulch, where delicate springtime flowers abound. Crossing a bridge over a tributary and another over the main creek, you leave this moist environment for a south-facing slope. Rounding a bend, you enter a drier open area. Tanoaks, cream bush, and even an evergreen oak or two flourish in a sunnier zone.

Then in Soda Gulch you return to deep forest, where circles of second-growth trees surround 5–6-foot diameter redwood stumps. One of the largest trees on the steep-sided trail is a towering, double-trunked redwood, whose scarred bark may indicate it was used to anchor cables for hauling logs uphill.

A handsome wooden bridge crosses the upper reaches of Soda Gulch Creek, full in spring, though sometimes dry by fall. Now more than halfway along the 2.5-mile Soda Gulch Trail, you leave the moist redwood forest to ascend open chaparral slopes. At a bend in the trail, you will find welcome shade under a lone, wide-spreading tanoak tree.

When you reach the Harkins Ridge Trail junction, it is 1.4 miles to the north parking area. Turn right (east) for a steep 0.3-mile climb on this wide service road, formerly known as the Harkins Fire Road. **Equestrians** and **bicyclists** now join **hikers** on this section of the Bay Area Ridge Trail. Low chaparral and a scattering of trees line the trail, which veers left and levels off to cross over the headwall of Whittemore Gulch. Looking west to the ocean, you can see breakers crashing on the beach near Half Moon Bay.

Past sizable redwoods, clusters of Douglas fir, and abundant flowers of the season, you come to the Whittemore Gulch Trail junction. Here, **equestrians** and **bicyclists** take the steep service road and **hikers** zigzag up through a fir and tanoak forest on a well-graded footpath.

At one of the bends in the footpath, look northwest toward other high points of the Santa Cruz Mountains—Montara Mountain, Scarper Peak and the long central Cahill Ridge in the San Francisco Watershed. Soon you reach the parking area at the crest of the Skyline ridge, having regained the 1,000 feet in elevation you lost in Purisima Creek Canyon.

On a beautiful day in May 1989, this 5.7-mile segment and the one just south, Wunderlich County Park to Huddart County Park, were dedicated. The occasion was marked by speeches congratulating all trail advocates and volunteers. There were hikes and rides on both legs of the Bay Area Ridge Trail, followed by refreshments for all.

From the northern terminus of this trail all the way to Sweeney Ridge, there is a 19-mile gap in the Bay Area Ridge Trail route. Negotiations for use of a gravelled service road on Cahill and Fifield ridges in the San Francisco Watershed are continuing. See *Sweeney Ridge to Milagra Ridge* for the next dedicated segment.∎

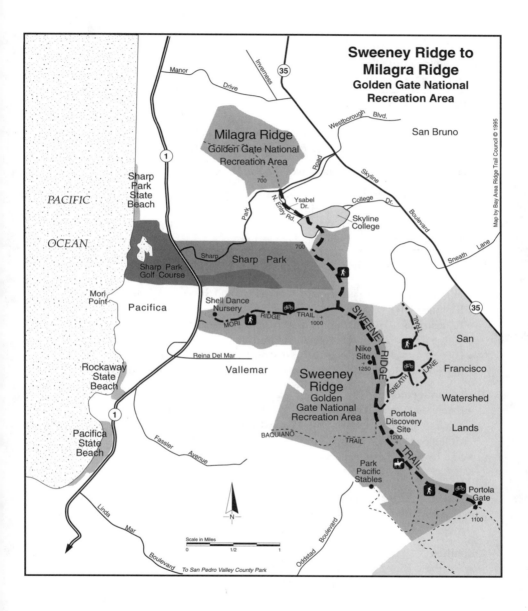

Sweeney Ridge to
Milagra Ridge
Golden Gate National
Recreation Area

Map by Bay Area Ridge Trail Council © 1995

San Bruno

Milagra Ridge
Golden Gate National
Recreation Area

700

Sharp
Park
State
Beach

PACIFIC

OCEAN

Manor

Drive

Inverness

35

Westborough   Blvd.

Road

Skyline

Park

N. Entry Rd.

Ysabel
Dr.

College   Dr.

Skyline
College

Boulevard

Sneath   Lane

Sharp   Park

Sharp

700

Sharp Park
Golf Course

Mori
Point

Pacifica

Shell Dance
Nursery

MORI   RIDGE   TRAIL
1000

SWEENEY RIDGE

TRAIL

35

San

Reina Del Mar

Vallemar

Nike
Site
1250

SNEATH   LANE

Francisco

Rockaway
State
Beach

Sweeney
Ridge
Golden
Gate National
Recreation Area

Watershed

Lands

1

Pacifica
State
Beach

Fassler

Avenue

BAQUIANO   TRAIL

Portola
Discovery
Site
1200

TRAIL

Park
Pacific
Stables

Portola
Gate

1100

Linda

Mar

Boulevard

Oddstad   Boulevard

N

Scale in Miles

0   1/2   1

To San Pedro Valley County Park

Sweeney Ridge To Milagra Ridge—GGNRA

From Portola Gate to Milagra Ridge Gate

The only Ridge Trail segment that traverses a college campus yields Bay and coast views, a visit to the San Francisco Bay Discovery Site, and a trip through unique coastal plant communities.

Length   From Sneath Lane to Discovery Site, including a round trip south to Portola Gate, and then north to Milagra Ridge gate—7 miles one way.
From Mori Ridge to Discovery Site, including a round trip to Portola Gate, and then north to Milagra Ridge gate—7.6 miles one way.

Location   In San Mateo County west of San Bruno and east of Pacifica.

Trail Characteristics   Sneath Lane to Nike site, paved road. All other trails wide, unpaved. Elevation gain to ridgetop from Sneath Lane 550 feet, from Mori Ridge 850 feet. No shade on trails, except at Skyline College. Sudden weather changes can bring cold wind and dense fog.

Ridge Trail Accessibility
- Hikers—All trails.
- Hikers only—From junction of Mori Ridge and Sweeney Ridge trails north to Skyline College.
- Equestrians—Horse trail from private Park Pacific Stables, and Sweeney Ridge trail to Discovery Site and to Portola Gate.
- Bicyclists—All trails, except from Mori Ridge/Sweeney Ridge trails junction north to Skyline College; use campus roads through Skyline College.

Trail Management
- Sweeney Ridge—GGNRA: 415-556-8642; 415-239-2366.
- Skyline College route—San Mateo Community College District, Skyline College: 415-355-7000.
- San Bruno City sidewalks—City of San Bruno: 415-877-8862.

Rules
- Sweeney Ridge—Open 8 A.M. to ½ hour after sunset; dogs on leash only.
- Skyline College—Open during college hours; no dogs; bicyclists use campus roads.

Amenities
- Sweeney Ridge—Bronze plaque and monument at Discovery Site, portable toilet at Nike site. No water or telephone.
- Skyline College—Vista point on west side of campus, telephone, water, benches, and restrooms.

Getting There

South entrance, Portola Gate—Not directly accessible by car.

Sneath Lane trailhead—From Skyline Blvd. (Hwy 35) in San Bruno go west on Sneath Lane to off-street parking at gate.

Mori Ridge trailhead—Going north on Hwy 1 in Pacifica, pass Reina del Mar Ave., turn abruptly right into the Shell Dance Nursery, and continue past nursery buildings to parking at end of dirt road. Going south on Hwy 1 in Pacifica, make a U-turn at Reina del Mar Ave. and go north, following directions above.

Skyline College—From Skyline Blvd. (Hwy 35) in San Bruno go west on College Dr., turn left at college entrance, and proceed to parking lot 2. Several spaces reserved for GGNRA trail use.

North entrance, Milagra Ridge—From Hwy 1 or from Skyline Blvd. (Hwy 35), take Sharp Park Rd., turn north on College Dr. Extension N. and continue to roadside parking at Milagra Ridge gate.

By Bus

SamTrans 20J and 21B to Skyline College weekdays and 30B daily except Sunday. SamTrans 32P to Sneath Lane/Monterey Dr. intersection weekdays. SamTrans 10S daily except Sunday and 1L daily on Hwy 1 to Westport Dr. or Reina del Mar Ave. near Mori Ridge trailhead in Pacifica.

On The Trail

The long, rounded Sweeney Ridge, which separates North Peninsula bayside and coastal communities, was once slated to be the I-380 route from Highway 101 to Highway 1. Since the GGNRA already held scenic and recreation easements on some 26,000 acres in San Mateo County, it purchased this 1,000-acre ridgetop in 1982 "to preserve the natural, cultural and recreation values of the ridge."

This segment of the Bay Area Ridge Trail on Sweeney Ridge has no southern entry point. Therefore, your trip begins with an ascent from Sneath Lane in San Bruno or from Mori Ridge in Pacifica. To start from the bayside, **hikers** and **bicyclists** go around the locked gate at the end of Sneath Lane and pick up the paved road that climbs through a dense growth of chaparral and coastal scrub. Curving into ravines and rounding shoulders of the ridge, your way is bordered with a rich variety of native shrubs—red-berried toyon, cream-colored Queen Anne's lace, coyote bush, arroyo willows, elderberry bushes,and blue-blossomed California lilac. At road's edge scarlet and yellow columbines, orange poppies, and lavender yerba santa brighten your way.

At the crest of the ridge the paved trail veers right (north), but to reach the Portolá Discovery Site, you turn left. Almost immediately you pass the Baquiano Trail going off to the right. This trail, named for Portolá's scout, Sgt. José Francisco Ortega, who was the first European to see San Francisco Bay, goes over private property at its western end and is open only to occasional ranger-led walks.

Continue a short distance beyond the Baquiano Trail to the Portolá Discovery

Site on a 1,200-foot knoll on your left, on the east side of the trail. Here are two commemorative monuments—the one on the left is a weathered serpentine boulder bearing a bronze plaque dedicated to the sighting of San Francisco Bay on November 4, 1769. The plaque states that Don Gaspar de Portolá's men first saw the Bay while searching for a land route to Monterey Bay. Portolá's commission was to establish a colony in Monterey to thwart British and Russian settlements in Alta California.

It was only later, when other expeditions recorded the vastness of the Bay's waters, that the Spaniards realized the importance of their find. They then charted the extensive harbor and in 1776 established their northern colony in present-day San Francisco on the shores of that Bay.

From this knoll Portolá's men could not see the Golden Gate, but they must have seen some Bay Area peaks and ridges. For today's explorers of this ridge, the monument on the right (south) side of the knoll shows the outlines and names of the Bay Area's major peaks etched on a black granite cylinder. Among the peaks shown are Mt. Tamalpais, Mt. Hamilton, Mt. Diablo, San Bruno Mountain, and Montara Mountain. Today, Bay Area Ridge Trail travellers see these landmark mountains from many ridgetops as they circle the Bay Area.

To reach the boundary between Sweeney Ridge and the San Francisco Watershed lands at the Portola Gate, you can make a 2.4-mile round trip south from the Discovery Site on the Sweeney Ridge Trail. It takes you past luxurious clumps of Douglas iris, beautiful blue or creamy-white blossomed in May, and beside a few springs seeping from winter to early summer. You can locate the springs in summer by the patches of sedges and tall grasses that prosper in the damp soil of the seep. Along this trail in late summer, you may be lucky enough to see, half-concealed under the shrubs, tall, slim flower stalks clustered with whitish-green blossoms— one of California's native orchids.

Enroute to the Portola Gate you pass the horse trail that leads to private stables in Pacifica outside the Sweeney Ridge property. **Equestrians** use this route to reach the Sweeney Ridge Trail and then go north to the Discovery Site or south to the Portola Gate.

Toward the south end of the Sweeney Ridge Trail, the crinkly-leaved ceanothus (California lilac) and orange-flowered twinberry have grown tall enough to provide a hedge and a modest but welcome windbreak. Soon, however, the vegetation opens up and you are in a clearing at the Watershed boundary. Here at the Portola gate a high fence and restrictive signs bar farther travel. However, the GGNRA rangers occasionally offer nature hikes and discovery walks in the Watershed to which the public is invited. The Watershed management requires advance reservations and a fee for these events.

On clear days you can see three long lakes filling the linear valley at the east base of the ridge. The northern one is San Andreas Lake, and south of it lie the Crystal Springs lakes. Still farther south the linear valleys continue, though not dammed for water storage. On a visit to California in the 1890s, Andrew Lawson, a pioneering geologist, recognized these linear valleys as typical of a rift zone and

The Sweeney Ridge Trail leads to the Portolá Discovery site.

after the 1906 San Francisco earthquake, named the great California earthquake fault for the valley containing the northernmost lake, the San Andreas Fault.

Water from the Hetch Hetchy Reservoir in the Sierra Nevada is transported through huge pipes and stored in these lakes, then purveyed to more than a million users in San Francisco and on the Peninsula. Drainage from the east side of Sweeney Ridge and those ridges to the south, Fifield and Cahill, mixes with the Hetch Hetchy water and is stored in these lakes. Local water runoff amounts to less than 5 per cent of the drinking water supplied by the San Francisco Water Department to its patrons.

Now retrace your steps to the Discovery Site and continue northward. You follow the paved service road with yellow fog line past defunct buildings of a former Nike site—the highest point on the ridge at 1,250 feet. As the trail swings west around the buildings, views of Mt. Tamalpais, Wolf Ridge in the GGNRA Marin Headlands, San Bruno Mountain, and the beautiful Bay open up. Even when fog lies in the valleys, the peaks can be visible, giving you the feeling of overlooking a vast, misty sea, pierced by isolated islands.

Soon the Sweeney Ridge Trail meets the Mori Ridge Trail, the coastside connector which reaches this junction by gaining 850 feet in elevation in 1.3 miles. In a series of steep pitches alternating with more gentle climbs, the Mori Ridge Trail offers magnificent views of the coast from San Pedro Point in the south to the tip of Point Reyes peninsula in the north. Lying southwest, Montara Mountain's long sweep to the sea stands dark against the sky, its many antennae piercing the blue.

Seen from the Mori Ridge Trail are many species of coastal scrub—from pungent sage to aromatic coyote mint—which cover the hillside. The moist ocean air enhances and intensifies the color of the plants' blossoms, particularly the blue-flowered lupine and the bushy yellow lizardtail. Crimson stalks of Indian paint-brush glow among the wind-sculpted coyote bush and California coffeeberry.

At the Mori Ridge/Sweeney Ridge trails junction **hikers** would veer right (northeast) to follow the Sweeney Ridge Trail to Skyline Community College and on to Milagra Ridge. However, at this writing this trail, through a very steep ravine between this junction and the college, is closed. By Fall 1995 the trail, for **hikers only**, will be redesigned to offer a safer grade, and will avoid native plants that host an endangered butterfly species. Until the trail is reconstructed and realigned, all trail users must return to their starting points.

On the other side of the steep ravine, the intact Sweeney Ridge Trail traverses a high ridge, where you see the coastline again. Clear days bring views of ocean waves crashing against the rocky cliffs and lapping at the sandy beaches. At your feet is evidence of the geologic beginnings of this land. Rocks of the Franciscan Formation, formed under water, then stressed and modified through the ages by action deep within the earth's crust and along the San Andreas Fault, are visible to the trained eye. A rounded basalt known as greenstone, some sandstone, and a red chert can be found. If you see white patches on some rocks, they are remnants of the Calera limestone, which is found in abundance in the Rockaway Quarry just west of here.

Continuing on the Bay Area Ridge Trail, **hikers** descend from the ridge to parking lot 2 at Skyline College, cross it, go down 78 broad steps through a tall conifer forest, and cross the road to a pretty plaza between the college buildings. On the left side of the plaza, which is sheltered by mature cypress trees in huge planters, is a large campus map, on which you can note the route through the inner campus.

Proceed through the plaza to the bookstore, turn left (west), mount a series of steps, and pass the north side of college Buildings 1 and 2. Between these buildings is another tree-filled plaza where, on October 12, 1994, the dedication of the Skyline College Ridge Trail Connection took place. Skyline College marked its 25th Anniversary by celebrating the completion of this important link between Sweeney and Milagra ridges and the opening of the first Bay Area Ridge Trail segment to pass through a college campus. Continuing past this plaza, pause at the north corner of Building 1 to read a bronze plaque commemorating Skyline College's dedication on May 17, 1970. Then turn right (north), pass Building 7, and cross the street to a bus stop, which is often crowded with children, college students, and Bay Area Ridge Trail travellers.

Now following the Bay Area Ridge Trail directional arrows placed high up on lamp posts and street signs, go around the corner, and veer right (north) on sidewalks beside College Drive. Shortly the Ridge Trail route shifts a few feet east onto parallel Ysabel Drive and continues north to Sharp Park Road. Signalized crossings take you to the opposite side of the street, where you use the road past a residential complex to continue north to the Milagra Ridge gate. You could park a shuttle car here or leave one at parking lot 2 on the college campus. A few places on the south side of this lot are reserved for those using the trail.

Negotiations are underway to complete a short gap between the northwest end of Milagra Ridge Preserve and city streets in Pacifica. However, you can take a brisk round trip along the trail that traverses the ridgetop to the end of the preserve. Notable along this route are the revegetation efforts of the National Park Service: the pampas grass, once so rampant here, is being curtailed; the lupine plant that is host to the Mission Blue butterfly is being protected; and new plants native to this region are being set out. On crisp, clear days, the fabulous views of ocean and coastline are well-worth a trip on this ridge.

Then retrace your route along College Drive North to parking at lot 2 at Skyline College, or have a shuttle car waiting to take you to Sneath Lane or Mori Ridge parking areas.

The next segment of the Bay Area Ridge Trail begins at Mussel Rock in Daly City, about 5 miles north of Milagra Ridge. See *Mussel Rock to Fort Funston— GGNRA.*   ■

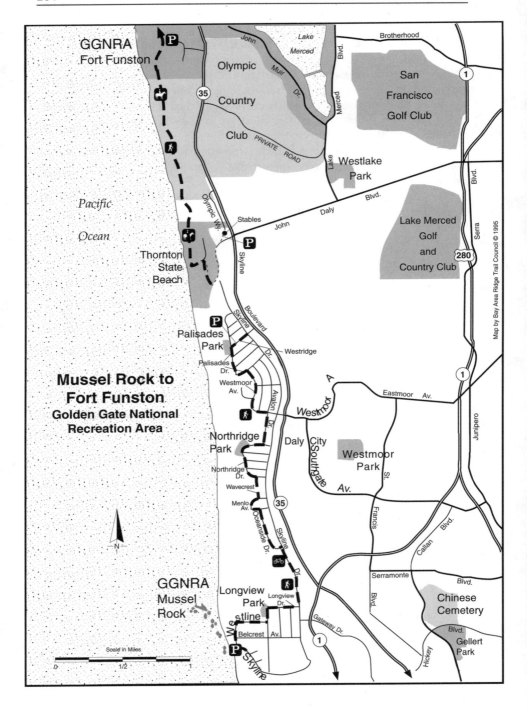

Mussel Rock to Fort Funston—GGNRA

From Vista Point through Daly City Neighborhoods and from Hang-Glider Viewing Deck over Sand Dunes

Starting from either end of this Bay Area Ridge Trail segment that hugs the Pacific shore, find coastal views from bluff-top parks and explore meandering trails over sand dunes at the edge of the surf.

Length Daly City Neighborhoods Trail—2.9 miles one way; Fort Funston Dunes Trail—1.2 miles one way.

Location In northern San Mateo and southern San Francisco counties on the coast west of Hwy 35.

Trail Characteristics Daly City streets and sidewalks are paved surfaces. Dunes Trail is sandy, sometimes overgrown with coastal scrub. No shade on entire route. Can be breezy and often foggy. Elevation gain of 550 feet in first ¾ mile. Elevation loss of 200 feet to Dunes Trail from Fort Funston.

Ridge Trail Accessibility
- Hikers—Entire route.
- Equestrians—Dunes Trail through Thornton Beach and Fort Funston.
- Bicyclists—Daly City streets.

Trail Management
- Streets and sidewalks—Daly City: 415-991-8097.
- Mussel Rock, Dunes Trail, and Fort Funston—Golden Gate National Recreation Area (GGNRA): 415-556-8371 or 415-239-2366.

Rules
- Daly City—Open during daylight hours. Dogs on leash only.
- Fort Funston—Open from sunrise to sunset. Dogs on leash or under voice control. Pick up pet litter.

Amenities
- Mussel Rock vista point—Parking.
- Palisades Park—Picnic tables, basketball court, children's play equipment, and unlimited streetside parking.
- Fort Funston—Visitor center, native plant nursery, hang-glider viewing deck with benches in protected nooks, hang-glider launching site, picnic tables, benches, restrooms, water, and telephone. The 1.2-mile Sunset Trail Loop is accessible to physically disabled.

Getting There
South entrance, Mussel Rock—Going south, take Skyline Blvd. (Hwy 35) to Westmoor Ave. in Daly City and turn right (west). Immediately turn left (south) on Skyline Dr. and continue 1¾ miles to Westline Dr. Make a short jog left

(southwest) on it and immediately turn right (northwest) on entrance road to Mussel Rock parking area.

Going north, take Hwy 1 to Manor Dr. exit in Pacifica, turn left at first stop sign, go two blocks, turn left on Manor Dr., and cross highway. Immediately turn right onto Palmetto Ave. and continue for almost 1 mile to Westline Dr. in Daly City. Turn left on Westline Dr. and then veer left on entrance road to Mussel Rock parking area.

North entrance, Fort Funston—Going south, take Skyline Blvd. (Hwy 35) to Lake Merced and after passing John Muir Dr., go 0.1 mile and turn right (west) into Fort Funston. At fork in road, bear right and continue to extensive parking area.

Going north, take Skyline Blvd. (Hwy 35) north to John Muir Dr., make a U-turn and go south on Skyline Blvd. 0.1 mile, turn right (west) into Fort Funston, and then follow remaining directions going south.

Equestrian entrance—Going south, take Skyline Blvd. (Hwy 35), turn right (west) on Olympic Way and proceed south to stables and equestrian parking.

Going north, take Skyline Blvd. (Hwy 35) to John Muir Dr., make a U-turn, and follow remaining directions going south.

By Bus
SamTrans 1L from Daly City BART Station serves Palmetto/Westline intersection daily. SamTrans 10S serves Daly City and Pacifica daily except Sunday from Serramonte Shopping Center.

On The Trail

This segment of the Bay Area Ridge Trail involves two trips—the first, from Mussel Rock north to Palisades Park in Daly City; and the second, a round trip from Fort Funston south to Thornton Beach State Park. The first can be taken as an approximately 6-mile round trip through Daly City neighborhoods or as a one-way 2.9-mile trip with car shuttle.

Before setting off on the first trip, your northward route through Daly City neighborhoods, walk from the Mussel Rock parking area to an opening in the fence from where a short trail leads to a small vista point high above the ocean. Just offshore lie several jagged, rocky islets, the largest of which, topped by a navigational marker, is Mussel Rock. These small, offshore islands, inhabited by black-coated, long-necked cormorants, present both a formidable boating hazard and a tempting destination for fishermen and adventurers. One islet is accessible by foot at low tide, but getting there is exceedingly dangerous because of erratic wave patterns off this coast.

From the vista point looking south along the gentle curve of beaches and rocky shoreline beyond the Pacifica pier, you can see Point San Pedro jutting into the sea. Just east of Pacifica lies the rounded flank of Sweeney Ridge in the 74,000-acre

Golden Gate National Recreation Area, where another segment of the Bay Area Ridge Trail traverses the 3-mile-long ridgeline.

North lies Fort Funston and beyond stretches San Francisco's Ocean Beach all the way to the Golden Gate. On a very clear day, the Marin Headlands and Point Reyes are visible farther north. Twenty-five miles offshore the Farallon Islands stand guard beyond the narrow entrance to San Francisco Bay.

Landward and immediately north of the vista point in a deep canyon is a former dumpsite, now replaced by the refuse transfer station housed in the large concrete building above the parking area. This canyon developed when heavy winter storms washed out great chunks of coastside bluffs. It is here that the San Andreas Fault enters the Pacific Ocean, to re-appear on the Point Reyes peninsula.

Almost hidden, north of the canyon on a shelf midway between the cliffs and the ocean, lies more testimony to the relentless force of Pacific Ocean storms. Here the northern leg of the Ocean Shore Railroad ran from 1907 until its demise in 1920. Although planned to connect San Francisco and Santa Cruz, the tracks never bridged the gap south of Half Moon Bay between Tunitas Creek and Davenport Landing. However, passengers were transported by Stanley Steamer on a scenic ride across the unfinished section. Your Bay Area Ridge Trail trip approximates the old railroad route north on a safer alignment.

**From Fort Funston's viewing deck Mussel Rock appears
at the outer curve of Daly City's coastline.**

After orienting yourself at this vista point above Mussel Rock, hikers and bicyclists go back along the entry road to the corner of Westline and Skyline drives and veer left. **Hikers** use the sidewalks on the left side of the street; **bicyclists** ride on the street. At each intersection a small Bay Area Ridge Trail marker on a signpost tells you which way to turn. For most of the trip north through Daly City, houses sit between you and the bluffs. However, occasional openings between the houses and at three cliff-top city parks offer ocean views.

In this Daly City neighborhood each home has its plot of lawn, often graced with small, rock-bordered flower beds of ferns and roses and accented by a palm tree.

You soon come to Longview City Park, where you'll find children's play equipment and convenient benches When you pass a water tower on the right at Fog Cap 3, you've reached the summit of your invigorating climb and it's downhill from here to the end of the first trip on this Ridge Trail segment.

At Daly City's Northridge Park there are picnic tables and benches, and playing fields and basketball courts stand ready for children's after-school or weekend play. On balmy days neighborhood residents relax in protected, sunny areas. Each of these city parks has fencing and hedges atop the bluff and a low, street-side fence to contain balls. Breaks in the hedges afford sea views. Even when it's foggy, the sound of the surf reminds the visitor of the ocean's incessant action below the cliffs.

The first trip ends at Palisades Park at the corner of Palisades Drive and Westridge Avenue. Beyond here is an uncompleted section of the Bay Area Ridge Trail. However, you can return to Mussel Rock on foot or bike or have a shuttle car waiting on Palisades Drive by this park.

Hikers start at Fort Funston to begin the second part of this Bay Area Ridge Trail segment. From the parking area walk seaward to the viewing deck to survey your coastal route south and watch the flotilla of hang-gliders on the wing or parked immediately adjacent to this deck. From the deck go back to the west edge of the parking area and take a trail that starts just left (south) of the hang-glider staging area. You make a dramatic descent from the bluff top to the dunes on a unique sand-ladder staircase, which is edged by a sturdy rope strung between 4x4 posts. When you reach the sand dunes, bear left (south) with the sight and sound of the waves nearby. There is a network of trails, and a few Bay Area Ridge Trail signs mark the route. In general, keep to the trail on top of the dunes.

If the tide is out, you can walk along the beach. But even from the dunes, you see shorebirds searching for sand crabs, grebes and terns diving for fish, and several kinds of seagulls resting on the sand. Overhead hang-gliders and para-gliders join long lines of pelicans riding the winds. At any time of the year a few wildflowers accent your way, but in spring the display of scarlet Indian paintbrush, lavender sea daisies, yellow lizardtail, and purple sand verbena makes this a colorful trip.

When the fog hangs over the shore, there is a sense of solitude here, broken only by the shrieks of gulls. When coastal breezes sweep in and the surf crashes on the beach, the closeness to nature's power makes this almost a wilderness experience. And on clear, sunny days with the glint of sunshine on the breaking waves, with flocks of shorebirds searching for clams, and with warm sand underfoot, this is truly a glorious place to be.

Shortly, the Bay Area Ridge Trail traverses an easement granted to the GGNRA by the Olympic Club. Along this stretch, look for a para-gliders' launching site on a leveled-off sand dune. From the launching site, these aerial adventurers rise above the beach, floating, suspended by ropes from a longitudinal sliver of double-layered, multi-colored parachute cloth.

As you rise to the crest of a long, high dune between a ravine and the shore, you approach a clump of windswept pine and cypress trees. Just before the trees, a sign directs you left down into the ravine and then another points right to two picnic tables in the lee of this high dune. These tables, the ravine, and the battered cliffs above you are all that remain of the former Thornton State Beach development, yet another example of the turbulent power of the sea.

Then continue south, up and down the dunes, through willow thickets and blackberry brambles, past clumps of red-orange Indian paintbrush and bright yellow succulents, always with the sea within sight or sound. You stroll through coastal scrub of creamy-blossomed coyote bush, red-leaved succulents, yellow and white yarrow, and bushy yellow beach lupines. **Hikers** may be joined on this route by **equestrians** who have descended from the stables on the deteriorating Thornton Beach road. Where this old road meets the dunes, about 1.2 miles from Fort Funston, hikers reverse direction and retrace their steps.

After trudging north along the dunes, look for a sign pointing to the first trail to the bluff top at Fort Funston. This is the equestrian trail, which hikers can also use. The next trail, 0.1 mile farther north, is the hikers' route, which involves a steady climb back to the bluff top on the sand ladder. Several landing platforms offer the chance to rest and to survey the round-trip route you just followed. The staircase terminates at the hang-glider staging area. Here behind the protection of wind-sculpted trees by the viewing deck, the parked hang-gliders look like a swarm of butterflies with outspread, brilliantly colored wings.

Bicyclists can join the **hikers** and dismounted **equestrians** here at the viewing deck built out over the bluff. Together you can look back over this spectacular coastline and over the dunes that the hikers and equestrians traveled. Watching the stream of ship traffic move in and out of the Golden Gate can test your knowledge of seagoing vessels. And especially on weekends, the brightly colored hang-gliders' silent take-off and flight above the strand can provide hours of vicarious aerial thrills. If the day is clear, you may want to stroll along the Sunset Trail or linger longer on the viewing deck for a picnic and more views of this dramatic coast.

The next leg of the Bay Area Ridge Trail starts here in Fort Funston—the first trip in this guidebook. See *Fort Funston to Stern Grove*, p 16. If you had begun your journey along the Bay Area Ridge Trail in Fort Funston and had followed all the trips in this guidebook described clockwise around San Francisco Bay, you would have traveled almost 200 miles along the ridges above the Bay. Each trip would have offered outstanding views and different perspectives on some very special features of the Bay Area.   ∎

APPENDIX 1

Bay Area Ridge Trail Council Trail Dedication Dates and List of Bay Area Ridge Trail Guide Pamphlets (indicated by **).

DATE	TRAIL SEGMENT
May 13, 1989	Wunderlich County Park to Huddart County Park ** San Mateo County
May 13, 1989	Purisma Creek Redwoods Open Space Preserve ** San Mateo County
September 21, 1989	Marin Headlands, Golden Gate Bridge to Morning Sun Trail ** Marin County
September 21, 1989	Mount Tamalpais State Park and GGNRA Shoreline Hwy. to Samuel P. Taylor State Park Marin County Includes: Shoreline Highway to Pantoll **
September 30, 1989	Fort Funston to Stern Grove** San Francisco County
October 7, 1989	Skyline Wilderness Park ** Napa County
October 14, 1989	Milagra Ridge and Sweeney Ridge San Mateo County
October 14, 1989	Sanborn County Park to Saratoga Gap ** Santa Clara County
October 21, 1989	Benicia Waterfront ** Solano County
June 23, 1990	Wildcat Canyon Regional Park to Cull Canyon Regional Park Includes: Tilden Regional Park to Redwood Regional Park ** Redwood Regional Park to Anthony Chabot Regional Park ** Anthony Chabot Regional Park ** EBMUD Lands to Cull Canyon Regional Recreation Area ** Contra Costa and Alameda Counties
October 13, 1990	Coyote Creek Park Chain (North) ** Santa Clara County

October 13, 1990   Mt. Burdell Open Space Preserve **
                      Marin County

October 20, 1990   Sugarloaf Ridge State Park **
                      Sonoma County

September 14, 1991   Santa Teresa County Park and Los Alamitos Creek Trail **
                      Santa Clara County

October 12, 1991   Carquinez Strait Regional Shoreline to John Muir National
                      Historic Site
                      Contra Costa County

June 6, 1992   Saratoga Gap, Long Ridge, Skyline Ridge,
                      and Russian Ridge Open Space Preserves **
                      San Mateo County

June 6, 1992   Windy Hill Open Space Preserve **
                      San Mateo County

September 19, 1992   Mussel Rock to Fort Funston
                      San Mateo County

October 3, 1992   Kennedy Grove Regional Recreation Area to Inspiration Point
                      Contra Costa County

October 3, 1992   Samuel P. Taylor State Park (Connector Trail)
                      Marin County

October 31, 1992   Cull Canyon Regional Recreation Area to Independent School
                      Alameda County

November 7, 1992   Stern Grove to the Presidio **
                      San Francisco County

April 24, 1993   Rockville Hills Community Park
                      Solano County

April 24, 1993   Mission Peak Regional Preserve to Ed R. Levin County Park **
                      Santa Clara County

May 22, 1993   Vallejo-Benicia Buffer
                      Solano County

October 17, 1993   Marin Headlands (Morning Sun Trail to Shoreline Hwy.)
                      Marin County

October 12, 1994   Skyline Comm. Coll. (Part of Sweeney Ridge to Milagra Ridge).
                      San Mateo County

April 30, 1995   Coyote Creek Park Chain (South)
                                        Santa Clara County

May 6, 1995   Annadel State Park and Connector Trails from
                      Howarth City Park and Spring Lake Regional Park
                                    Sonoma County

May 21, 1995   Pinole Valley Park (Connector Trail) and
                      Sobrante Ridge Regional Preserve,
                                    Contra Costa County

APPENDIX 2

Information Sources for Parks and Preserves on Bay Area Ridge Trail Route

Agencies Responsible for Bay Area Ridge Trail Segments

National Park Service, Golden Gate National Recreation Area	415-556-0560
Fort Mason	
San Francisco, CA 94123	
South District—Fort Funston, Sweeney and Milagra ridges, and Phleger Estate	415-239-2366 or 415-556-8642
The Presidio	415-556-1874
North District—Marin Headlands and Muir Woods	415-331-1540
Point Reyes and Olema Valley	415-663-1092
John Muir Historic Site	510-228-8860
State of California, The Resources Agency	
Department of Parks and Recreation	916-653-8803
Box 942896	
Sacramento, CA 94296-0001	
Mt. Tamalpais State Park	415-388-2070
Samuel P. Taylor State Park	415-488-9897
Petaluma Adobe State Historic Site	707-778-4303
Annadel State Park	707-539-3911
Sugarloaf Ridge State Park	707-833-5712
Benicia State Recreation Area	707-745-3385
East Bay Regional Park District	415-635-0135
2950 Peralta Oaks Court	
P.O. Box 5381	
Oakland, CA 94605-0381	
East Bay Municipal Utility District	510-254-3778
500 San Pablo Dam Rd.	
Orinda, CA 94563	
Midpeninsula Regional Open Space District	415-691-1200
330 Distel Circle	
Los Altos, CA 94022	
San Francisco Recreation and Park Department	415-666-7200
McLaren Lodge, Golden Gate Park	
501 Stanyan St.	
San Francisco, CA 94117	
Marin County Open Space District	415-499-6387
Marin County Civic Center	
San Rafael, CA 94903	

Sonoma County Parks Department 2300 County Center Dr. Santa Rosa, CA	707-527-2041
Greater Vallejo Recreation District 395 Amador St. Vallejo, CA 94590	707-648-4600
Santa Clara County Parks and Recreation Department 298 Garden Hill Dr. Los Gatos, CA 95030	408-358-3741
San Mateo County Parks and Recreation Department County Government Center 590 Hamilton St. Redwood City, CA 94063	415-363-4020
City of Petaluma	707-778-4380
City of Fairfield	707-428-7428
City of Benicia Recreation Department	707-746-4285
City of San Jose Parks Department	408-277-4000

Transportation Agencies Serving Parks and Preserves on the Bay Area Ridge Trail Route

BART	415-992-2278
	510-465-2278
San Francisco Municipal Railway—MUNI	415-673-6864
Golden Gate Transit	
From San Francisco and Southern Marin County	415-332-6600
From Central and Northern Marin County	415-453-2100
From Sonoma County	707-544-1323
AC Transit	800-559-4636
Santa Clara County Transportation Agency	800-894-9908

Organizations Sponsoring Group Hikes, Bicycle and Horseback Rides, Nature Trips, Trail Maintenance Days

Many public agencies offer docent-led nature walks and occasional trail maintenance days. Consult the agency near you from the above list. In addition, local and statewide nonprofit groups sponsor outdoor trips for environmental education and enjoyment. Consult your telephone directory for the Bay Area office of the following groups:

American Youth Hostels
Audubon Society—Bird walks

Bay Area Orienteering Club

Bay Area Ridge Trail Council—Publishes a quarterly Outings Calendar of
  docent-led trips

Bicycle Groups, e.g., Bicycle Trails Council of Marin, California Association of
Bicycle Organizations—East Bay Bicycle Coalition, ROMP, Western Wheelers

California Native Plant Society

Community Colleges—Some offer group hiking classes

Environmental Museums, e.g., California Academy of Sciences, Coyote Point
  Museum, Oakland Museum

Golden Gate National Park Association

Hiking Clubs

Horsemen's Associations

The Nature Conservancy

Santa Cruz Mountains Natural History Association

Santa Cruz Mountains Trail Association

Senior Centers—Offer group walks

Trail councils and clubs, e.g., East Bay Area Trails Council, Santa Cruz Mountains
Trail Association

The Trail Center—A 4-county trail information and trail maintenance clearing-
  house, based in Los Altos

Youth Groups—Boy Scouts, Girl Scouts, and Campfire Girls units

Sierra Club—Local chapters around the Bay Area offer hiking, bicycling,
  backpacking, climbing and kayaking trips.

APPENDIX 3

A BAY AREA RIDGE TRAIL SAMPLER
Trips for Many Reasons

"Bag a Peak" on the Ridge Trail Route

Stern Grove to The Presidio—Twin Peaks

Mt. Tamalpais State Park—Mt. Tamalpais' East Peak is 4+ miles from Pantoll
and 1,200' feet higher

Mt. Burdell Open Space Preserve—Burdell Mountain

Sugarloaf Ridge State Park—Bald Mountain

Tilden Regional Park to Redwood Regional Park—Vollmer Peak

Redwood Regional Park to Chabot Park—Redwood Peak

East Bay Municipal Utility District Lands to Cull Canyon Regional
Recreation Area—Dinosaur Ridge

Mission Peak Regional Preserve and Ed R. Levin County Park—Mission Peak

Santa Teresa County Park and Los Alamitos/Calero Creek Park Chain—
Coyote Peak

Skyline Ridge Open Space Preserve and Russian Ridge Open Space Preserve
—Borel Hill and Mt. Melville

Windy Hill Open Space Preserve—Windy Hill summit

For Ocean Views—On a clear day without fog over the Pacific

Fort Funston to Stern Grove—See the Farallones from the hang-glider viewing deck

Stern Grove to The Presidio—From Twin Peaks and adjoining streets

Marin Headlands—From Golden Gate Bridge North to Tennessee Valley
From Tennessee Valley to Shoreline Highway

Mt. Tamalpais State Park—From Shoreline Highway to Pantoll

Mt. Tamalpais State Park and Golden Gate National Recreation Area
From Pantoll to Bolinas-Fairfax Road

Golden Gate National Recreation Area and Samuel P. Taylor State Park

Kennedy Grove to Tilden Regional Park—From Inspiration Point

Tilden Regional Park to Redwood Regional Park—From Sea View Trail

Sanborn County Park and Castle Rock State Park—Monterey Bay

Saratoga Gap Open Space Preserve to Skyline Ridge Open Space Preserve—
From Long Ridge OSP

Skyline Ridge Open Space Preserve and Russian Ridge Open Space Preserve

Windy Hill Open Space Preserve—Windy Hill summit

Purisima Creek Redwoods Open Space Preserve—From Harkins Ridge Trail

Sweeney Ridge To Milagra Ridge—From Mori Ridge and the Discovery Site

Mussel Rock to Fort Funston—From both ends of the trail

For San Francisco Bay Views—Sparkling blue or fog-shrouded,
it's always impressive

Stern Grove to The Presidio—From Twin Peaks

San Francisco Presidio—Especially Golden Gate, Richardson Bay and Alcatraz

Marin Headlands—From Golden Gate Bridge North to Tennessee Valley—
From Tennessee Valley to Shoreline Hwy.—Richardson Bay and Angel Island

Mt. Tamalpais State Park—From Shoreline Highway to Pantoll
Mt. Burdell Open Space Preserve—From the summit of Burdell Mtn.
Sugarloaf Ridge State Park—From Bald Mtn.
Skyline Wilderness Park—See Napa Marshlands
Vallejo/Benicia Buffer—All along the trail
Benicia Waterfront—On the Trail West
Carquinez Strait Regional Shoreline to John Muir National Historic Site
    —San Pablo Bay
Kennedy Grove to Tilden Regional Park—From Nimitz Way
Tilden Regional Park to Redwood Regional Park—From Sea View Trail
Mission Peak Regional Preserve and Ed R. Levin County Park
Skyline Ridge Open Space Preserve and Russian Ridge Open Space Preserve
Windy Hill Open Space Preserve—Up and down the Bay from the summit
Sweeney Ridge To Milagra Ridge—Here Portolá discovered the Bay

For a Child's Ridge Trail Birthday Party—Picnic tables
and restrooms nearby

Fort Funston to Stern Grove—Several picnic areas
Stern Grove to The Presidio—Many parks along the Ridge Trail route with
    picnic facilities; restrooms at Stern Grove and Golden Gate Park only
Mt. Tamalpais State Park—Rock Spring or Bootjack Picnic Areas
Golden Gate National Recreation Area and Samuel P. Taylor State Park—
    Walk or ride on Cross Marin Trail and picnic in the park
McNear Park to Petaluma Adobe State Historic Park—Picnic at either end
    or at parks along the way
Annadel State Park—Picnic at Spring Lake Park and Walk or Ride
    the Connector Trail to Annadel State Park
Sugarloaf Ridge State Park—Round trip on Stern Trail and picnic by
    Sonoma Creek
Benicia Waterfront—Walk, bike, or roller-blade on level, paved trail
    and picnic at one of several park sites along the way
Kennedy Grove to Tilden Regional Park—Picnic sites and level trail at both ends
Tilden Regional Park to Redwood Regional Park—Many sites at several entry
    points; Steam Trains at Tilden
Redwood Regional Park and Anthony Chabot Regional Park—At Redwood Bowl
    beside the Ridge Trail less than 1 mile from Redwood Regional Park's
    Moon Gate; other sites available at Redwood Gate and at Bort Meadow
East Bay Municipal Utility District Lands to Cull Canyon Regional Recreation
    Area—Cull Canyon Recreation Area especially suited to birthday parties
Mission Peak Regional Preserve and Ed R. Levin County Park—Sandy Wool
    Lake picnic sites and children's play area
Coyote Hellyer County Park to Metcalf City Park—Walk or ride bikes along
    the trail and return to birthday treats at several parks along the trail
Santa Teresa County Park and Los Alamitos/Calero Creek Park Chain
    —Work off extra energy before the party on a short Ridge Trail trip from
    Santa Teresa Pueblo Group Area
Skyline Ridge OSP and Russian Ridge OSP—Hike the trail before picnicking
    at Horseshoe Lake or Alpine Pond
Windy Hill OSP—Picnic area adjacent to Skyline Boulevard; no restrooms

Mussel Rock to Fort Funston—Neighborhood parks along the trail in Daly City. Watch the hang-gliders and picnic on the viewing deck at Fort Funston

For Spring Wildflowers' Beautiful Blossoms—Especially in the Grasslands

Marin Headlands—From Golden Gate Bridge North to Tennessee Valley
—From Tennessee Valley to Shoreline Highway
Mt. Tamalpais State Park and Golden Gate National Recreation Area
Mt. Burdell Open Space Preserve
Annadel State Park—White fritillary
Sugarloaf Ridge State Park—Lewisia
Rockville Hills Community Park
Vallejo/Benicia Buffer
Carquinez Strait Regional Shoreline to John Muir National Historic Site
Anthony Chabot Regional Park—Trillium garden
Mission Peak Regional Preserve and Ed R. Levin County Park
Santa Teresa County Park and Los Alamitos/Calero Creek Park Chain
—Stile Ranch Trail
Saratoga Gap OSP to Skyline Ridge OSP—Masses of blue and cream-colored iris
Skyline Ridge OSP and Russian Ridge OSP—Acres of wildflowers,
especially on Russian Ridge.
Windy Hill Open Space Preserve—Blossoms persist late into summer.
Wunderlich County Park to Huddart County Park—Especially Clintonia and
bleeding heart
Purisima Creek Redwoods Open Space Preserve—Shade-loving plants
Sweeney Ridge To Milagra Ridge—Native orchids and host plants for
Mission blue butterfly
Mussel Rock to Fort Funston—Seaside flowers

Trips with an Overnight Camp or Hostel Nearby
—Not more than 2 miles away

Stern Grove to the Presidio—San Francisco International Hostels
Marin Headlands—Golden Gate Hostel, Hawk and Haypress Backpack Camps
Mt. Tamalpais—Pantoll and Shansky Backpack Camps
Golden Gate National Recreation Area and Samuel P. Taylor State Park—
Car Camping at Samuel P. Taylor State Park and Horse Camp at Devils Gulch;
Pt. Reyes Hostel (5 miles from Olema Hill parking)
Mt. Burdell OSP—Group camping by reservation
Annadel State Park—At adjoining Spring Lake Park
Sugarloaf Ridge State Park—Campsites near creek; corrals for horses
Kennedy Grove to Tilden Regional Park—Youth group camps by reservation
at Wildcat and Tilden parks
Tilden Regional Park to Redwood Regional Park—Youth group camps
by reservation only
Redwood Regional Park and Anthony Chabot Regional Park—Youth group camps
by reservation only at Redwood and Family camping at Anthony Chabot
Anthony Chabot Regional Park—Year-round family camping
Mission Peak Regional Preserve and Ed R. Levin County Park—Group camping
at Ed R. Levin County Park
Sanborn County Park and Castle Rock State Park—Hostel and walk-in

camps in Sanborn County Park and backpack camp at Castle Rock State Park.
Wunderlich County Park to Huddart County Park—Group camping
   at Huddart County Park by reservation only

To Historic Sites—Ranches, homes, forts, and inns

Fort Funston to Stern Grove—Military site and Trocadero Inn
San Francisco Presidio—Historic Spanish military site and American military base
McNear Park to Petaluma Adobe State Historic Park—Victorian homes
   and General Vallejo's ranch house
Annadel State Park—Former Rancho Los Guilicos
Vallejo/Benicia Buffer and Benicia Waterfront—Former General Vallejo rancho;
   former state capital
Carquinez Strait Regional Shoreline to John Muir National Historic Site
   —John Muir's home
Mission Peak Regional Preserve and Ed R. Levin County Park
   —Former Mission San Jose lands
Santa Teresa County Park and Los Alamitos/Calero Creek Park Chain
   —Joaquin Bernal's former Rancho Santa Teresa
Skyline Ridge OSP and Russian Ridge OSP—Former "summer capital" of
   California Governor James Rolph; historic logging road from west side
   forests to Bay
Windy Hill OSP—Former Rancho El Corte de Madera
Sweeney Ridge to Milagra Ridge—First sighting of San Francisco Bay
   by Portolá's scouts; World War II military sites

Almost Level Trails—And mostly paved

Fort Funston to Stern Grove
McNear Park to Petaluma Adobe State Historic Park
Benicia Waterfront
Kennedy Grove to Tilden Regional Park—The Nimitz Way segment from
   Wildcat Canyon Regional Park gate to Inspiration Point
Coyote Hellyer County Park to Metcalf City Park
Santa Teresa County Park and Los Alamitos/Calero Creek Park Chain—
   Segment on Los Alamitos/Calero Creek Park Chain

Short Trips—Less than 5 miles one way with shuttle

Fort Funston to Stern Grove
San Francisco Presidio
Marin Headlands—From Golden Gate Bridge North to Tennessee Valley
Marin Headlands—From Tennessee Valley to Shoreline Highway
Vallejo-Benicia Buffer
Benicia Waterfront
Carquinez Strait Regional Shoreline to John Muir Historic Site
Kennedy Grove to Tilden Regional Park
Windy Hill OSP
Mussel Rock to Fort Funston

Trips of 5 to 10 miles—one way with shuttle

Stern Grove to The Presidio

Mt. Tamalpais—From Shoreline Highway to Pantoll
Mt. Tamalpais and GGNRA
McNear Park to Petaluma Adobe
Annadel State Park
Tilden Regional Park to Redwood Regional Park
Redwood Regional Park to Anthony Chabot Regional Park
Anthony Chabot Regional Park
East Bay Municipal Utility District Lands to Cull Canyon Regional Park
Mission Peak Regional Preserve and Ed R. Levin County Park
Coyote Hellyer County Park to Metcalf City Park
Santa Teresa County Park and Los Alamitos/Calero Creek Park Chain
Sanborn County Park and Castle Rock State Park
Saratoga Gap OSP to Skyline Ridge OSP
Wunderlich County Park to Huddart County Park
Purisima Creek Redwoods OSP
Sweeney Ridge to Milagra Ridge

—or round trip on the Ridge Trail
Mt. Burdell Open Space Preserve
Sugarloaf Ridge State Park
Skyline Wilderness Park
Rockville Hills Community Park
Skyline Ridge and Russian Ridge OSP
Windy Hill OSP

Long Trips—More than 10 miles one way with shuttle, or round trip on same trail
Stern Grove to Presidio round trip.
Mount Tamalpais State Park—From Shoreline Highway to Pantoll round trip
Mount Tamalpais State Park and GGNRA—From Pantoll to Bolinas-Fairfax Road round trip
GGNRA and S.P. Taylor State Park—From Bolinas-Fairfax Road to State Park Entrance one way
Tilden Regional Park to Redwood Regional Park round trip
Coyote Hellyer County Park to Metcalf City Park round trip

Linger by a Lake on a Ridge Trail Trip
Fort Funston to Stern Grove—Lakes Merced and Pine Lake
Mt. Burdell OSP—Seasonal
Annadel State Park—At Spring Lake Park
Skyline Wilderness Park—At trail's end
Rockville Hills Community Park
Vallejo/Benicia Buffer
Kennedy Grove To Tilden Regional Park
Anthony Chabot Regional Park—Short distance off the trail
East Bay Municipal Utility District Lands to Cull Canyon Regional Recreation Area—Swimming in season, too
Mission Peak Regional Preserve and Ed R. Levin County Park
Coyote Hellyer County Park to Metcalf City Park

Saratoga Gap to Skyline Ridge OSP
Skyline Ridge OSP and Russian Ridge OSP

Trips With Bus Connections—Take the bus to a Ridge Trail entrance, hike as far as you like and return to the bus stop*
Stern Grove to The Presidio—At each end
Marin Headlands—At north end of Golden Gate Bridge
Mt. Tamalpais State Park—At Pantoll
GGNRA to Samuel P. Taylor State Park—At State Park on Cross Marin Trail
Mt. Burdell OSP—In town of Novato
McNear Park to Petaluma Adobe State Historic Park
    —Downtown Petaluma connections
Carquinez Strait Regional Shoreline to John Muir Historic Site—To historic site
Kennedy Grove to Tilden Regional Park—Weekends and holidays
Tilden Regional Park to Redwood Regional Park—To Tilden on weekends
    and holidays
Mission Peak Regional Preserve and Ed R. Levin County Park
    —Climb the peak from Ohlone College and return there
Santa Teresa County Park and Los Alamitos/Calero Creek Park Chain
    —Connections near both ends of trail
Sweeney Ridge to Milagra Ridge—To Skyline College frequently
Mussel Rock to Fort Funston—By BART and bus to several locations in Daly City

Or by combining Bay Area Ridge Trail segments with adjoining park trails, hikers, equestrians, and bicyclists can make many fine loop trips and return to trailhead bus stops or car parking.*

"Fault-y" Trips and Serpentine Strolls
Along the San Andreas Fault
    Trips from Sanborn County Park north through Huddart County Park lie
        close to the west side of the fault on the Pacific Plate
    Sweeney Ridge to Milagra Ridge on Pacific Plate
    At Mussel Rock the fault drops into the Pacific Ocean, and then re-appears in
        Marin County
    Marin County Ridge Trail trips from the Golden Gate Bridge north to Samuel P.
        Taylor State Park lie on the east side of the fault on the North American Plate

Along the Hayward Fault
    East Bay trips through ridgetop parks parallel the Hayward fault, which lies
        to the west

More Faults
    St. John Mountain Fault in Sugarloaf Ridge State Park
    Rodgers Creek Fault lies west of Annadel State Park

---

* Phone bus company to verify schedules and stops.

From Rockville Hills Community Park look down to Green Valley where
a known fault exists

Serpentine Strolls

Large area of serpentine outcrops on Ecology Trail side trip in San Francisco
Presidio
Santa Teresa County Park has two areas of serpentine outcrops
See serpentine on trip to Bald Mountain in Sugarloaf Ridge State Park
Weathered serpentine column at Portolá Discovery Site on Sweeney Ridge

Three or More Contiguous Ridge Trail Segments	**Total Miles**
Fort Funston to Stern Grove	
Stern Grove to The Presidio	13 smiles
The Presidio	
Marin Headlands—From Golden Gate Bridge to Tennessee Valley	
" " —From Tennessee Valley to Shoreline Highway	32.6 miles
Mt. Tamalpais State Park	
Mt. Tamalpais State Park and GGNRA	
GGNRA and Samuel P. Taylor State Park	
Kennedy Grove to Tilden Regional Park	
Tilden Regional Park to Redwood Regional Park	
Redwood Regional Park and Anthony Chabot Regional Park	35.3 miles
Anthony Chabot Regional Park	
East Bay Municipal Utility District Lands and Cull Canyon Reg. Recreation Area	
Sanborn County Park and Castle Rock State Park	
Saratoga Gap OSP to Skyline Ridge OSP	18.6 miles
Skyline Ridge OSP and Russian Ridge OSP	

APPENDIX 4

Selected Readings

History

Arbuckle, Clyde, and Rambo, Ralph. *Santa Clara County Ranchos*. San Jose: Harlan-Young Press, 1968.

Avina, Rose H. *Spanish and Mexican Land Grants in California*. Berkeley: Thesis, University of California, 1932. Reprinted, R. E. Research Associates. Saratoga and San Francisco: Robert D. Reed, Publisher, 1973.

Bogart, Sewall. *Lauriston; an Architectural Biography of Herbert Edward Law* Portola Valley: Alpine House Publications, 1976.

Brewer, William H. *Up and Down California in 1860–1864: the Journal of William H. Brewer*. Edited by Francis P. Farquhar. Berkeley: University of California Press, 1974.

Bruegmann, Robert. *Benicia, Portrait of an Early California Town*. San Francisco, New York: 101 Productions, 1980.

Costansó, Miguel. *The Discovery of San Francisco Bay: the Portolá Expedition of 1769–1770: the diary of Miguel Costansó, in English and Spanish*. Edited by Peter Browning. Lafayette, CA: Great West Books, 1992.

Cowan, Robert G. *Ranchos of California, A List of Spanish Concessions, 1775–1822 and Mexican Grants 1822–1846*. Fresno: Academy Library Guild, 1956.

Gilliam, Harold. *The San Francisco Experience*. Garden City: Doubleday, 1972.

Gudde, Erwin G. *California Place Names, A Geographical Dictionary*, 3rd ed. Berkeley: University of California Press, 1969.

Hart, James D. *A Companion to California*. 2nd ed. Berkeley: University of California Press. 1987.

Kyle, Douglas E.; Hoover, Mildred B.; Rensch, Hero E.; Rensch, Ethel G.; and Abeloe, William N. *Historic Spots in California*. Rev. 4th ed. Stanford: Stanford University Press, 1990.

Krumbein, William. *A Teacher's Guide for Annadel State Park*. Glen Ellen: Valley of the Moon Natural History Association, 1990.

Lara, Adair H. *History of Petaluma, a California River Town*. Petaluma: Self-published, 1982.

Mason, Jack. *Earthquake Bay, A History of Tomales Bay*. Inverness: North Shore Books. 1976.

——, and Park, Helen Van Cleave. *Early Marin*. Jack Mason Publications: Marin County 1971.

McCarthy, Francis F. *The History of Mission San Jose, California, 1797–1835*. Fresno: Academy Library Guild, 1958.

Richards, Rand. *Historic San Francisco: a concise history and guide*. San
    Francisco: Heritage House Publishers, 1991.

Stanger, Frank. *South From San Francisco. San Mateo County, California,
    Its History and Heritage*. San Mateo: San Mateo County Historical
    Association, 1963.

——. *Sawmills in the Redwoods*. San Mateo: San Mateo County Historical
    Association, 1967.

Stein, Mimi. *A Vision Achieved, Fifty Years of East Bay Regional Park District*.
    Oakland: East Bay Regional Park District. 1984.

Woodbridge, Sally B., and Woodbridge, John. *Architecture—San Francisco: The
    Guide*. San Francisco, New York: American Institute of Architects,
    San Francisco Chapter: 101 Productions. 1982.

Natural History

Bakker, Elna S. *An Island Called California*. Berkeley: University of California
    Press, 1971.

Johnston, Verna R. *California's Forests and Woodlands: A Natural History*.
    Berkeley: University of California Press, 1995.

California Natural History Guides, Berkeley: University of California Press.
    Berry, William D., and Berry, Elizabeth. *Mammals of the San Francisco
        Bay Region*, 1959.
    Gilliam, Harold. *Weather of San Francisco Bay Region*, 1966.
    Metcalf, Woodbridge. *Native Trees of the San Francisco Bay Region*, 1959.
    Sharsmith, Helen D. *Spring Wildflowers of the San Francisco Bay Region*, 1965.
    Stebbins, Robert, D. *Reptiles and Amphibians of the San Francisco Bay Region*,
        1960.

Conradson, Diane R., *Exploring Our Baylands*. Point Reyes: Coastal Parks
    Association, 1982.

Evens, Jules G., *The Natural History of the Point Reyes Peninsula*. Point Reyes:
    Point Reyes National Seashore Association, 1988.

Murie, Olaf J. *A Field Guide to Animal Tracks*. Boston: Houghton Mifflin,
    2nd ed. 1974.

Pavlik, Bruce M. and Pamela Muick, Sharon Johnson and Marjorie Popper,
    Oaks of California. 3rd ed. Los Olivos: Cachuma Press, Inc. and California
    Oak Foundation, 1991.

Peterson, Roger Tory, *A Field Guide to Western Birds*. 3rd ed. Boston: Houghton
    Mifflin, 1990.

Scott, Shirley, *Field Guide to the Birds of North America*. Washington, D.C.:
    National Geographic Society, 2nd ed. 1987.

Thomas, John Hunter, *Flora of the Santa Cruz Mountains of California*. Stanford:
    Stanford University Press, 1961.

Uvardy, Miklos D. F., *The Audubon Society Field Guide to North American Birds*. New York: Alfred A. Knopf, 1977.

Guidebooks

Bakalinsky, Adah, *Stairway Walks in San Francisco*. 3rd ed. Berkeley: Wilderness Press, 1995.

California Coastal Conservancy. *San Francisco Bay Shoreline Guide.* Berkeley: University of California Press, 1995.

Doss, Margot P. *San Francisco at Your Feet.* New York: Grove Press, Inc., 1984

——. *The Bay Area at Your Feet,* Rev. ed. San Francisco: Don't Call It Frisco Press, 1987.

Hubbard, Doni. *Favorite Trails of Northern California Horsemen.* Redwood City: Hoofprints, 1980.

Jackson, Ruth A. *Combing the Coast: San Francisco to Santa Cruz.* San Francisco: Chronicle Books, 1985.

Margolin, Malcolm. *The East Bay Out: A Personal Guide to East Bay Regional Parks.* 2nd ed. Berkeley: Heyday Books, 1988

Newey, Bob. *East Bay Trails: A Guide for Hikers, Runners, Bicyclists and Equestrians.* 4th ed. Hayward: Footloose Press, 1981.

Rusmore, Jean, and Spangle, Frances. *Peninsula Trails.* 2nd ed. Berkeley: Wilderness Press, 1989.

Spangle, Frances, and Rusmore, Jean. *South Bay Trails.* 2nd ed. Berkeley: Wilderness Press, 1991.

Spitz, Barry. *Tamalpais Trails.* 3rd ed. San Anselmo: Potrero Meadows Publishing Co., 1995.

Suttle, Gary. *California County Summits.* Berkeley: Wilderness Press, 1994.

Taber, Tom. *The Expanded Santa Cruz Mountains Trail Book.* 7th ed. San Mateo: Oak Valley Press, 1994.

Whitnah, Dorothy. *An Outdoor Guide to the San Francisco Bay Area.* 5th ed. Berkeley: Wilderness Press, 1989.

Whitnah, Dorothy, *Point Reyes*, 3rd ed. Berkeley: Wilderness Press, 1995.